COMPARING SOCIAL POLICIES

Exploring new perspectives in Britain and Japan

Edited by Misa Izuhara

The POLICY
PP
PRESS

First published in Great Britain in February 2003 by

The Policy Press
34 Tyndall's Park Road
Bristol BS8 1PY
UK

Tel +44 (0)117 954 6800
Fax +44 (0)117 973 7308
e-mail tpp-info@bristol.ac.uk
www.policypress.org.uk

British Library Cataloguing in Publication Data

A catalogue record for this book is available from the British Library

ISBN 1 86134 366 3 paperback

A hardcover version of this book is also available

Misa Izuhara is a Research Fellow at the School for Policy Studies, University of Bristol.

Cover design by Qube Design Associates, Bristol.

Front cover: photograph of Tokyo subway kindly supplied by Shigeo Kogure.

Printed and bound in Great Britain by Henry Ling Limited,
at the Dorset Press, Dorchester, DT1 1HD

Contents

List of tables and figures

Tables

Figures

Acknowledgements

This volume emanated from the Anglo-Japanese workshop on 'Social Policy in the Twenty-first Century' held at the School for Policy Studies, University of Bristol, UK in March 2000. I would like to acknowledge the institutional support provided by the School combined with funding by the Great Britain Sasakawa Foundation, which enabled us to bring scholars from the opposite side of the globe to participate in the workshop. It required a great effort to bring the papers together given the differences in language and academic culture. As an editor, I am very grateful to all contributors for working with the deadlines and revising their respective chapters carefully.

I would like to thank two anonymous referees for their intellectual advice and valuable comments on the drafts, Stuart Gallagher for his skilled copy-editing, and Karen Bowler, Dawn Rushen, Dave Worth and the staff of The Policy Press for their strong support of this project.

The photograph on the front cover was kindly supplied by Shigeo Kogure. This photo, taken in the subway of Shinjuku Station in Tokyo, captured well the divided and transitional nature of Japanese society – hundreds of cardboard houses made by homeless people on one side and commuters on the other. After a tragic fire in 1998, these cardboard houses were removed permanently from the site.

Finally, my special thanks go to Professor Masami Iwata who spent her sabbatical year at Bristol when I was editing this book. I am very thankful for her intellectual advice (filling a gap in my knowledge) and her continued friendship.

November 2002

Glossary of Japanese terms

B

bataya   Rubbish collectors' shabby dormitories; work places to sort and sell rubbish

burakumin   Descendants of an outcast group under the caste system of the feudal era

D

danchi   Multi-family Housing Corporation housing estates

F

fukushi gan-nen   'Welfare Year One'

G

gakko hoken ho   School Health Law

gan   Cancer

goju-nen kankoku   Recommendation for social security system 1950

H

Heisei   Current regime period under Emperor Akihito (1989 to present)

hoshu tanka   Fee schedule for services

I

ie   Family, household, lineage, home or house: *ie seido* (the family system [lineage which is conceptualised as continuously succeeding from generation to generation])

J

Jido-fukushi ho   Child Welfare Act

Jukkyu Kisoku   Regulation for Relief

K

kigyo-gata fukushi shakai   Corporate-centred welfare society

kokumin hoken   National health insurance

kokumin kiso nenkin   Basic pensions for all the nation

kosei nenkin   Occupational pension

koshu eisei   Public health

koteki fujo   Public assistance

koteki kaigo hoken   Long-term care insurance

kumiai hoken   Society-managed health insurance

kyosai kumiai hoken   Mutual aid associations health insurance

kyugo ho	Public Assistance Act

M

mokuchin	Privately rented multi-family housing in a wooden structure

N

nagaya	Wooden terraced housing constructed prior to the Second World War.
Nihon-gata fukushi	Japanese-style welfare state
ningen dokku	Human dry dock
ni-setai jutaku	Two-household housing

P

pachinko	Pinball game

R

rodo anzen eisei ho	Industrial Health and Safety Law
rodo-ryoku seisaku	Labour policy
rojin hoken ho	Health and Medical Service Law for the Elderly

S

seifu kansho hoken	Government-managed health insurance
seikatsu hogo	Livelihood protection, public assistance
seikatsu hogo ho	Public Assistance Act
shakai fukushi	Social welfare
shakai fukushi hojin	Social welfare corporations, quango
shakai hoken	Social insurance
shakai hosho	Social security
shakai hosho seido shingi-kai	Advisory Council for Social Security systems
shakai seisaku gakkai	Japanese Association of Social Policy
shin-gata tokuyo	New type of nursing home
shinryo hoshu	National fee schedule for medical care

T

tokubetsu yogo rojin home	Nursing home

Y

yoseba	Where casual labourers gather to live in mass flophouses (and with an open-air labour market mainly for construction and transportation industries)
yuai-kai	Workers' organisation for mutual assistance

Notes on contributors

Lesley Doyal is Professor of Health and Social Care in the School for Policy Studies, University of Bristol. She has published widely in the area of gender, health and health care and acts as a consultant on related issues to WHO, the UN and the Global Forum for Health Research. Her recent publications include *What makes women sick: Gender and the political economy of health* (Macmillan, 1995) and *Women and health services: An agenda for change* (Open University Press, 1998).

Yosuke Hirayama is Associate Professor of Housing and Urban Studies at Kobe University, Japan. His research work and numerous publications focus on the postmodern housing system, deconstruction of housing policy and spatial politics of urban restructuring. He also engages in housing and neighbourhood developments as a planner. He was awarded academic prizes by the City Planning Institute of Japan, Architectural Institute of Japan, and Tokyo Institute of Municipal Research.

Masami Iwata is Professor of Social Welfare at Japan Women's University in Tokyo, Japan. She is engaged in a wide range of research and has published widely, with particular interests in poverty, social needs, social exclusion, household economy and social policy in Japan. Her recent work concerns the issues and policies of homelessness. She is a member of the social security council in a central government ministry, and the chief editor of the *Journal of Japanese Society for the Study of Social Welfare*.

Misa Izuhara is a Research Fellow at the School for Policy Studies, University of Bristol. Her research interests include ageing and gender issues in welfare state, housing, urban and social change. She is the author of *Family change and housing in post-war Japanese society* (Ashgate, 2000). Her current project is *'Generational contract' between care and inheritance in Japan and Britain*, funded by the UK Economic and Social Research Council.

Patricia Kennett is Lecturer on Comparative Social Policy at the School for Policy Studies, University of Bristol. Her interests include global governance and international social policy, comparative welfare systems, housing and urban policy, homelessness, citizenship and social exclusion and social theory. She is the author of *Comparative social policy: Theory and research* (Oxford University Press, 2001) and joint editor of *Homelessness: Exploring the new terrain* (The Policy Press, 1999). Patricia is also currently the editor of the journal *Policy & Politics*.

Mark Kleinman is the author of *Housing, welfare and the state in Europe* (Edward Elgar, 1996) and *A European welfare state? EU social policy in context* (Palgrave, 2001), and joint author of *Working capital: Life and labour in contemporary London* (Routledge, 2002). A Professor with the School for Policy Studies, he is currently on secondment to the Prime Minister's Strategy Unit.

Hilary Land is Professor Emeritus of Family Policy and Child Welfare at the School for Policy Studies, University of Bristol. Her main research interests are family policies from historical and comparative perspectives, feminist theories and social policy, social security (especially pensions), and lone parents returning to education and 'welfare-to-work'. Her publications include (with K. Kiernan and J. Lewis) *Lone motherhood in the twentieth-century* (Oxford University Press, 1998).

Ellen Malos is a Senior Lecturer and founder member of the Domestic Violence Research Group at the School for Policy Studies, University of Bristol. She has been active in the Women's Aid movement for 30 years. Her published collaborative research on domestic violence includes *Domestic violence and housing* (Women's Aid Federation England and School of Applied Social Studies, University of Bristol, 1993), *Multi-agency work and domestic violence* (Women's Aid Federation England and School of Applied Social Studies, University of Bristol, 1996), *Children, domestic violence and refuges* (Women's Aid Federation of England, 1996), and *Children's perspectives on domestic violence* (Sage Publications, 2002). Her other publications include *Politics of housework* (Allisona Busby, 1980, reprinted New Clarion Press, 1995) and *Domestic violence: Action for change* (with Gill Hague) (New Clarion Press, 1993, reprinted 1998).

Kristiina Martimo (MA, University of Kent) is currently working as a Research Assistant on the Economic and Social Research Council 'Growing Older' Programme at the University of Sheffield. She is also pursuing doctoral research in active ageing and sociology of the older body. Her interests include quality of life and media representation of older people.

Yoko Shoji is Professor of Sociology at the Faculty of Social Relations, Rikkyo University, Japan. Her teaching and research interests include family sociology, child welfare and issues of domestic violence. She is co-author of *Shakai fukushi-ron* [*Theory of social welfare*] (Yuhikaku, 1993) and *Kazoku jido fukushi* [*Family and child welfare*] (Yuhikaku, 1998).

Miyako Takahashi is Assistant Professor of School of Health Sciences and Nursing at the University of Tokyo, Japan. Her main research interests are psychosocial care for people with cancer, multidisciplinary collaboration in clinical settings, and qualitative research methodology. She has published in these fields. Miyako also works as a physician at some hospitals in Tokyo. She is currently working on a project on Japanese surgeons' attitudes towards breast reconstructive surgery.

Kingo Tamai is Professor of Social Policy at Osaka City University, Japan. His main research interests are the history of Japanese social policy in the 20th century, and ageing society and social policy in the 21st century. He is the author of *Bouhin nosouzou* [*Against poverty*] (Keibunsha, 1992). He is currently a chief of Kansai Office for the Study of Social Policy in Japan.

Alan Walker is Professor of Social Policy at the University of Sheffield and Director of the Economic and Social Research Council 'Growing Older' Programme and the UK National Collaboration on Ageing Research. He has been writing and researching in the fields of social policy and social gerontology for over 30 years. His most recent publications include *The new generational contract* (UCL Press, 1996), *Ageing Europe* (Oxford University Press, 1997), *The politics of old age in Europe* (Oxford University Press, 1999) and *The social quality of Europe* (The Policy Press, 1998).

Introduction

Misa Izuhara

Comparing Britain and Japan

This volume aims to provide a new perspective on social policy in Britain and Japan, by comparing policies shared between the two countries. Existing comparative research on welfare, welfare states and social policy tends to focus on European and/or English-speaking countries, such as the US and Australia, reflecting the dominance of a 'western paradigm' in academic and popular discourses (see Walker and Wong, 1996). However, Japan has an established but somewhat different welfare system from Britain, with well-practised occupational, family and community welfare. Therefore, interesting contrasts can be drawn with East Asia by comparing such dissimilar cultures and socioeconomic situations, despite work on East Asian welfare systems being still at a relatively early stage, since some characteristics regarding policy developments between East and West are common to both.

It has been more than a decade since Esping-Andersen's *The three worlds of welfare capitalism* (1990) first provoked academic debate on comparative welfare systems. Although this volume does not intend to expand debate on welfare typologies, it is worthwhile looking briefly at where each of the two countries stand. According to his regime typologies – using *decommodification* (the degree to which the welfare state can help individuals achieve independence from the market and strengthen their citizenship rights) and *social stratification and solidarity* (the degree to which the welfare state can help build solidarity among citizens) as the main criteria for evaluation – Esping-Andersen classified Britain and Japan in different regime models. Britain was described, along with the US, as being close to the 'liberal' regime (characterised by means-tested assistance, limited universal transfers and social insurance schemes). Japan was closer to the 'conservative–corporatist' regime model along with Germany and other Continental European countries in which social rights are based on employment and contributions and the responsibility for welfare is placed on families rather than the state.

In most cases, analysis has sought to place Japan into one of a variety of existing welfare regime models conceptualised from a Western framework rather than examining it in its own terms (Goodman and Peng, 1996). Since it does not often sit comfortably in such regime models, a compromise results whereby the Japanese welfare system is described as 'unique' or 'exceptional'. Responding to many critiques, Esping-Andersen (1997) later re-examined the Japanese regime. By highlighting some similarities with familialistic welfare societies of Southern European countries, he suggested that Japan might be a 'hybrid' of the liberal–residual and the conservative–corporatist models. As with other East Asian countries – such as Korea and Taiwan, whose systems have been partly based on the Japanese model – a new typology of welfare states, an 'East Asian welfare model' or 'Confucian welfare state', has also been suggested (see for example, Rose and Shiratori, 1986; Jones, 1993; Goodman and Peng, 1996; Kwon, 1997). Other critiques include those by feminists who bring up a gender (and family) blind analysis in the original 'three worlds' model. This led to the proposal of the fourth 'familial' regime model of Mediterranean countries (but Japan is also sometimes grouped in this model). Esping-Andersen argues (1999) that although none of the elements (such as family and occupational welfare, social insurance, and so on) are uniquely Japanese, the peculiar mix is not easily compatible with a simple trichotomy of welfare regimes. The peculiarities of cases in Japan, Australia or Southern Europe are, however, "variations within a distinct overall logic, not the foundations of a wholly different logic *per se*" (Esping-Andersen, 1999, p 92).

This is also the case for contemporary Britain, which Esping-Andersen (1990) noted a "rather uneasy mix of universalism and the market" (Cochrane et al, 2001, p 19). It reflects the dynamic nature of a welfare state being shaped and reshaped since 1945, accompanying the changing roles of different sectors in the provision of welfare services. This captures well one of the shortcomings of the regime-typology approach despite the merit of comparative analysis that clustering various welfare states together aids. Typologies can be problematic since they usually refer only to one point in time and do not take mutation of welfare states into account (Esping-Andersen, 1999). And countries such as Britain, an example of 'regime-shifting', tend to fall into this trap. Another shortcoming, which is also true in cross-national work involving non English-speaking countries in particular, is its dependency on aggregated, quantitative data and its tendency of emphasising convergence in social policy development across nations (see for example Kennett, 2001).

Goodman, White and Kwon (1998, p xv) also point out shortcomings of cross-national comparison between East and West thus:

> Most studies of East Asian welfare systems have either been written by members of those societies, have drawn largely on local sources and often have been subject to only minimal comparative analysis, or else have been written by Western scholars often unable to use the indigenous sources, written or spoken, and hence heavily reliant on English-language sources and on Western-derived analytical tools which may not always be appropriate to internal debates.

In this context, what can this volume contribute to the world of comparative social policy? For the last decade, the inclusion of Japan, as an East Asian country, along with Britain in such comparative analysis has gained increasing popularity, but often the systems were examined with a single perspective (for example, Esping-Andersen, 1990, 1999; Gould, 1993; Mishra, 1999). British social policy has also been keenly studied by Japanese scholars, introducing its history, issues and theories with Japanese perspectives (Osawa, 1986; Mouri, 1990; Takegawa, 1999). Some scholars still protect the uniqueness of Japanese policy and practice by hanging on to existing analytical tools developed in Japan. However, there is a new breed of Japanese academics who have started examining (and re-examining) Japanese social policy using a framework adopted from British social policy (see for example, Takegawa, 2001). Moreover, there are international comparisons of welfare states and social policy and various collections of work involving different national perspectives (Esping-Andersen, 1996a; Alcock and Craig, 2001a; Cochrane et al, 2001). Japan is sometimes included in such collections of work, but authors are often required to follow a western-derived framework for analysis (see for example, Uzuhashi, 2001).

This volume does not belong to any of these categories of existing literature. It is a new style of academic text, containing six 'paired chapters' written from both British and Japanese perspectives in the selected fields of social policy. The point made by Goodman, White and Kwon earlier in this introduction perhaps explains the reason why the term *comparing* was chosen over *comparative* for the title of this volume.

The following chapters do not strictly compare policy processes and issues between the two countries. Rather, each chapter provides country-specific analyses using empirical data and a theoretical and conceptual framework, but can also be read comparatively with its paired Japanese or British chapter. Indeed the strength of the volume lies in the materials collected, analysed and written by scholars in these fields, whose research experiences and insights are embedded in their own cultural and policy context.

Drawing mainly on national research, this volume recognises divergence in terms of policy development, focuses on current issues and debates in various policy areas, and is sensitive to national and cultural specificity. It is, however, perhaps the first attempt by British and Japanese scholars to present their cases side by side, not compromising their own understanding in order to 'fit in' the analytical framework set by other national perspectives. Yet, each paired chapter displays similar themes; therefore, similarities and differences of the chosen policy fields are emphasised. This volume also aims to address the dearth of Japanese social policy materials written in English.

This is not a comprehensive textbook on social policy: by reading this volume, one cannot expect to ascertain comprehensive views on issues of all the major social policy arenas in the two countries under investigation. Instead, reflecting current trends and situations of the new millennium, this volume selected topical and contemporary areas of social policy by compromising some of the 'classic' policy areas, such as employment and education. Some areas (such as employment and the labour market) are examined across related and overlapping disciplines, and are discussed in various chapters of this volume.

In order to set out a context of social policy, Chapters One and Two provide an overview of social policy development with particular reference to social security in Britain and Japan, respectively. These chapters are followed by an analysis of five specific policy areas. Chapters Three and Four examine the implications of population ageing for intergenerational relations. Chapters Five and Six explore how domestic violence is perceived in Britain and Japan, respectively, in the context of family relations and socio-legal changes. The operation of the housing system and how housing policy contributes to the creation of social inequality are explored in Chapters Seven and Eight. Chapters Nine and Ten analyse the meaning and causes of homelessness and examine policy responses in the context of recent economic and labour market changes. Finally, Chapters Eleven and Twelve present broader and specific issues involving women's position in health and health services.

The style of pairing varies across the chapters. Some of the imbalance in pairing perhaps explains crucial points of difference between nations. For instance, the chapters on domestic violence (Chapters Five and Six) do not appear so well paired; it may be that this imbalance illustrates the different stages of policy development, understanding and recognition of the problem in the two societies. The pairing of chapters on women and health (Chapters Eleven and Twelve) is also of a different kind. Chapter Eleven provides a comparison between the two countries on women and their health concerns, while Chapter Twelve explores a very detailed and brave example of this issue through her own qualitative research.

What is social policy in Britain and Japan?

The definition and content of social policy are understood differently in British and Japanese academic debates. Social policy is perhaps a more developed discipline, or field of study, in Britain than in Japan, evidenced in a larger and growing body of academic literature (see for example, Titmuss, 1956; Marshall, 1967; Townsend, 1976; Alcock, 1996; Alcock et al, 1998; Ellison and Pierson, 1998; also *the Journal of Social Policy*). Alcock defined the term 'social policy' as describing actions aimed at promoting the welfare and wellbeing of individuals and society collectively, and also the academic study of such action:

> Although social policy is about values and how needs are met within economic constraints, it is also about services and the roles that welfare services play within the social process. (Alcock, 1996, p 18)

Other definitions focus more narrowly on the activities of the welfare state; that is, "the range of government policies and social services used to enhance the welfare of citizens within a country" (Alcock et al, 2000, p 1). Since welfare services are often provided by multiple sources of public and private as well as other sectors, such narrow definitions can be misleading.

In the study of social policy, key concepts – such as social needs and rights – are often debated, and the intellectual foundations to debates (that is, perspectives from the left, right, and feminists) are explored in Britain. Those who provide and deliver social welfare are another focus of social policy debate, examining the role of the four main sectors – the state, the market, the informal sector, and the voluntary sector. In terms of the content of social policy in the postwar period, this largely resulted in the introduction of the first system of comprehensive state provision for the prevention of social deprivation (or tackling the 'five giant social evils' identified by the 1942 Beveridge report) in a capitalist economy. The classic contents therefore included health care, education, social security, housing, and employment. Compared with other policy areas, however, housing occupies a unique position in social policy in Britain as well as in Japan. With the postwar expansion of owner–occupation (approximately 60% of citizens in Japan and 70% in Britain were homeowners in the late 1990s), housing is identified as "neither fully part of the welfare state, nor fully part of the free market" as Kleinman explores in Chapter Seven of this volume.

We now live in a society characterised by a growing sense of risk and insecurity (Beck, 1992; Giddens, 1998) associated with the global concerns of environmental disaster, for example. Management of risk and exploring alternative ways to respond to such risks has also become new policy debates.

Despite the myth (or misconception) of underdeveloped welfare provision or social policy in Japan, which lags behind its postwar economic development when compared with other industrial societies (Lee, 1987), the history of Japanese social policy, interestingly enough, can be traced back to the late 19th century as discussed by Tamai in Chapter Two. From such times, the leading welfare models of Western societies were eagerly studied by the Japanese government and scholars when developing their own systems.

In Japan, labour policy (*rodo-ryoku seisaku*) and social security (*shakai hosho*) have been the two main pillars of social policy among academic debate (see Tamai, 1997; Nishimura and Aramata, 1999). In terms of evaluating the Japanese welfare system, Peng (2000) pointed out the exclusive use of the corporate-centred welfare society approach (*kigyo-gata fukushi shakai*) by Japanese scholars (see Osawa, 1993; Kumazawa, 1997, 2000), contrasting with the welfare regime typology approach, which is the dominant framework used by Western scholars. Indeed, in Japan it is generally agreed that labour policy was the starting point of social policy debates, and the two terms were used almost interchangeably in earlier periods (Tamai, 1997). It is misleading, however, to say that labour policy was the only facet of social policy considering company-based social security schemes had already existed since pre-war times. Given that access to the scheme was made exclusively through employment, it is however debatable whether the developing social security system could be considered as part of labour policy rather than standing on its own right. The discipline of social policy was reinforced by theories developed by Kazuo Ohkouchi in the 1930s and 1940s. He argued the importance of locating economic theory within social policy debates, placing an emphasis on the role of social policy in the production and maintenance of the labour force. Social policy therefore continued to focus upon employment and labour market policies concerning the wages and working conditions of workers.

Compared with Britain, social security (*shakai hosho*) is defined more widely including social insurance (*shakai hoken*), public assistance (*koteki fujo*), public health (*koshu eisei*) (in Britain health care stands on its own as one significant area of social policy), and social welfare (*shakai fukushi*). Indeed the term 'social security' is sometimes used interchangeably with 'social welfare' (see for example, Ichien, 1993; Jinushi and Hori, 1998). Housing and education are usually not considered as part of social policy in Japan. Although strong state intervention exists to regulate the market, housing has been left mainly to individual responsibility, assisted by companies. In Chapter Eight, Hirayama explores how the operation of the housing system and housing policy has contributed to the creation of social inequality.

Along with many other economic and policy reforms in Japan, the widening scope of social policy was typically driven by external forces when the OECD requested a comprehensive report on social policy in the 1970s (Tamai, 1997). Since then, a shift has been made from mere labour policy – targeting only adult male workers as a client group – to achieving more comprehensive provision of welfare to wider sections of society.

Social change, welfare mix and social policy

Social policies (or more narrowly, welfare states) develop in different ways in different social, economic and political contexts. Policy also changes over time responding to the dynamic nature of society and economy. Observational differences in welfare systems between Britain and Japan are therefore inevitable. For instance, there is variation between the roles of different sectors (the state, the market, the family and the voluntary sector) in the provision of welfare services in different societies and such balances also change within a society over time. As Alcock and Craig argue (2001a), political struggles, economic changes and ideological conflicts all result in welfare policy changes. The changing balance of the mixed economy of welfare, and the different (and changing) role played by the state are indeed some of the key themes explored throughout this volume. This introduction paints an overall picture of how the 'welfare mix' differs between Britain and Japan, and highlights changing policy directions through postwar socioeconomic changes. At the same time, some similarities between the two welfare systems are also explored.

In Britain, the creation of the welfare state was a significant focus of the mid-20th century, guaranteeing to meet the welfare needs of all citizens. The postwar welfare state was indeed closely associated with the establishment of universal, redistributive, and national welfare services represented by a National Insurance (NI) scheme for social security (means-tested public assistance was originally intended to play a minor role), comprehensive free health and education services, and state support for full (male) employment. Since the early postwar period saw the expansion of state welfare, the role of the state as a welfare provider was a primary concern of social policy. An expansion of state expenditure was also apparent. Between 1951 and 1976, welfare spending on education, health and social security grew from 11% to 22% as a proportion of gross domestic product (GDP) (Alcock and Craig, 2001b). Despite the principle of universal provision, however, in practice social barriers – including gender, ethnicity and disability – have prevented all citizens from pursuing the full range of services on offer (see Williams, 1989; Campbell and Oliver, 1996; Sainsbury, 1996). Moreover, during the 1960s, Beveridge's principle of flat-rate benefits in return for flat-rate contributions was replaced with earnings-related contributions for NI. In Chapter One, Land provides detailed discussion on such policy changes with particular reference to social security in the context of postwar socioeconomic changes.

The postwar welfare states in both societies were founded on the assumptions of steady economic growth to fund public (and in the Japanese case, occupational) welfare. Following the global economic recession of the 1970s, the government's commitment to further expand state welfare was jeopardised, and therefore economic and political priorities were altered. In Britain, significant reforms to privatise and marketise welfare provision, together with changes to the structure and operation of state welfare services, took place during the 1980s after Margaret Thatcher's 'new right' government came into power. In social security, for instance, targeted (means-tested) provision such as Income Support replaced universal (but contributory) provision of NI benefits. Statutory sick pay was transferred to employers. Through the Right-to-Buy campaign, supply-side ('bricks and mortar') subsidies of council housing was replaced with demand-side support of housing benefit (means-tested support for rent payments) with an increasing reliance on the private sector for housing provision (Forrest and Murie, 1991; see also Chapter Seven of this volume). Such a shift from the direct provision of public services and facilities to private market provision supported by means-tested public subsidies was also evident in other areas such as residential care for older people. The Thatcherite principle of a 'free economy and a strong state' also re-emphasised the role of the family in welfare provision. Despite the cutbacks of the 1980s, however, the principle of universalism has remained strong in some areas of state welfare, such as health care and education, although the quality of the services can be debatable.

Moreover, diversity exists in the public–private balance across welfare categories. For example, 70% of people own their own home while only 7% of children were educated in fee-paying schools in the late 1990s.

The voluntary sector has been playing a significant role in the development and delivery of welfare services in Britain, reaching the needs which other sectors cannot meet (Alcock, 1996). Voluntary (or charitable) organisations vary in size, activity, and type of funding, and range from small local self-help groups to large national organisations such as Shelter and Age Concern. The significant and independent role played by the voluntary sector in pre- and inter-war periods was lessened with the creation of the welfare state in the 1950s and 1960s. They are now frequently referred to as the 'agencies of the state' due to the increased state funding available and the compromised position they find themselves in to accommodate the needs of the state to deliver a wide range of welfare services. Public support in welfare provision now operates increasingly in partnership with the private as well as voluntary sectors subsidised by the taxpayers. A similar approach is also adopted in Japan in the provision of nursing care under the new Long-Term Care Insurance (LTCI) scheme (see Chapter Four of this volume for more discussion).

At the turn of the century, the British New Labour government shifted and reinterpreted the 'social contract' for welfare between the state and the individual. The notion of rights to welfare has shifted from that in the 'classical' welfare state. Now, rights match responsibilities, echoing to some extent the Victorian values at the end of the 19th century. Consequently, people increasingly need to draw welfare through paid-work. The promotion of 'welfare-to-work' and the New Deal programme reinforced the role of labour market participation as the major means for tackling the problems of poverty and welfare dependency (Alcock and Craig, 2001b). In Chapter Nine, in the context of broader structural factors such as changes in the economy, the labour market and a reorientation of the welfare state, the issue of homelessness is discussed by Kennett. These initiatives highlight how Britain is currently moving towards a new and more mixed economy of welfare.

In Japan, on the other hand, family dependency and the strong role of the corporate sector through established occupational welfare have characterised the postwar welfare mix. And in a sense, the establishment in 1961 of the social insurance schemes of 'health insurance for all nations and pensions for all nations' marked the beginning of a welfare state (the issue of non-Japanese residents in welfare provision still remains in contemporary policy debate). Unlike Britain, the role of the state in the postwar period had been developed not to replace the existing functions of the family and companies. Rather, it was to build upon and enclose existing resources within the state umbrella, as Tamai argues in Chapter Two using the social insurance system as an example.

Japan has favoured social insurance over other means of financing such as taxation-based or pay-as-you-go schemes. This is also apparent in the more recent policy development to fund growing nursing care costs in ageing society (see Masuda, 2001). The contemporary occupational welfare system had evolved in parallel with the increasing comprehensiveness of the postwar public welfare system. Instead of achieving egalitarian redistribution of resources, however, such state-corporate 'dualism' in welfare provision has been a cause of social stratification (see Esping-Andersen, 1997). Non-employed workers such as farmers and the self-employed, employees of small firms with fewer than five regular workers, and non-regular employees such as part-timers and casual labourers, usually insure themselves (and their family) via public or other private schemes. Also, the gap in welfare benefit levels among workers in different sized companies has been widening, especially in the areas of health-related and retirement schemes since the mid-1970s (Osawa, 1993). Women's access to social security is often made through their dependant status within the family as wives (discussed later in this introduction).

The 1970s was also a dramatic decade for the Japanese welfare state with increased public pressure on this arena. *Fukushi Gannen* (Welfare Year One) sought to introduce more welfare and a better quality of life in 1973 but soon altered its direction due to the oil crisis. The slogan of 1973 was gradually replaced by 'reconsider welfare', 'welfare state disease', or 'Japanese-style welfare state'. The concept of welfare re-emphasised individual responsibilities, re-establishing traditional practices of mutual aid within the family, local communities and the workplace. This idea was to avoid following the path of Western welfare states towards public welfare dependency and instead to only use public assistance to supplement welfare provided by other sectors (see Rudd, 1994). Although Japan started to face similar problems as Britain (such as the population ageing in the 1980s), the 'Japanese model' of welfare provision survived without making any drastic changes, partly due to the 'bubble' economy up to the early 1990s (see Chapter Two of this volume).

Since the economic bubble burst in the early 1990s, the Japanese economy has lost its momentum, suffering its worst recession since the Second World War. Many Japanese corporations now find it necessary to seek alternative ways of cutting costs and achieving greater productivity in order to compete and survive in both domestic and international markets. The new global economy and the 'post-bubble' recession are indeed causing the breakdown of the unique practice of the Japanese employment system. Some companies are beginning to question their conventional 'firm-as-a-family' model, characterised by lifelong employment and the seniority system, and are adopting more contractual, flexible, individualistic and competitive arrangements in areas such as hiring practices, salary structures, and occupational benefits.

Indeed, the prolonged recession, as well as social and demographic changes, have brought new social problems and also started bringing some existing ones into harsher light at the turn of the century. Japan is now one of the fastest ageing societies in the world. The number of newspaper articles reporting domestic violence doubled between 1997 and 1999. And the increasing precariousness of the labour market as well as the social structure has made rough sleepers more visible in many Japanese cities (Chapter Ten includes original quantitative research data). Today, people are unlikely to believe in the myth that Japan is a stable and homogeneous society. Instead, it has become more fragmented and unequal due to the increasing risks in the economy, changing employment practises, and increased diversity in society. Facing similar problems as other industrial societies, the uniqueness of Japanese social policy may also be diminishing.

Changing families and the state

Another overarching policy theme of this volume is the state–family relationship. Changes in family formation and functions are one of the contributory factors for eroding the capacity of the family to support other members. How does the state respond to such changes? In both societies, the postwar welfare system was originally developed on the basis of the male breadwinner family model. In Britain, this model was most fully operated in the late 19th century protecting male employment (and with increasing middle-class values) backed up by the notion of a 'family wage' (see Land, 1980; Lewis, 1992). In Japan, marriage was once considered as a 'permanent employment' providing a means of survival for women (see Sodei, 1979). The male breadwinner model reinforced gender roles in married couples by sustaining unpaid female domestic workers in order to enhance available resources within the family, which in turn generated an economic bond between couples. The gender division of labour – differentiating positions of men in the 'public' realm of the labour market and women in the 'private' sphere of family life – tends to create a power relationship within couples. Domestic violence born out of such gender relationships is often hidden in the private sphere of the family. (This issue is explored in Chapters Five and Six of this volume.) Compared with Britain, the underdeveloped policy and research on domestic violence in Japan are coined with the myth that such social problems were 'absent' in society.

In Japan, the social security and tax systems have been developed based on the 'family-as-a-unit' rather than on the individual. The discriminatory tax treatment of two-income households, for instance, discourages wives from taking full-time employment. Many married women try not to exceed the maximum earning limit and stay in a dependant status in order to benefit fully from the taxation and welfare system. Therefore the rise in female workers since the Equal Opportunity Act 1986 has been concentrated on fringe work, such as part-time jobs, without full occupational benefits (Osawa, 1993). The feminisation of the workforce is an increasingly common practice in post-industrial societies including Britain, but again the expansion is accounted for by part-time employment with short hours and few benefits.

In-built institutional constraints, ranging from the shortage of collective and affordable social services including childcare and care for vulnerable adults, to the lack of maternity rights, are other contributing factors in both societies. In Japan, consequently, women's labour force participation has been typically characterised as 'M-curve employment', the drop from the first peak resulting from marriage and childbirth and the drop from the second peak due to the necessity of taking care of elderly parents (and in-laws). Esping-Andersen (1997) argued that the paradox of a familialistic welfare state in a post-industrial order prohibits family formation. Social and employment structures are insufficiently developed to allow women to become working mothers, so that many women must choose between a career and childbearing. Decreasing fertility rates, combined with increased longevity, indeed help accelerate societal ageing. Responding to the ageing of the population has become an important policy agenda in both societies. Societal ageing poses a considerable challenge to the family and the state partly due to the increasing need for nursing care, limited financial resources, and decreasing capacity of family to care. In contrast, the British pattern of childbearing is now called 'twin peak' with increasing teenage pregnancy, which itself has become a new social issue. (The implication of population ageing for relations between the generations is explored in Chapters Three and Four of this volume.)

Recent changes in family structure and living arrangements in both societies have started to undermine the expected role that families have played in providing care and maintenance for children, older people and other vulnerable family members. Britain has experienced changes in family patterns and formation in recent years despite the promotion of marriage and family values by successive governments. As Land argues in Chapter One, the male breadwinner model has become further removed from the reality of most families' lives as the 'individual-worker' model replaces it. Increasing divorce rates, especially after the 1969 Divorce Law Reform Act, mean significant increase in remarriage forming many 'reconstituted' families which subsequently produced a complex web of responsibility among members. Over the past 20 years, the incidence of relative poverty among children has tripled. This is caused by increasing inequality in earnings, an expansion of lone-parent households over the last 30 years, and also an increased share of households with children with no working adult. Lone parents indeed challenge the traditional family model due to its structure, division of labour, and moral supremacy (see Lewis, 1997). An attempt was made under the Child Support Act 1991 to shift responsibility for children from the state back to absent parents (often, but not always, fathers) due to the increased number of lone parents on state benefits. The Labour Government has also responded by adopting as a policy objective ending child poverty by 2020 with both direct and indirect financial support to families with children such as the Working Families' Tax Credit (WFTC). For lone mothers as well as for young people, access to welfare is now increasingly sought through paid-work under the New Deal programme.

Compared with British families, Japanese families are often legally obliged to provide support to their members. Such obligation often extends vertically up and down three generations. For example, when a person applies for *seikatsu hogo* (livelihood protection or public assistance), the local government assesses the income, assets, and 'support ability' of the household first, and then of the extended family members, even when they live separately. Although the extended family is usually approached, in practice the authority cannot enforce support from them. Instead, what they do is reduce the amount of assistance – or not grant it at all – if they realise that other family members are 'able' to support the applicant. The interpretation of the family obligations varies across local government offices. Although extended family living arrangements provide a perfect structural context for exchanging family support, family nuclearisation has accentuated for the last few decades and started to alter the idealised notion of reciprocity within extended families. These structural changes do not always undermine functional aspects of family relations. However, changes are likely to require different policy responses in the area of care provision.

This volume presents an up-to-date and detailed account of how these areas of social policy have developed in the postwar period in Britain and Japan. It is hoped that future comparative study in this area will be founded on the issues explored and policy responses examined here.

References

Alcock, P. (1996) *Social policy in Britain: Themes and issues*, Basingstoke: Macmillan.

Alcock, P. and Craig, G. (eds) (2001a) *International social policy*, Basingstoke: Palgrave.

Alcock, P. and Craig, G. (2001b) 'The United Kingdom: rolling back the welfare state?', in P. Alcock and G. Craig (eds) *International social policy*, Basingstoke: Palgrave, pp 124-42.

Alcock, P., Erskine, A. and May, M. (eds) (1998) *The student's companion to social policy*, Oxford: Blackwell.

Alcock C., Payne, S. and Sullivan, M. (2000) *Introducing social policy*, Harlow: Pearson Education.

Beck, U. (1992) *Risk society*, London: Sage Publications.

Beveridge, W. (1942) *Report on social insurance and allied services*, Cmd 6404, London: HMSO.

Campbell, J. and Oliver, M. (1996) *Disability politics*, London: Routledge.

Cochrane, A., Clarke, J. and Gewitz, S. (eds) (2001) *Comparing welfare states* (2nd edn), London: Sage Publications.

Ellison, N. and Pierson, C. (1998) *Developments in British social policy*, Basingstoke: Macmillan.

Esping-Andersen, G. (1990) *The three worlds of welfare capitalism*, Cambridge: Polity Press.

Esping-Andersen, G. (ed) (1996a) *Welfare states in transition: National adaptations in global economies*, London: Sage Publications.

Esping-Andersen, G. (1996b) 'Welfare state without work: the impasse of the continental European model', in G. Esping-Andersen (ed) *Welfare states in transition: National adaptations in global economies*, London: Sage Publications, pp 66-87.

Esping-Andersen, G. (1997) 'Hybrid or unique? The Japanese welfare state between Europe and America', *Journal of European Social Policy*, vol 7, no 3, pp 179-89.

Esping-Andersen, G. (1999) *Social foundations of postindustrial economies*, Oxford: Oxford University Press.

Forrest, R. and Murie, A. (1991) *Selling the welfare state: The privatisation of public housing*, London: Routledge.

Giddens, A. (1998) *The third way: The renewal of social democracy*, Cambridge: Polity Press.

Goodman, R. and Peng, I. (1996) 'The East Asian welfare states: peripatetic learning, adaptive change, and nation-building', in G. Esping-Andersen (ed) *Welfare states in transition: National adaptations in global economies*, London: Sage Publications, pp 192-224.

Goodman, R., White, G. and Kwon, H.-J. (eds) (1998) *The East Asian welfare model: Welfare orientalism and the state*, London: Routledge.

Gould, A. (1993) *Capitalist welfare systems: A comparison of Japan, Britain and Sweden*, London: Longman.

Ichien, M. (1993) *Mizukara kizuku fukushi* [*Self-help welfare*], Tokyo: Ministry of Finance Press.

Jinushi, S. and Hori, K. (1998) *Shakai hosho dokuhon* [*Social security: Reader*], Tokyo: Toyo Keizai Shinpou.

Jones, C. (1993) 'The Pacific challenge: confucian welfare states', in C. Jones (ed) *New perspectives on the welfare state in Europe*, London: Routledge, pp 198-217.

Kennett, P. (2001) *Comparative social policy: Theory and research*, Buckingham: Open University Press.

Kumazawa, M. (1997) *Noryoku shugi to kigyo shakai* [*Ability based company society*], Tokyo: Iwanami.

Kumazawa, M. (2000) *Josei roudou to kigyou shakai* [*Female labour force and company society*], Tokyo: Iwanami.

Kwon, H.-J. (1997) 'Beyond European welfare regimes: comparative perspectives on East Asian welfare systems, *Journal of Social Policy*, vol 26, no 4, pp 467-84.

Land, H. (1980) 'The family wage', *Feminist Review*, vol 6, pp 55-78.

Lee, H.-K. (1987) 'The Japanese welfare state in transition,' in R. Friedmann, N. Gilbert and M. Sherer (eds) *Modern welfare states: A comparative view of trends and prospects*, Brighton: Wheatsheaf Books, pp 243-63.

Lewis, J. (1992) 'Gender and the development of welfare regimes', *Journal of European Social Policy*, vol 2, no 3, pp 159-73.

Lewis, J. (ed) (1997) *Lone mothers in European welfare regimes: Shifting policy logics*, London: Jessica Kingsley.

Marshall, T.H. (1967) *Social policy in the twentieth century* (2nd edn), London: Hutchinson.

Masuda, M. (2001) 'Kaigo hoken seido no seisaku keisei katei no tokucho to kadai: kanryo soshiki ni okeru seisaku keisei katei no jirei' ['Characteristics and issues of the policy-making process for the long-term care insurance system: a case in the Japanese bureaucracy'], *The Quarterly of Social Security Research*, vol 37, no 1, pp 44-58.

Mishra, R. (1990) *The welfare state in capitalist society: Policies of retrenchment and maintenance in Europe, North America and Australia*, London: Harvester Wheatsheaf.

Mishra, R. (1999) *Globalization and the welfare state*, Cheltenham: Edward Elgar.

Mouri, K. (1990) *Igirisu fukushi kokka no kenkyu: Shakai hosho hattatsu no shokakuki* [*Study of the English welfare state*], Tokyo: Tokyo University Press.

Nishimura, H. and Aramata, S. (1999) *Shin shakai seisaku wo manabu* [*New: Study of social policy*], Tokyo: Yuhikaku.

Osawa, M. (1986) *Igirisu shakai seisaku-shi: Kyuhin-ho to fukushi kokka* [*English social policy history: Poor Law and the welfare state*], Tokyo: Tokyo University Press.

Osawa, M. (1993) *Kigyo chuusin shakai wo koete: Gendai Nihon wo gender de yomu* [*Beyond the corporate-centred society: An examination of modern Japan from gender perspectives*], Tokyo: Jiji Press.

Peng, I. (2000) 'A fresh look at the Japanese welfare state', *Social Policy and Administration*, vol 34, no 1, pp 87-114.

Rose, R. and Shiratori, R. (1986) 'Introduction: welfare society: three worlds or one?', in R. Rose and R. Shiratori (eds) *The welfare state East and West*, Oxford: Oxford University Press.

Rudd, C. (1994) 'Japan's welfare mix', *The Japan Foundation Newsletter*, vol 22, no 3, pp 14-17.

Sainsbury, D. (1996) *Gender, equality and welfare states*, Cambridge: Cambridge University Press.

Sodei, T. (1979) 'Fujin-mondai no nakano chukonen-mondai' ['The issue of middle/older people among women's issues'], in *Chukonen Joseigaku* [*Study of middle-aged older women*], Tokyo: Kaikiuchi Shuppan.

Takegawa, S. (ed) (1999) *Igirisu senshin shokoku no shakai hosho* [*England – social security of developed countries*], Tokyo: Tokyo University Press.

Takegawa, S. (2001) *Fukushi shakai: shakai seisaku to sono kangaekata* [*Welfare society and social policy*], Tokyo: Yuhikaku.

Tamai, K. (1997) 'Shakai seisaku kenkyu no keifu to konnichi-teki kadai' ['History of study of social policy and current issues'], in K. Tamai and M. Ohmori (eds) *Shakai seisaku wo manabu hito no tame ni* [*For those who study social policy*], Kyoto: Sekai Shisou Sha.

Titmuss, R. (1956) *The social division of welfare: Some reflections on the search for equity*, Liverpool: Liverpool University Press.

Titmuss, R. (1968) *Essays on the welfare state*, London: Allen & Unwin.

Townsend, P. (1976) *Sociology and social policy*, Harmondsworth: Penguin.

Uzuhashi, T.K. (2001) 'Japan: bidding farewell to the welfare society', in P. Alcock and G. Craig (eds) *International social policy*, Basingstoke, Palgrave, pp 104-23.

Walker, A. and Wong, C.-K. (1996) 'Rethinking the western construction of the welfare state', *International Journal of Health Services*, vol 26, no 1, pp 67-92.

Williams, F. (1989) *Social policy: A critical introduction*, Cambridge: Polity Press.

ONE

Issues and theories of social policy in Britain: past, present and future

Hilary Land

Introduction

Richard Titmuss, the first professor of social administration in Britain, was also the first to set out a comprehensive research agenda for social policy (Titmuss, 1958). He was strongly committed to an infrastructure of universal services because it "provides a general system of values and a sense of community" (Titmuss, 1968, p 135). However, he was well aware that "universalism was not by itself alone, enough" (1968, p 135). His own work, along with that of Peter Townsend, Brian Abel-Smith, and Tony Lynes, had revealed that poverty among pensioners, as well as sick and disabled people, low-wage earners and their families, and lone parents, had not been eradicated despite full employment and the general growth in affluence in the 1950s and 1960s. Moreover, inequalities in the distribution of income and wealth remained, despite being tempered by the tax and benefit systems. In practice there was unequal access to – and effective use of – the social services. In particular, the middle classes made fuller use of the education and health care systems. As universalism has been watered down, particularly since 1980, the challenge today is how to re-establish universality in the context of growing reliance on the private for-profit sector heavily subsidised by the taxpayer. Or, perhaps, the challenge in fact is to find an alternative way to sustain a sense of community and social solidarity. This chapter explores some of the key issues involved, looking first at some of the main changes which have occurred since the 1950s.

During the 1960s, Beveridge's principle of flat-rate benefits in return for flat-rate contributions had been abandoned, and both National Insurance (NI) contributions and benefits had become earnings related (up to a ceiling set at one and a half times average male earnings). A tax credit scheme to tackle the problem of the inadequacy of the basic state pension had been considered in the mid-1960s and abandoned (for a detailed account, see Webb, 1975). Instead, attention focussed in the short term on making means-tested supplementary benefits (now Income Support) more acceptable to pensioners, and in the longer run developing a 'partnership' between public and private providers which would form the basis of reforming state pensions. In this partnership (which took until 1975 to reach the statute book because of two intervening general elections), employers, with their occupational pension schemes, had a significant role to play. The 1975 Pensions Act introduced a flat rate basic state pension together with a state earnings-related pension (SERPS). This set the standard for all occupational pension schemes; that is, if employees wanted to opt out of the SERPS, the scheme they joined had to be based on a defined 'benefit' and the pension paid had to be at least as good as the state scheme, including adequate provision for widows. It was intended that all occupational pension schemes would include trade union as well as employer representatives among the trustees. However, the Labour government's majority was dependent upon Liberal Party support and they did not agree to confine employee representation to trade union members.

For the first time, women's entitlement to benefits was independent of their marital status and full-time carers of both children and adults with additional health or disability needs had their pension rights protected. The NI scheme funding remained based on the same three pillars as Lloyd George's first social insurance scheme in 1911, namely contributions from employers, employees and the state. In other words, risks were still being pooled and SERPS was based on a formula that advantaged the below-average earner. All long-term social insurance benefits were to be index-linked to earnings or prices, whichever was the higher, thereby giving long-term benefit claimants a share in rising national prosperity. At this time the trade union movement was powerful enough to insist on improved state pensions.

The new Conservative government in 1980 interpreted 'selectivity' rather differently. They reverted to flat-rate benefits but kept earnings-related contributions, with heavier contributions levied on the average and below-average earner. Benefits were linked to prices instead of earnings. The range of earnings over which NI contributions for employees are levied, is linked to the level of the state pension. The upper contribution limit has fallen and, at the time of writing, is close to average male earnings. By the end of the 1980s, the state's contribution to the NI scheme had been abolished. Personal pensions were introduced and minimum standards were based on defined 'contributions'; that is, the risk of there being insufficient funds to pay an adequate pension was shifted to the individual. Most significantly the link between earnings and state pensions was severed and as a result, 20 years later, the basic state pension is 30% lower than it would have been had the link been maintained. Privatisation of the utilities meant large public sector pension funds passed into private hands with little or no trade union representation. Personal pensions were sold to many who would have been better off staying in SERPS or their occupational scheme, and there was a major scandal over their widespread mis-selling.

The Conservative government had to take equal treatment of men and women in the social security system seriously because of a number of EC/EU directives. This was achieved by levelling benefits downwards, raising the pension age to

65 for women, generally eroding the contributory benefit system, and increasing dependence on means-tested income support. Those who could afford to do so made private provision assisted by generous rebates and tax relief. Claimants on social security became increasingly stigmatised and labelled 'passive' and 'dependent'. Individuals were being blamed for the consequences of major demographic and economic changes.

Changing families and households

The postwar British welfare state was based on a mix of family and market, as well as state, provision. The principle of universalism was not intended to usurp either 'the family' or 'the market'. Indeed, the success of the welfare state depended on fully functioning two parent nuclear families and labour markets which delivered full employment. For example, Beveridge was very clear that a comprehensive social insurance scheme could not be sustained without full employment (at least for men). He was also explicit about the different responsibilities of men and women within marriage: men had a 'duty' to support their wives and children by taking paid employment (they could be imprisoned for failing to do so). Women had a 'duty' to give the care of their husbands and children priority over any activity in the labour market. He had held this model of the family for many years:

> The problem of unemployment lies, in a very special sense, at the root of most other social problems. Society is built up on labour; it lays upon it members responsibilities which in the vast majority of cases can be met only from the reward of labour; it imprisons for beggary and brands for pauperism; its ideal unit is the household of man, wife and children maintained by the earnings of the first alone. The household should have at all times sufficient room and air according to its size – but how, if the income is too irregular always to pay the rent? The children, till they themselves can work, should be supported by the parents – but how, unless the father has employment? The wife, so long at least as she is bearing and bringing up children, should have no other task – but how, if the husband's earnings fail and she has to go out to work? Everywhere the same difficulty recurs. Reasonable security of employment for the bread-winner is the basis of all private duties and all sound social action. (Beveridge, 1909, p 1)

It was a model which had been established as *normative* in the 19th century (Bosanquet, 1915). Therefore, the strong version of the male breadwinner model (Lewis, 1997) became deeply embedded in the British tax and social security systems as they developed in the 20th century, challenged by feminists (Rathbone, 1924) and some socialists (Wells, 1911) who recognised that women's dependence on men was a major impediment both to women achieving equality in the labour market and in civil society and to protecting the welfare of children. Family allowances paid directly to mothers were a challenge to this model and it is significant that this was not only controversial in 1945 when family allowances were introduced, but also in 1976 when child benefits replaced family allowances and child tax allowances (Land, 1976) and again in 1987 and 1999, when first a Conservative government and then a Labour government proposed paying benefits for children to the main (that is, male) breadwinner in order to 'make work pay'. In the 2002 Budget, the Chancellor of the Exchequer made it clear that benefits and the new credits for children would, after all, be paid to their main carer, usually the mother. He was convinced by the research evidence and the lobbying of women's groups that the children are more likely to benefit from the money if it is paid to the person caring for them. However, this is being done in the context of a joint assessment of parental income, thereby undermining the principles of independent taxation introduced in 1990.

The male breadwinner model of the family has become even further removed from the reality of most families' lives than it was when Beveridge was writing. He assumed only one in eight married women would have paid employment in the 1950s. Paradoxically it was the expansion of the health, education and social welfare services in the 1950s and 1960s that provided so many more women with job opportunities. Over 80% of the workforce in these services was, and still is, female. During the 1950s the government encouraged the public sector to offer part-time employment to married women and at the same time actively encouraged workers from the New Commonwealth to join the full-time workforce of the National Health Service (NHS). Since 1990, when individual taxation removed the tax penalty on higher earning married women, more and more mothers have been returning to employment within months of confinement (compared to a 15-year break when Titmuss was writing). Although most return to part-time employment, there are increasing numbers working full-time while they have pre-school children. Two-parent families are now more likely to have two *earning* parents. At the same time there has been a growth in lone parent families: at the end of the 1990s, 28% of children under 12 years-of-age were in households with one parent. At first the rise was accounted for by increasing divorce rates, and since the mid-1980s by the increase in never-married mothers. Unable to combine employment with the care of their children, the majority became dependent on means-tested benefits from the early 1980s. Today children are more likely to be in a household with either no earner or two earners than with one male breadwinner. Those in households with no one in employment are likely to be poor. Child poverty rates increased from one in ten children in 1979 to over one in three 20 years later. It is not surprising that both child poverty *and* the issue of childcare have moved up the government agenda. However, providing good and safe care outside of the family is a complex undertaking and a challenge in a secular society, which emphasises *individual* responsibility. Titmuss saw social policy as having an integrative function, encouraging solidarity between the social classes as well as the generations. The old male breadwinner, full-time housewife model for providing maintenance and care for young and old no longer seems widely applicable as it is replaced by the individual-worker model. Who now provides care for the young and the old, and on what terms? Who determines its standards?

Changing labour markets

Women make up nearly half the labour force in Britain but many are employed part-time. Britain has one of the highest proportions and numbers of part-time employees in the EU, and four out of five are women. Men combine part-time employment with education or early retirement; women with family responsibilities. In the early postwar years only one in 20 employees worked fewer than 30 hours a week. By the early 1990s this had increased to over one third. European Union directives have improved the rights of part-time employees to pensions, sick pay and holiday pay but they are still found in the periphery rather than at the core of the labour market. Over the years there has been a shift in the occupational structure of the employed population towards highly paid non-manual occupations and away from low-paid manual occupations. The manufacturing sector has declined and continues to do so, while the service sector has grown. Britain industrialised early in the 19th century and the agricultural sector was already small (15%) by the beginning of the 20th century.

It has become increasingly important to have educational qualifications, and as the numbers participating in further and higher education increases (from a low base), those with no qualifications are further disadvantaged in the labour market. Unemployment is not spread evenly across the country: areas in which heavy industry has declined have high rates among both young and older men. As trade union membership has fallen from over half in the late 1970s to just over a quarter in the 1990s, and national wages agreements have been abandoned and 'flexible' contracts increased, it has become harder to earn 'a family wage'. Families increasingly need two earners, or at least one-and-a-half earners, to meet their basic needs. The introduction of a minimum wage and the Working Families' Tax Credit by New Labour recognises these inadequacies of the wages system which is no longer expected to deliver a family wage for the lower paid.

New Labour and social policies in the 1990s

The New Labour government has not reversed the trend towards targeting or 'selective' benefits and services. Employment is the route out of poverty for all of working age men and women, mothers and fathers. Looking increasingly to the US and its neoliberal policies rather than to the EU, 'work for those who can and security for those who cannot' is the new slogan, which is embodied in the New Deal programmes to help young, old, disabled people and lone parents back into the labour market.

As Tony Blair explained in a speech in Singapore before he became Prime

Minister (and before the Asian crisis), "the system will only flourish in its aims of promoting security and opportunity across the life cycle if it holds the commitment of the whole population, rich and poor" (Blair, 1996, p 1). In contrast to the postwar British welfare state, which Blair asserts was seen "simply as universal cash benefits", he argues for "a more active conception of welfare based on services as well as cash: childcare as well as child benefit, training as well as unemployment benefit" – or, as he later described it, "a hand up not a hand down". Whatever the limitations of this analysis of the postwar welfare state (and there are many), at least there is a recognition that the expectations of the citizen of the state and the state of the citizen have changed. More recently in September 2000 in their reply to the Select Committee on Social Security's *Report on the contributory principle*, the government expressed the view that "the welfare system should support a number of objectives: delivering work from those who can, helping those who need it most – families with children and the poorest pensioners" (DSS, 2000, para 5). This is the focus of their policies "rather than concentrating on the merits of universal, means-testing or contributory benefits" (DSS, 2000, para 6). They made it clear that they disagreed with the committee's view that "there are structural reasons inherent in means testing which run the risk of undermining key objectives of the present government of tackling poverty, making work pay and equipping people to take control over their lives" (DSS, 2000, para 107).

In his book *The politics of uncertainty* (1996), Peter Marris also draws attention to the impact of dwindling security of employment and eroding social benefits which undermine – but also make more urgent – claims to social protection:

> The old arguments for comprehensive social security no longer convince, because both their economic assumptions and the political consensus to which they appeal have been undermined. Yet the emerging ideologies which seem to take the claims of global economic organisation at their own valuation, and displace the blame for growing insecurity onto the poor, the marginal and the failures of government can only promote greater uncertainty and social disintegration. (Marris, 1996, p 3)

The central theme of Marris's book is "the interaction between the personal construction of a sense of agency and social organisation of powers of control" (Marris, 1996, p 1). In developing this theme he draws out connections between the intimacy of family life and the structures of government and corporate power. His aim is to understand better how a more hopeful "politics of collaboration and reciprocity" (Marris, 1996, p 1) might be developed. This in turn must involve articulating a moral consensus to sustain it.

The New Labour government is clear that the relationship between the state and citizen, which underpinned the postwar welfare state in Britain, has changed and is changing still. The government also wants to 'modernise' the relationship between the state and the private for-profit sector. Twenty-five years of cutting and under-funding the public sector has left it unable to meet the needs and expectations of the public. The private for-profit sector is presented as being more efficient and more able and willing to provide cost-effective services of a higher quality and more attuned to the demands of citizens who are increasingly conceived of as consumers rather than citizens.

The speed and extent of the privatisation and marketisation of education, health and welfare services has increased rather than diminished since the election of New Labour in 1997. The model-informing policy is close to the neoliberal models adopted in the US, Australasia and Japan in the 1990s. The private sector is heavily subsidised by the taxpayer through private finance initiatives (PFI) or public private partnerships (PPP). In effect the infrastructure of the welfare state is being separated from service delivery. As a result the relationships between public services and their users and their workers are being marketised. Titmuss would not be surprised at the impact of what he called, in his analysis of the growing private insurance industry in the 1950s, "a retreat into irresponsibility" (Titmuss, 1958, p 215). Although he was writing before the removal of exchange controls and the free movement of finance capital, he warned against ignoring these trends, already visible in the 1960s, and anticipated that their growth was likely to accelerate:

> The growth of a 'pressure group state' generated by more massive concentrations of interlocking economic, managerial and self-regarding professional power, points in other directions: towards more inequality; towards the restriction of social rights and liberties and the muffling of social protest among large sections of the population. (Titmuss, 1968, p 157)

These developments, together with the growing diversity, complexity and fluidity of society, means that establishing and maintaining trust is more important were social cohesion to be achieved, but at the same time it is more difficult. For those who have lived through this period of change there are particular and urgent problems for social policies to address because their expectations of – and trust in – government policies were forged in an earlier age. Therefore, research is needed to enable both policy makers and practitioners to develop policies sensitive to this. For example, one of the key issues on the social policy agenda is how best to support and care for the older generation who remember Beveridge's promise of support from the cradle to the grave.

Solidarity between the generations

In Continental Europe, debates about pension policies appeal explicitly to the need to recognise 'solidarity' between the generations. The older generation has claims on the younger generation for support because of previous contributions made – and paid – as workers and, in the case of those aged over 75, because of military service. 'Solidarity' is not a term that slips easily off the tongue in debates on pensions in Britain; nevertheless, there was a clear understanding that the postwar social security system would deliver adequate state pensions. The care and health services that might be needed in the future would be there on the basis that they (or in the case of women, their husbands) had contributed and paid taxes all their working lives. The continuing fall in the value of the basic state pension relative to average earnings since 1980 and the growing practice of distinguishing between personal care which must be paid for and health care which is still free, has left the older generation feeling disillusioned and betrayed. The recent report by the Royal Commission on Long-Term Care, *With respect to old age* (1999), provides several examples of this sense of betrayal:

> I am 80 and for years I and my firm paid our contributions in the belief that I was providing as Beveridge had stated for all necessary care from cradle to grave .... Only recently have the rules been changed. I regard this as a blatant breach of contract by Government who took my money promising care and reneged on the contract after I had paid all my dues. To my mind this is a fraud. (Royal Commission on Long-Term Care, 1999, p 37)

There are also problems in the social care sector concerning young children. Here there is a strong line drawn between education (which is universal and free) and childcare (which must be paid for and is closely linked to the employment status of the parent[s]). The New Labour government launched its National Childcare Strategy early in its first term. It has invested heavily in creating childcare places, for it was understood that without childcare, mothers, and lone mothers in particular, could not return to or stay in the labour market. As the Japanese government has done, the Labour government has used the private for-profit sector to increase the capacity of this sector by giving them generous start-up grants. However, it has recognised that the market will not provide childcare in poorer areas, so there are a number of schemes targeted on deprived areas. However, funds for these are time-limited, and in any case will only reach a minority of poor children. At the same time it has provided financial assistance for parents in employment by paying a credit up to a maximum of 70% of the cost of a childcare place in the formal sector. There is no support for informal carers, who are often grandparents.

The number of places has increased from one in nine for every child under 8 years-of-age in 1999 to one in seven in 2001. The rate of growth in 2001 was only 2% and provision remains unevenly distributed over the country. A major constraint on expansion is the difficulty in recruiting and retaining staff. The childcare sector has to compete with nursing, teaching and social work in a dwindling pool of young women who now expect reasonable pay and a progressive career structure. In contrast to Britain's EU partners, the childcare sector provides neither. The US relies heavily on poorly paid immigrant labour to provide care for children and the frail elderly. Is this the solution that Britain is going to choose?

Frank Field, meanwhile, argued in his book, *Making welfare work: Reconstructing welfare for the millennium* (1995), for a funded pension scheme "completely independent of politicians' sticky fingers" (1995, p 176) on the grounds that it would be impossible to rebuild SERPS because it "has received such a political mauling since 1979 that it would be difficult to convince taxpayers – even if some politicians convinced themselves – that their benefit rights were secure" (1995, p 176). However, pension schemes in the private sector are not necessarily safe from the sticky fingers of those who manage their funds or indeed from HM Treasury, which transferred money out of the pension funds of the nationalised industries when they were privatised. At least this has put the management and control of these huge funds on the political agenda. However, the experience of the mis-selling fiasco by personal pensions advisers means there is little confidence among the older generation that they will receive what they need *and* feel entitled to. Among the younger generation there is little trust in any of the sources of advice, public or private. The recent troubles of the oldest (200 years old) and most reputable mutual society, Equitable Life, whose membership included senior members of all professions, illustrates how much the principle of mutuality has been eroded. The demise of the social insurance system and its underpinning contributory principle, means that in Britain we have devalued and are losing an important mechanism for transferring resources between the generations. Unlike Japan (see Goodman and Peng, 1996), family values in Britain today place less emphasis on obligations towards the older generation than was formerly the case (the legal obligation to maintain elderly parents was abolished in 1948). There are some important research and policy questions here which both historical and comparative perspectives might illuminate. The question is not only what will replace the contributory system but also how can any mechanism be trusted and involve the contributors? It is ironic that an interest in mutual and friendly society models of participation and control are occurring just at the time when so many of those formed 100 years ago and more are turning into banks. Unless a broader sense of social cohesion and solidarity between the generations in the wider society is established, this necessary trust will not be rebuilt. How can this be done?

Time

Flexibility, uncertainty, fragmentation: each implies short or disrupted time horizons. Linear time and cyclical time associated with natural processes have never been in step, but the rhythms of working life and family life are changing more rapidly and not in ways which necessarily fit easily or well together or lead to greater social cohesion in the workplace and the home:

> It's the time dimension of the new capitalism, rather than high-track data transmission, global stock markets or free trade which most directly affects people's emotional lives outside the workplace. Transposed to the family realm 'no long term' means keep moving, don't commit yourself, and don't sacrifice. (Sennett, 1999, p 25)

Time can be considered as a resource. Time budgets can be as important as money budgets and just as we talk of work-rich and work-poor households, we can also talk of time-rich and time-poor households. The time of poorer families and individuals is often taken for granted. Work-rich families may be time-poor as the need for two earners to earn what was once the family wage earned by the male breadwinner has become necessary for growing numbers of households in Britain and the US in particular. As Esping-Andersen comments:

> A hallmark of new emerging family forms is that they suffer from a scarcity of time. As the conventional family disappears so does the supply of unpaid domestic labour. The new 'atypical' families, be they single person or dual-earner households, may be income rich but they also crave services because they lack time. (2000, p 57)

However, unless subsidised by the state, only those who can command high earnings can afford to purchase the services necessary for daily living which were once provided by full-time housewives. The preparation and eating of meals – or fast food – outside the home is much more common and the market for domestic and caring services has grown in countries such as Britain and the US where state provision is low. Esping-Andersen argues that it is unrealistic to expect men to do more in the home. Instead the solution lies outside the household in either the market or the state. Richard Scase's report *Britain towards 2010* (1998) describes the future circumstances of three households. Duncan and Kim, the affluent two-earner couple with one ten year-old child have a family home which "is full of modern technology which has replaced many traditional household tasks. *But they still employ a cleaner on a weekly basis and a live-in au pair*" (p 4, emphasis added). Kim's mother is presumably living in her own home and currently "Kim orders on-line her mother's shopping needs. It's so much more convenient than having her living with them". But what will happen if, and when, her mother becomes so frail that she needs daily personal care? Technology will be of rather less help in that eventuality.

The current welfare-to-work policies devalue and obscure activities within the home which until recently were regarded, if not as work, than at least giving rise to legitimate claims on the state for support. In the postwar welfare state, lone mothers (and, since the early 1970s, lone fathers) were not required to register for employment as a condition of receiving means-tested social assistance until their children reached 16 years of age. As the Supplementary Benefit Commission, responsible until 1980 for the supplementary benefit system, the predecessor of income support, said in their 1980 Annual Report:

> We stress that our support for better working opportunities for lone parents is not based on the view that they *ought* to be supporting themselves. Many lone parents believe it is better to concentrate their efforts exclusively on

the difficult and important task of bringing up children single-handed, and they are entitled to do that. Thus it is important to raise benefits to a level at which lone parents do not feel compelled to take a job to support their families. Freedom of choice should be the aim. (1980, p 12)

The objective of social policies today is to get more lone parents, partners of the unemployed, and over-50s off benefit and into the labour market (even to look after other people's children). It is likely that in the near future lone mothers with a school-age child(ren) will be *required* to register for employment as a condition of receipt of benefit. There is in any case a benefit penalty if they fail to attend an annual compulsory interview to discuss future employment prospects. Under the Pensions Act 1975 women (and men) who were out of the labour market because of their caring responsibilities had their future entitlement to state pensions protected. In the proposed new Carers Pension, these claims will only be protected while they have a child of *pre*-school age. These are examples of where claims on resources are being linked more firmly to time spent *in* the labour market.

Time spent on certain activities gives us claims on resources; but how much – if any – will depend not only on what these activities are but where they take place and who does them? Many activities that attract resources are conventionally called 'work'. However, as Peattie and Rein argued, in their study of how women's claims for resources on family, employment and the state have changed in the past 150 years:

> It is possible to treat 'work' itself as part of that body of social conventions which Polanyi saw as the construction of a new social reality. In this extended view 'work' is no more self-evidently a claim on consumption than any other: the concepts of 'work' and 'wage' may be seen as social conventions which, rather arbitrarily, put some institutionally determined claims on consumption into a special status. (1983, p 20)

What we conventionally call 'working lives' are getting shorter as young people stay in education longer, older people retire earlier and life expectancy has increased. The pension entitlement of different cohorts of old people can vary quite considerably depending on the length of their working life, experience of unemployment as well as their level of earnings. Heavier reliance on money purchase schemes means that in future a woman's pension will be affected by the timing of motherhood. Those who delay having a child into their 30s will have time to build up a pension fund maturing over a longer period than those who have children in their early 20s and therefore start contributing later. The state earnings-related pension (SERPS) was originally based on the best 20 years earnings, thereby removing the disadvantages of a period of part-time or low-paid employment. Since 1988, SERPS has been calculated on the whole of one's working life. The mechanisms for distributing earnings and resources over an individual's lifetime are changing along with the mechanisms for redistributing resources between the generations discussed above. Young people must be more willing to take responsibility for their future wellbeing – by taking out loans to acquire education and saving early for old age. Despite the significant research on student debt, more could be done on young people's attitudes towards savings, as well as investments in their future welfare, and what shapes their time horizons. An emphasis on short-termism is not conducive to making long-term plans, although that is what social policy makers expect. It would appear that the current policy framework is in danger of going against the grain of everyday life.

As the 'working life' is shortening, working days and weeks are lengthening. There is a greater coincidence of *both* parents working their *longest* hours at the point at which they have responsibility for young children. In Britain, this is not a new phenomenon for fathers. However, over the past ten years the biggest increase in full-time employment rates has been among mothers of pre-school children. (Full-time employment rates for mothers of school-age children have remained almost constant throughout the postwar period.) An analysis of the 1998 Labour Force Survey (Harkness, 1999) found that fathers were working on average 47 hours per week (two hours more than a decade ago) and a third were working over 50 hours a week (compared with a quarter a decade ago). Among mothers, the change has been more dramatic, for although mothers are more likely than women without children to be working part-time than full-time, 7% work more than 50 hours (compared with 3% a decade ago) and the proportion working more than 40 hours has increased from 19% to 33%. Much of this increase is due to an increase in working overtime, which, in the case of women, is unpaid:

> Ten years ago women worked little overtime compared to men, but by 1998 while women were as likely as men to be working overtime it was much more likely to be unpaid. (Harkness, 1999, p 107)

This is because women full-time workers are now found in occupations which Lewis Coser (1974) described as "greedy institutions" – notably the professions. When mothers of schoolchildren worked full-time in the 1950s (the proportion fell subsequently and it was not until the mid-1990s that the proportion reached 1950s levels once again), they were more likely to be working-class women employed in traditional occupations such as clothing and textiles. The hours were predictable and fixed and there was a tradition of sharing childcare within the family and neighbourhood. Moreover they worked close to home. In the 1960s over half of all married women in employment worked within a ten-minute journey from home. Nowadays, the average journey to work is nearly half an hour *plus* the majority of primary-school children have to be escorted to school. In other words, family lives and working lives are increasingly dislocated (literally), and synchronising the two is becoming harder. There is much discussion about family-friendly social and employment policies, but much more fundamental changes are necessary, certainly beyond introducing parental leave and a childcare tax credit. At the same time, one in five children in Britain are growing up in workless households: the highest rate in OECD countries (Gregg et al, 1999). Labour market studies and studies of family life need to be developed *together* and the patterns and rhythms of time studied in relationship to each other. Only then can policies which take account of their findings be devised.

On a theoretical level, there is scope for refining and developing the perspective of time, building, for example, on the concept of the life-course first developed by the historian Tamara Hareven (1978). Using the concepts of 'individual time' (the timing of transitions into marriage, parenthood or retirement, for example) and 'family time' (the ways in which the individual timetables of members of a family group are woven together in order to keep the family unit viable), Hareven examined how the alignment of 'individual' and 'family' time has changed over historical time. She concluded that the economic circumstances in the 20th century have made this alignment less necessary. Janet Finch (1989) has argued that this does not mean it has become unnecessary. Moreover, the idea of normative timetables:

> ... helps us to generate some interesting empirical questions about contemporary family obligations. Do people still feel under any pressure to schedule their own life changes with reference to the needs of their kin; if so, which kin? Under what conditions does this happen or conversely become irrelevant? Do women feel under more pressure than men to bring their own individual time into line with family time? Also there are important issues about how much this varies for different ethnic and cultural groups. (Finch, 1989, p 176)

Jane Lewis' research with Jessica Datta and Sophie Sarre for the Lord Chancellor's Department, *Individualism and commitment in marriage and cohabitation* (1999), shows how the issues of time allocation and individual time were more important for younger couples than older couples. Moreover, these issues required negotiation and "it was the process of negotiation that was difficult and often brought tensions to the relationship, *more in relation to time than money*" (1999, p 89, emphasis added). Overall the women wanted both the chance to develop individually and to invest time in relationships with other family members, but their behaviour had changed less than what Lewis calls their 'mentalities'. Women still saw themselves as mother-workers whereas the men were worker-fathers and the division of labour within the home was still unequal. However, it was with respect to an *awareness* of the tensions between investment in own time and in other related activities, tensions which made communication important that most distinguished the younger generation from the older generation and particularly men from their fathers (Lewis et al, 1999, p 59). The picture describing the older couples was much closer to that revealed by Elizabeth Roberts' oral histories of working-class women in the early and mid-20th century. They upheld a set of mores which were clearly understood but rarely discussed: "They saw little distinction between their own good and that of their families" (Roberts, 1994, p 203).

This movement towards a new culture of time, and the changing understanding of time between the generations as well as between men and women is also affected by household structures and the timing of transitions from the parental household to a different household. As more young people leave the parental home earlier and establish non-familial households, pressures to conform to family norms about the 'proper time' for childbearing and marriage, for example, may be changing, although these pressures may be overshadowed by economic considerations. As Gershuny shows using data from the British Household Panel Survey:

> The rate of co-residence of 16-25 year olds with friends or other adults trebled over the last quarter century, and grew sixfold for those aged 26-35. Just one fifth of all adults below the age of 36 now live in this form of household. (Gershuny, 2000)

It is to early to tell what impact this and the growing incidence of living alone will have on patterns of reciprocity over time and between generations within families. Gershuny is surprised that unemployment encourages movement away from the family home, but for the last 15 years Britain has had a housing benefit system which *penalises* co-residence if parents or adult children are unemployed and encourages co-residence with non-kin, particularly for the under-25-year-olds. Therefore traditional familial strategies for saving on housing costs during times of poverty have been undermined by social policies in Britain.

Currently there are significant differences between Japan and Britain with respect to the proportions of young people and older people who are co-resident with their families (Table 1.1). These changes in household composition also make the study of poverty and its *dynamics* much more complex:

> The individuals who make the economic decisions on employment and earnings are being continuously sorted into different household groups .... The aggregate poverty rate for a group of individuals depends on the earnings available to the group, and how the group organises itself into households. The central components are labour market factors such as labour supply and earnings generation, household formation and dissolution processes such as marriage, divorce and fertility. These are the economic processes that constitute the poverty transition process and on which future research will need to focus. (Burgess and Propper, 1999, p 274)

There is a growing interest in the dynamics of poverty both by policy makers as well as researchers.

Table 1.1: The intensity of family welfare provision

	% aged living with children (mid-1980s)	Unemployed youth living with parents as a share of total (1991-93)	Weekly unpaid hours, women (1985-90)
Liberal regimes			
Canada	–	27	32.8
UK	16	35	30.0
US	15	28	31.9
Social democratic regimes			
Denmark	4	8	24.6
Norway	11	–	31.6
Sweden	5	–	34.2
Continental Europe			
France	20	42[a]	36.0[a]
Germany	14	11	35.0
Netherlands	8	28	38.7
Southern Europe			
Italy	39	81	45.4
Spain	37	63	45.8
Japan	65	–	33.1

[a] Estimated average from INSEE (1990, Figure 1).

Source: Esping-Andersen (2000, p 63, Table 4.3)

Table 1.2: A summary overview of regime characteristics

	Liberal	Social democratic	Conservative
Role of			
Family	Marginal	Marginal	Central
Market	Central	Marginal	Marginal
State	Marginal	Central	Subsidiary
Welfare state			
Dominant mode of solidarity	Individual	Universal	Kinship Corporatism Etatism
Dominant locus of solidarity	Market	State	Family
Degree of decommodification	Minimal	Maximum	High (for breadwinner)
Modal examples	US	Sweden	Germany Italy

Source: Esping-Andersen (2000, p 85, Table 5.4)

Conclusion

In his latest book, *The social foundation of postindustrial economics* (1999), Esping-Andersen takes the family rather more seriously than in his first, *The three worlds of welfare capitalism* (1990). He summarises the characteristics of the three regimes identified in his first book in relation to the role of family, market and state as well as the dominant sources of solidarity (Table 1.2).

Esping-Andersen concludes that a social democratic regime has relatively flexible labour markets, but even when the labour market is in turmoil, it maintains a strong social security and welfare programme. The conservative regime attempts to minimise labour market turmoil and the responsibility for welfare is placed on families rather than the state. The liberal regime is characterised by failing families combined with a scaled back welfare state which does not ensure security (Esping-Andersen, 2000, p 142). While acknowledging that Japan does not 'fit' one of the three regimes which were based on an analysis of the experience of Western industrialised welfare states (see Goodman and Peng, 1996, for a full discussion of a distinctively Asian welfare regime), Esping-Andersen suggests that Britain has less market regulation than Japan, and Japan has a familialist regime compared with Britain's non-familialist regime. He includes Japan among the social insurance based welfare regimes and Britain with a mix of residual and universalist services. He identifies as a key question, "how to maximise, or at least to maintain existing standards of equality and social citizenship while, simultaneously, generate more jobs and less exclusion" (1999, p 168). This means looking at the welfare state not just in terms of its coverage but how successful it is in sustaining "well-functioning, welfare-producing labour markets and families" (1999, p 168). To do this – as Titmuss wrote over 30 years ago – "we can no longer consider welfare systems solely within the limited framework of the nation state" (Titmuss, 1968, p 127).

References

Beveridge, W. (1909) *Unemployment: A problem of industry*, Harlow: Longmans Green and Co.

Blair, A. (1996) 'Towards a welfare state in a stakeholder's society', *Fabian Review*, vol 108, no 1, pp 1-4.

Bosanquet, H. (1915) *The family*, Basingstoke: Macmillan.

Burgess, S. and Propper, C. (1999) 'Poverty in Britain', in P. Gregg and M. Wadsworth (eds) *The state of working Britain*, Manchester: Manchester University Press, pp 259-75.

Coser, L. (1974) *Greedy institutions*, London: Unwin.

DSS (Department of Social Security) (2000) *Report on the contributory principle*, reply by the Government to the Fifth Report of the Select Committee on Social Security, 1999-2000 HC 56.

Esping-Andersen, G. (1990) *Three worlds of welfare capitalism*, Cambridge: Polity Press.

Esping-Andersen, G. (ed) (1996) *Welfare states in transition*, London: Sage Publications.

Esping-Andersen, G. (2000) *Social foundations of postindustrial economics*, Oxford: Oxford University Press.

Field, F. (1995) *Making welfare work: Reconstructing welfare for the millennium*, London: Institute of Community Studies.

Finch, J. (1989) *Family change and family obligations*, Cambridge: Polity Press.

Gershuny, J. (2000) *Household and family structure: Issues for the future*, Swindon: ESRC.

Goodman, R. and Peng, I. (1996) 'The East Asian welfare states: peripatetic learning, adaptive change and nation building', in G. Esping-Andersen (ed) *Welfare states in transition*, London: Sage Publications, pp 192-224.

Gregg, P., Hansen, E. and Wadsworth, M. (1999) 'The rise of the workless household', in P. Gregg and M. Wadsworth (eds) *The state of working Britain*, Manchester: Manchester University Press, pp 75-89.

Hareven, T.K. (ed) (1978) *Transitions: The family and the life course in historical perspective*, London: Academic Press.

Harkness, S. (1999) 'Working 9-5?', in P. Gregg and M. Wadsworth (eds) *The state of working Britain*, Manchester: Manchester University Press, pp 90-108.

Land, H. (1976) 'The child benefit fiasco', in K. Jones (ed) *Yearbook of social policy 1976*, London and New York: Routledge, pp 116-31.

Land, H. (1999) 'New Labour, new families?', *Social Policy Review*, no 11, Social Policy Association, pp 127-44.

Lewis, J. (1997) 'Gender and welfare regimes: further thoughts', *Social Politics*, vol 4, no 2, Summer, pp 160-77.

Lewis, J. with Datta, J. and Sarre, S. (1999) *Individualism and commitment in marriage and cohabitation*, London: Lord Chancellor's Department.

Marris, P. (1996) *The politics of uncertainty*, London and New York: Routledge.

Peattie, L. and Rein, M. (1983) *Women's claims: A study in political economy*, Oxford: Oxford University Press.

Rathbone, E. (1924) *The disinherited family*, London: Unwin.

Roberts, E. (1994) *A woman's place*, Oxford: Blackwell.

Royal Commission on Long-Term Care (1999) *With respect to old age*, Cm 4192, London: The Stationery Office.

Scase, R. (1998) *Britain towards 2010*, Swindon: ESRC.

Sennett, R. (1999) *The corrosion of character*, Cambridge: Polity Press.

Supplementary Benefit Commission (1980) *Annual Report for 1979*, Cmnd 8033, London: HMSO.

Titmuss, R.M. (1958) *Essays on the welfare state*, Allen & Unwin.

Titmuss, R.M. (1968) *Commitment to welfare*, London: Allen & Unwin.

Webb, A. (1975) 'The abolition of national assistance', in P. Hall, H. Land, R. Parker and A. Webb (eds) *Change, choice and conflict in social policy*, London: Heinemann, pp 410-71.

Wells, H.G. (1911) *The new Machiavelli*, Basingstoke: Macmillan.

TWO

Development of social policy in Japan

Kingo Tamai

Introduction

Japan has a long history of social policy making, dating back to the end of the 19th century. *Shakai seisaku gakkai* – the Japanese Association of Social Policy – was established for social policy research as early as 1897 after Japanese scholars had studied foreign social policies (Tamai, 1997). Since its earliest days, *Shakai seisaku gakkai* has been holding conferences and publishing its findings. These materials are indeed valuable, enabling us to document the upsurge in discussion and debate on the development of social policy in the early part of the 20th century.

The activities of the association in its early years significantly influenced developing ideas towards social policy. In Western societies, such as Britain and Germany, the nature of social policy had already begun to shift from poverty relief to poverty prevention (Thane, 1996). Although policies and practices to *relieve* poverty were not yet developed fully in Japan at that time, Japanese society enthusiastically pursued ideas of *poverty prevention* by adapting it to the Japanese model of welfare provision (Tamai, 1992). This Japanese model had two major characteristics:

- to strengthen the role and function of the family and communities in order to prevent poverty;
- the important role of individual companies.

In this context, the role of the state had been developed not to replace the existing functions of the family and companies, but to build upon and enclose existing resources within the state umbrella (Tamai, 2001). Social insurance schemes are a case in point, and a point that this chapter explores in detail.

The development process of social policy in the period immediately following the Second World War was again influenced by Western forces, mainly due to the US occupation, which resulted in the introduction of new schemes to enhance social rights among employees and Japanese people in general. Regardless of the strong foreign influence, however, the core of social policy has remained stubbornly unchanged following the pre-war ideal of the Japanese model.

A century has now passed since the dawn of social policy making. At the beginning of the new millennium, Japan is now facing new problems with the breakdown of the pre-existing welfare provided by the family, the community, and companies. The current recession, as well as the structural problems in the Japanese economy and society, has focused attention once more on the debate of establishing a 'social safety net system' appropriate to the 21st century (see, for example, Tachibanaki, 2000). Such debate, however, tends to be carried out without considering the complexity of the Japanese model of welfare provision. Therefore, it is worthwhile re-examining the historical structure of the Japanese welfare system.

This chapter examines the history of social policy making, focusing on the development of the social insurance schemes. The analysis focuses on four rough chronological periods: the pre-war period; the 1940s to 1950s; the 1960s to the 1980s; and the 1990s to the present.

Historical perspectives

The pre-war period

In the pre-war period, and in the 1920s in particular, company welfare systems adopted by large corporations to maintain their industrial relations spread very quickly throughout Japan. It was, however, only large corporations such as Kanegafuchi Spinning Company and Tokyo Spinning Company that established the 'Japanese-style industrial relations' with the provision of occupational welfare. Conversely, trade union-based welfare systems were never developed in Japan to the same extent as in other developed nations. This was not only because the central government suppressed the activities of trade unions, but also because most of the working-class population was earning such a low income that they could not afford to contribute to the schemes. Although a workers' organisation for mutual assistance, *Yuaikai*, was established in 1912, similar to a British friendly society, it was not successful due to political divisions and fierce oppression by the central government.

A series of social insurance schemes were established throughout the chronological periods studied in this chapter. At the national level, the Health Insurance Act, which mainly covered manual workers, was enacted as the first social insurance measure in 1922. It was followed by the National Health Insurance Act in 1938, covering mainly farmers and the self-employed. In addition, in 1931 the Industrial Injury Assistance Act was enacted, covering unemployed casual labourers working mainly in construction sites. In 1940, social insurance for seamen was established and it was in 1941 that the first Pension Act for employees was enacted. However, there was no unemployment insurance in the pre-war period since the principle of 'self-help' was still dominant in Japanese society, and there was still an option for many of those who lost their jobs to return to agricultural areas to do farm-related work. In terms of public assistance, on the other hand, the first regulation for relief, *Jukkyu Kisoku*, was enacted in 1874 but with little effect. In fact, it was only 1929 when *Kyugo ho* (Public Assistance Act) was introduced to replace the regulation with more comprehensive measures. At this time, social policy and practices were becoming formalised at both regional and local levels. In cities, in particular, social reform activities, and facilities for the protection and welfare of employees such as job centres, nurseries, and small retail shops (pawnshops, and so on), began operating. Overall, although various social insurance and public assistance schemes were developed in the pre-war period, these were not comprehensive in terms of their coverage and level of benefit.

The early period of social security systems was often viewed as insufficient, traditional, and 'pre-modern' compared with those developed in other advanced countries. In fact, Japan was not the only society whose schemes were underdeveloped: the early history of social security in most advanced countries is often less than admirable. Nevertheless, it is important to remember that the core of the Japanese model, which was far from 'pre-modern', remained even in the postwar development of the country's welfare schemes.

In the period immediately following the Second World War, the proportion of farmers in the working population was still very high at over 50%. It was therefore crucial for the Japanese government to take the farmers position into account in developing new social security systems. This industrial structure is perhaps one of the major differences between Japan and Britain when comparing the development process of the welfare system. In Japan, there was a significant amount of debate over how to develop the system of both national health insurance and pension schemes particularly for farmers and the self-employed. Indeed, the issue of those engaged in the agricultural industry significantly influenced the creation of the Japanese-style social insurance system. In such farming communities, mutual help among family and community members remained strong. Therefore, the development of the public system was required to take such existing resources into account. Although Japan adapted some ideas from both the 1942 Beveridge Report and the New Deal policy of the US in general, the Japanese government seemed to have retained the Japanese model when it came to the details (Kondo, 1963a).

The development of postwar welfare systems (from the 1940s to the 1950s)

Following the publication of the 1942 Beveridge Report, *Shakai Hosho Seido Shingi-kai* – the Advisory Council for Social Security – was established in 1949. In October 1950, the advisory council published a recommendation for a social security system – *goju-nen kankoku* – addressing issues of:

- social insurance;
- national assistance;
- public health and medical care;
- social welfare;
- administration and finance (Kondo and Yoshida, 1950).

The introduction consisted of three main items:

1. Since there were a great number of causes of poverty among Japanese people, the state should provide various measures for the welfare of the nation. However, the state should not undermine the self-help nature of the nation. In this sense, the primary means of social security should be a social insurance system based on contributions;
2. In the unusual conditions of the period immediately after the Second World War there were a great number of people below the poverty line who could not be catered for through the insurance system. Hence, the state should directly assist them and secure their national minimum. Indeed, this measure is considered the last resort. Therefore, the national assistance system should be subordinate to the social insurance system, as the latter was extended; and
3. The social security system was however not to operate only through the above measures. The state should provide the administration and facilities for the public health service, which will in turn promote national health. In addition, the administration of social welfare should be extended to maintain the standard of living. (Shakai Hosho Kenkyu Sho, 1975, pp 189-90)

The introduction emphasised four pillars of the social security system: social insurance, national assistance, public health, and social welfare. Consequently, this plan was considered very similar to the Beveridge Report. In fact, some commissioners of the advisory council argued the merit of putting more emphasis on developing *national assistance* rather than solely focusing on social insurance. As a result, the advisory council had to reconcile two views of the social security system. After a long debate, a majority of members of the advisory council agreed to adapt the Beveridge approach of social insurance rather than the residual approach of the US. In particular, Bunji Kondo, Professor at Osaka City University, was very active in drawing up a plan and repeatedly stressed the importance of social insurance to the advisory council. Being an expert in social insurance, he was very aware of the many advantages that Japanese people would enjoy from an entitlement to benefit. In this respect, his view was similar to that of Beveridge, and he subsequently became known as the 'Japanese Beveridge' (Tamai, 1987).

Kondo drew up the recommendation document almost entirely by himself. It is, however, important to note that he did not immediately adopt the assumptions about social security, emphasised by Beveridge. In particular, he rejected the ideas of a universal national health service and family allowance. He was probably aware of the difficulty in implementing the schemes under the tight fiscal conditions of the period. Instead, his recommendation adopted the minimum wage system as one of its assumptions.

The advisory council stressed that although his recommendation was far from the ideal plan that the central government should adopt, it should nevertheless be enforced as soon as possible. Despite the strong recommendation by the council, the government completely rejected it. The political instability surrounding the Korean War in the 1950s appeared to be the main reason preventing the decision. Indeed, the advisory council fiercely criticised the attitude of the central government for not taking it forward. In Britain in 1951, Aneurin Bevan resigned as Minister of Labour. Although in the case of Britain this meant only a small retreat from the existing social security system, the rejection by the central government was a major setback in Japan. It was not until 1961 that Japan began to establish a comprehensive social security system in line with the earlier recommendations.

Regarding the national health insurance and pension schemes, Kondo divided the nation into two main categories: employees, and farmers/self-employed. In the development of public pension schemes, his view was that, although insurance for the whole nation would be established, insurance for employees ought to be extended and integrated in the future. On the other hand, however, he stressed that the temporary non-contributory pension system for farmers and the self-employed should be introduced only if the fiscal budget would permit it. It is notable that a non-contributory pension system was recommended for this group of workers, although it was temporary. Since farmers and the self-employed tended to be in poverty and therefore often unable to contribute anything at all, the idea of a non-contributory pension scheme was indeed radical. These plans were not enacted, however, partly due to the tight fiscal conditions that Japan faced during the period. The gap between idea and reality was significant.

The function of the family was one of the legacies of this era. For example, in the case of farmers, children (and the eldest sons in particular) used to inherit the property intact from their parents and became heads of the household once they had grown up. Such a family system was one of the characteristics of Japanese society. Since ageing parents were expected to reside with their son (and grandsons) and his family for life, the institution of the family largely substituted state social security.

In addition, there was another institution − company welfare. Since some workers in large corporations were covered by company welfare in the pre-war period, those workers were able to receive benefits from both the state and their companies. Company welfare was often substituted for state welfare, however, and became compulsory for some workers to contribute. Therefore, after the end of the Second World War it was impossible to ignore the established roles that the family and companies had been playing. The development of postwar social security systems, however, stressed that state welfare was the most essential. Therefore, it was difficult to establish the effective balance of welfare among the state, the family, and private companies.

From the 1960s to the 1980s

In 1961, Japanese social policy reached a decisive turning point: the central government established a new social security system – national health insurance and pension schemes. The progress of social security development resulted in the extension of the schemes, which, in 1961, granted coverage for farmers and self-employed workers. Eligibility for the new system was now based on residency in local government jurisdictions, which were also administering the schemes. Since the percentage of farmers was almost half the total working population in the 1950s, this shift was inevitable. In fact, among those who were supposed to be covered by the local-based insurance scheme, some could not contribute to the scheme and were consequently not covered by the scheme. For a long time, these people managed to live without public welfare provision due to the support provided by their families and the community.

Certainly, the establishment of the 1961 system made a significant contribution to Japanese social security since all Japanese people were finally covered under the social insurance schemes. Yet it was also true that the establishment of the 1961 system was not a radical reform, since social insurance covering employees and civil servants had existed since the pre-war period. Indeed, the 1961 reform did not have any effect on these groups of workers. In other words, instead of having a universal scheme for all, two parallel insurance schemes were then in operation: one for employees and civil servants (an occupational-based scheme), and the other for farmers and the self-employed (a local-based scheme) (Kondo, 1963b).

Moreover, the 1960s were well known as a period of high economic growth in Japan. Japan experienced dramatic social and economic changes, especially between 1955 and 1973. Within ten years of the earlier legislation, in order to respond to new problems facing those just above the poverty line, a new division needed to be created. In 1962, the Advisory Council of Social Security published a new recommendation and pointed out several emerging issues. This time, the council suggested that Japan be divided into three income groups: middle-income, lower-income (those in or just above the poverty line), and poor-income groups (those below the poverty line), as opposed to the two previous categories of 'employees' and 'others' as suggested in the 1950 recommendation. In particular, the emergence of the lower-income group was a phenomenon, which the council had to refer to. The 1962 recommendation, therefore, emphasised the significance of social welfare work to deal with the problems in this particular group of low-income earners.

Furthermore, the advisory council argued the necessity of cross-subsidisation in social insurance schemes, in particular in health insurance in its 1962 recommendation. This was related to the fact that once again there existed two health insurance systems in Japan: an occupational-based scheme, and a local-based scheme, as was mentioned earlier. In the 1960s, however, the fiscal gap between the two insurance systems had widened. On the other hand, the rapid economic growth in this period undermined the need to adopt the 1962 recommendation. The government thought that the rapid economic growth would produce sufficient fiscal resources and gradually reduce the gap between the two schemes. Despite the suggestion, the integration of the two social insurance schemes hardly progressed during the 1960s.

The year 1973 marked a further watershed in the history of social security provision, since the central government enacted significant reforms in both health insurance and pension schemes. Certainly, it raised the level of both its benefits and services. However, no action had yet been taken to integrate the two systems. It was also a dramatic turning point in the Japanese economy as the rapid economic growth was approaching its end. In the meantime, the state welfare system had been extended between 1961 and 1973, while family and community welfare had weakened. Despite the very important role played by company welfare, the trend shifted towards the lesser expenditure of company welfare schemes.

In terms of demographic changes, 1970 was another significant year: Japan met the UN definition of an 'ageing' society (7% of the total population comprised of people aged 65 years and older). Despite the fact that the Welfare Act for Older People was enacted in 1963, the measures had not necessarily been sufficient. The 'arrival' of an ageing society aroused national interest in state welfare for older people, in particular in the areas of health/medical care and pensions. These factors influenced the 1973 reform on health and pension insurance. After the 1973 reform was enacted, however, rapid economic growth slowed down, preventing the government from further increasing fiscal resources for state welfare for older people. In addition, we should bear in mind that the rapid economic growth drastically changed the industrial and employment structure of the country – for instance, the proportion of farmers in the total working population rapidly decreased to a figure below 20%.

In this context, the central government of the 1970s realised the need to drastically reform social security. Above all, locally based health insurance (predominantly covering farmers and the self-employed) and national pensions began to pose serious fiscal problems. The national health insurance covered not only farmers and the self-employed, but also the increasing number of older people who were retired. This meant that most of the older people depended on this scheme for their medical care services. The central government came to enact the new Health Act for Older People in 1982 in order for the national health insurance system to escape the fiscal crisis of the 1970s.

A similar crisis occurred in the national pension system. Costs and benefits in the national pension scheme had been out of balance from the start of the scheme. In particular, some farmers and self-employed people were often unable to make regular contributions to the scheme, since they were on low incomes. Moreover, the end of the rapid economic growth prevented an increase in pension resources. From the 1970s onwards, the number of beneficiaries of pensions increased, while that of contributors decreased. The national pension fund peaked in 1983, after which it declined in monetary terms. In 1985, the central government adopted a new act regarding the provision of public pensions in order to avoid a fiscal crisis in the national pension system. It was therefore inevitable that Japan had gone through two important reforms in social insurance in the 1980s.

Common to reforms in both national health insurance and national pensions were measures of introducing cross-subsidisation, a type of income transfer. In order to save the national health insurance system for the self-employed, the health insurance system for employees was required to transfer additional resources to care for older people. This allowed a reduction of the burden of contributions on individuals in the national health insurance system. In those days, health insurance for employees could afford to contribute more, but in recent years the health insurance fund has faced a serious fiscal crisis due to a rapid increase in payments for older people. After the health insurance fund had supported national health insurance for two decades, the system is now on the verge of breaking down.

As for the national pensions system, the 1985 reform was remarkable among postwar public pensions, and provides a good example of the Japanese model of welfare – the public system built upon including other sector provisions. Consequently, the two systems that had previously run parallel to one another were merged into a two-tiered system. The first tier consisted of *Kokumin kiso nenkin*, basic pensions for all Japanese people (flat-rate contribution and benefits). The second tier was made up of *Kosei nenkin*, the occupational component with contributions based on incomes. Many people appreciated the new system, since it finally established the basic pension benefit for all. To support the national pension fund, however, other pension funds were required to make additional contributions. In particular, thanks to *kosei nenkin*, which suffered from heavy fiscal burdens, the national pension fund was able to escape from an acute fiscal crisis. Since the 1990s, however, the national pension fund is facing a new fiscal crisis partly due to the contributions sabotaged by young people despite the mandatory contribution for all Japanese nationals aged 20 years and over. Some young people either cannot afford to pay their contributions because of their student or unemployed status or are unwilling to do so due to strong doubts about the viability of the future public pension system.

The 1990s to the present

In order to ascertain the characteristics of the development of social policy in Japan, it is necessary to scrutinise employment policy. In the early 1980s, for instance, the central government began to implement employment policies, especially for older workers. In 1983, the Fifth Basic Employment Plan built in some important measures for older workers, including the setting of the retirement age at 60 with provision for moratorium periods up to age 65 (for example, for an extension of contract, or re-employment schemes). The new provisions took effect in 1986. The retirement age was originally set at 55 following the Second World War; however, during the 1980s it had been shifted rapidly upwards until it was finally set at 60 in the 1990s. The main policy of the central government was therefore supporting people to remain employed until the age of 65. This approach seems to reflect factors such as the strong work ethos of older workers, the pensionable age, which is related to the rapid ageing of the population, and the shortage of young workers. Many older workers hope to continue working as long as possible, well into their old age. To illustrate this point, according to an opinion survey conducted by the Management and Coordination Agency in 1998, 30% of older respondents expressed their wishes to work well into their 70s. A new law in 1994 started the increase of the pensionable age from 60 to 65. This change is to be phased in over a 12-year period from 2001 to 2013 for male workers and from 2006 to 2018 for female workers. It is clear that the central government is eager to combine increased employment among older workers by rising their retirement age.

In addition, the central government forecasted that the number of young workers would begin to decline in the first decade of the 21st century. Therefore, older workers were expected to take their places in the workforce. We should bear in mind these factors in discussing employment policies for older workers. In 1997, the central government proposed a new plan for the employment of workers over the age of 60, including the establishment of a retirement age at 65 and the concept of an 'ageless' society – enabling people to be active in society regardless of age. In particular, the central government regarded the former as more important than the latter. It is difficult however to establish the retirement age at 65 in a short period, considering the fact that it had taken approximately 30 years to shift the retirement age from 55 to 60. Moreover, associations of large corporate employers rejected the government's proposal, instead proposing a more flexible retirement age.

Another notable factor in employment is the working conditions since the 1980s, especially with the growth of part-time work. Those who are engaged in part-time work are primarily women. The typical pattern of women's employment is to leave jobs following marriage and to re-enter the labour market after finishing childrearing. Since women's working conditions tended to be poor, the central government established the first set of guidelines for part-time work in 1984 (and revised in 1989). The guidelines helped to improve working conditions for part-time workers to some extent. In the 1990s, the proportion of part-time workers in the labour force grew faster than in the 1980s, rising from approximately 10% in 1980 to over 21% in 1997 (Management and Coordination Agency, 1980, 1997). In addition, the range of part-time jobs steadily diversified. Some part-time workers, for example, require high skill levels, such as in the IT industry and supervisory positions in the service industry. One establishment exists, where all employees are working part-time. Clearly, part-time workers now play a very important role in the Japanese economy.

However, serious problems regarding the growth of part-time work go hand-in-hand with the social security system. For example, the particular work schedule of part-time workers usually determines whether or not they are eligible for social insurance. The standard qualification is that they should work at least three quarters of the hours of regular workers. Therefore, this rule divides part-time workers into two groups: those who qualify for *company-based* social insurance benefits, and those who do not. In 1995, 35.8% of part-time workers were covered by *company-based* pension and health insurance schemes and the same percentage of those were also covered by employment insurance (Ministry of Labour, 1995). The proportion of part-time workers in the workforce is expected to grow continuously in the 21st century. It is highly likely that there will be households in which each person in a couple will be engaged in part-time work. The central government established a new law based on previous codes of guidance to govern part-time work in 1993. Although it may have reduced the disparity between part-time and full-time workers to some extent, it certainly did not meet the needs of workers in terms of wages, working conditions, and welfare benefits. Indeed, in recent years, many employers prefer to employ part-time workers instead of regular (full-time) employees in order to cut labour costs. Since this tendency is expected to continue, there is an increasing need for the central government to take immediate action to establish basic labour standards for part-time workers.

Once Japan's 'bubble economy' burst, the country spent the 1990s in a severe recession. Many large corporations dismissed employees in the process of restructuring. Such industrial restructuring primarily affected middle-aged and older workers, partly due to the large number of excess workers in this age group and also the higher salary and welfare burdens which older workers posed under the Japanese seniority system. Although Japan had maintained a unique employment system in the postwar period, even the lifelong employment system is now threatened (see, for example, Saguchi, 2001). The 1990s have indeed brought a turning point in Japanese industrial relations. The extreme case of casual labour symbolised in day labourers is often found in major cities in Japan. In particular, Osaka has the largest labour market for day labourers. Largely due to the current recession, the growing numbers of people who are unemployed are further increasing the numbers of the homeless population in Osaka, which have reportedly grown by approximately 10,000 people in 2001 (Iwata, 2000; Chapter Ten of this volume).

Furthermore, the unemployment rate in Japan has increased to over 5% (December 2001), and is currently headed towards 6%. The central government now proposes emergency employment measures, which include the provision of new training schemes and subsidies to local governments. It has also established a new Unemployment Insurance Act that has reformed the duration of jobless benefits. For instance, the new system differentiates the level of benefits between those who left a job voluntarily and those who were made redundant. It is easy to blame factors such as globalisation, the overseas transfer of manufacturing, and the IT revolution that have contributed to the recession; however, domestic factors, such as the number of bad debts in the Japanese economy, contribute to the problem.

Conclusion

The family and companies have played very important roles in welfare provision in the pre-war period in Japan. Although the state began to replace some of their functions after the end of the Second World War, it was impossible for it to ignore the roles of both the family and companies in establishing a new system of social security. The fact that the central government has taken into account the functions of the family and companies in developing the new system explains why the Japanese welfare system has become so complex (Tamai, 2001).

The oil crisis of 1973 drastically changed conditions in Europe, bringing pervasive economic stagflation and high unemployment rates. It is evident that many European countries began to tackle the establishment of the new welfare state after the 1970s. In Britain, the Conservative Party defeated the Labour government in the 1979 general election, and Margaret Thatcher, upon becoming Prime Minister, criticised the extension of the public sector and the increased social security burden, and pursued strongly market-oriented principles. She hoped to construct a new welfare state and revive the British economy. Other European countries also tried to overcome economic and social issues and thereby lay the foundations of a new welfare state. During the 1980s, the major European countries, including Britain, France and Italy, experienced high unemployment rates, and the rapid ageing of society. Therefore, both employment and social security measures were inevitably given high priority. It goes without saying that each country had to seek new measures to reinforce old structures – the introduction of career counselling, reforming job training, and so on. Indeed, the 1980s were an important turning point towards the foundation of the new European welfare state.

Japan faced similar problems during these periods. However, without making any drastic changes, the *Japanese model* of welfare provision survived. The characteristics of the Japanese model lies on the fact that family and company welfare was built within the state umbrella. The complexity of interdependency and the nature of coexistence made reform difficult to carry out (Tamai, 2001).

Since the 1990s, and with the current prolonged economic recession, Japanese social policy has entered its third stage. The functions of the family and companies, which made up the core of the Japanese model of welfare provisions, have significantly weakened. As for the family, the model based on the male family breadwinner and full-time housewife has been changing with increasing rates of labour participation among married women (Nakagawa, 2000). The current recession has indeed resulted in a number of closures, bankruptcies and mergers of companies, which again considerably weakened the provision of previously defined company welfare schemes. Companies have started replacing full-time workers with part-time workers in order to reduce the cost of salaries and welfare payments. Consequently, the labour market has started to fluctuate more widely. In this context, what measures should the central government take in the field of social policy? It is apparent that it has become increasingly difficult to sustain the Japanese model, which has survived through turmoil in the past. There is no going back to the self-help option. The newly emerged concept of a 'safety net', currently the focus of much debate among scholars, still needs wider and further consideration before it can be introduced into a welfare system suitable for the 21st century.

References

Beveridge, W. (1942) *Social insurance and allied services*, London: HMSO.

Iwata, M. (2000) *Homuresu/gendai shakai/fukusi kokka* [*Homeless people in contemporary Japan*], Tokyo: Akasi Shoten.

Kondo, B. (1950) *Shakai hosho e no kankoku* [*Recommendations for social security*], Tokyo: Shakai Hoken Hoki Kenkyukai.

Kondo, B. (1963a) *Shakai hosho no rekisi* [*The history of social security*], Tokyo: Zensharen Koho Shupanbu.

Kondo, B. (1963b) *Shakai hoken* [*Social insurance*], Tokyo: Iwanami Shoten.

Kondo, B. and Yoshida, H. (1950) *Shakai hosho kankoku no seiritu to kaisetsu* [*Publication and comment on the recommendation of social security*], Tokyo: Shakai Hosho Chosakai.

Management and Coordination Agency (1980, 1997) *Rodo-ryoku chosa* [*Survey of Japanese workforce*], Tokyo: Bureau of Statistics.

Ministry of Labour (1995) *Part-time rodo sha sogo jittai chosa* [*Survey of conditions of part-time workers*], Tokyo: Ministry of Finance Printing Office.

Nakagawa, K. (2000) *Nihon tosi no seikatu hendo* [*History of urban family life in Japan*], Tokyo: Keisou Shobou.

Saguchi, K. (2001) 'Koyo ryudoka ron no rekishi teki imi' ['The current situation of Japanese internal labour markets'], *Shakai-seisaku gakkai shi* [*Journal of Social Policy and Labour Studies*], no 5, pp 17-32.

Shakai Hosho Kenkyu Sho [Social Development Research Institute] (1975) *Nihon shakai hosho shiryo I* [*Historical documents of Japanese social security I*], Tokyo: Shiseido.

Tachibanaki, T. (2000) *Safety net no keizaigaku* [*Economics of a safety net*], Tokyo: Nihon Keizai Shinbun Sha.

Tamai, K. (1987) 'A note on Japanese social security planning: the impact of the Beveridge report and American social security', *The Quarterly Journal of Economic Studies*, vol 9, no 4, pp 25-36.

Tamai, K. (1992) *Bohin no sozo* [*Against poverty*], Kyoto: Keibunsha.

Tamai, K. (1997) 'Shakai seisaku kenkyu no keifu to konnichi-teki kadai' ['History of study of social policy and current issues'], in K. Tamai and M. Ohmori (eds) *Shakai seisaku wo manabu hito no tame ni* [*For those who study social policy*], Kyoto: Sekai Shisou Sha.

Tamai, K. (2001) '20 seiki to fukusi sisutemu' ['Japanese welfare system in the 20th century'], *Shakai-seisaku Gakkai Shi* [*Journal of Social Policy and Labour Studies*], no 5, pp 33-48.

Thane, P. (1996) *Foundations of the welfare state* (2nd edn), London: Longman.

THREE

Ageing and intergenerational relations in Britain

Alan Walker and Kristiina Martimo

Introduction

The main aim of this chapter is to examine the implications of population ageing for relations between the generations. In line with Chapter Four of this volume, our main focus is on intergenerational caring relationships between kin rather than the macro-social contract on which the funding of pensions and health and social care are based. However, a key theme of this chapter is that, what society does by way of social policy has a critical bearing on the nature and experience of generational relations. In other words, a sharp distinction between micro-level interpersonal relations and macro-social and economic policy is misleading. Similarly what Mannheim (1952) called the 'problem of generations' or the popular press call 'generational war' should not be viewed as purely intrinsic qualities of generations in isolation from their social and economic context (Walker, 1996).

With these caveats in mind, this chapter covers three topics. First of all, changing demography and the key policy challenges it raises and, particularly, the implications for care needs. We then discuss the nature of the social contract in Britain and, finally, how and why intergenerational relations are changing.

Policy issues facing an ageing society

As a result of the combination of declining fertility and increasing longevity, Britain is ageing, although the pace of this change differs between regions. Between 1951 and 1991 the numbers aged 65+ increased by 66% while those aged 85+ rose by 300%. Over the next 50 years the proportion of people aged 65+ will rise from nearly 16% to nearly 25%. The most intense rate of growth is among very old people (and 80+) and their numbers will rise by 10% between 2000 and 2005 alone.

Britain shares population ageing with other EU countries and, like them, several regions saw their populations stop growing before the end of the last century. By 2015 this will apply to a majority of regions. Other EU countries are experiencing a more rapid ageing of their populations than Britain. For example, between 2000 and 2005 the increase in numbers aged 80+ will be above 25% in Belgium and France, and almost as much in Italy and Austria. The average increase in the EU will be 18.6%. The Eastern European countries are also experiencing demographic ageing. All of them, except Poland, will see a decline in the total population (and that of working age) before 2010. The EU shares demographic ageing with other world regions; with Japan, however, it has the most pronounced trend over the next 20 years.

It is important not to fall into the demographic trap of thinking that policy is determined by figures such as these. The policy implications of demographic change are *not* just a matter of the absolute numbers in different age groups. First of all it must be remembered that increasing longevity is an indicator of social and economic progress: the triumph of science and public policy over many of the causes of premature death which truncated lives in earlier times. Therefore, we should not bemoan the emergence of more balanced age structures; rather, we should recognise that this unique phenomenon is one of the great achievements of the 20th century. At the same time it presents challenges to policy and practice in all sectors of society. Secondly, there is not a simple linear relationship between demographic change and demand for spending on social protection, still less with the levels of such spending. For example, with regard to health and social care, the level of need for formal (paid) care depends not only on health status but a range of social factors. In Britain, as in all EU countries (though to different degrees of intensity), it is the family that provides the first response to the need for help and support. Therefore, the demand for formal care, public and private, is a function of both health status and family relationships such as marriage patterns, fertility, household composition, and living arrangements. The primary sources of care are unpaid family and friends, including the care provided by older people themselves to their spouses and others.

The number of disability-free years is predicted to increase in this century (Tallis, 1992) but the evidence so far is inconclusive (Bebbington, 1991; Department of Health, 1992; Dunnell, 1995; Wordsworth et al, 1996). Other population trends are more certain. Older people living alone tend to make greater use of formal services than those living with others (partly because of the correlation between advanced old age and living alone) and there is an increasing proportion of both older and younger people living alone (Figure 3.1).

The increase in one-person households since 1961 has been particularly notable. The numbers of one-person households have more than doubled among those over pension ages, and for those under pension ages the numbers have trebled. The most marked growth in living alone has happened among the population aged 75 years and over. In 1973, 24% of men and 48% of women aged 75+ were living alone. By 1994 these figures had risen to 33% of men and 59% of women (Haskey, 1996). There has been a decline in the numbers of women and men living as married partners, and also in the numbers

Figure 3.1: One-person household as percentage of all households (England and Wales)

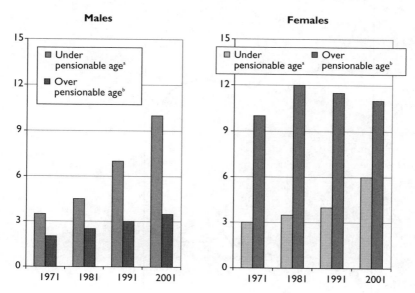

Males   Females

[Bar charts for Males and Females showing percentages from 1971 to 2001, with categories "Under pensionable age[a]" and "Over pensionable age[b]"]

[a] Current pensionable age: 65 for men; 60 for women.

[b] Projections.

Source: DoE (1995)

of cohabiting couples. Often seen as part of the growing numbers of lone parents, this decline can also be attributed to the increasing tendency to live alone or with others, not with the nuclear family.

Also, given the primacy of family care, it is likely that the growth in family breakdown and divorce among both older people and their children will have an impact on the demand for formal care but, again, the evidence is inconclusive (Figure 3.2).

The British divorce rate is the highest in the EU, almost twice the average of other member states. Similarly the increased participation of women in the labour force is likely to have affected the ability of the family to provide care; certainly it has increased the strains experienced by the primary carers – women.

Although more and more older people today have children than in previous generations, family size has declined dramatically over the course of this century. Consequently, the pool of potential family carers has shrunk. Over the next decade or so, however, there will be a slight rise in the number of those aged 45-64, the main age group from which family carers are drawn.

Therefore, the need for paid care is, to a large extent, the outcome of the interaction between health status and family relationships. In certain instances

Figure 3.2: Marriages and divorces in Britain (1971-92)

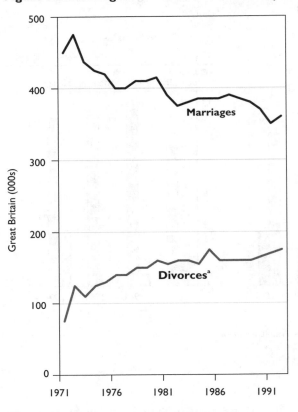

ª Including annulments.

Source: OPCS (1995); General Register Office (Scotland)

there is a more direct connection between health in old age and the demand for formal services, including acute episodes such as stroke and long-term impairment such as dementia. Cognitive impairment is one of the main reasons why older people enter long-term institutional care. The prevalence of moderate or severe cognitive impairment rises steeply with age – from 2.3% in those aged 65-74, to 7.2% in those aged 75-84, and to 21.9% in those aged 85+. Undoubtedly, dementia causes acute problems for family carers, and there is a need for special measures to support the care of this group.

Similar points about the policy implications of demographic change can be made briefly with regard to pensions, since they are beyond the scope of this chapter. Crude age-dependency ratios would suggest increasing tax burdens on the working population. However, that pessimistic scenario rests on the classic economic obfuscation *ceteris paribus* [other things being equal] which freezes present trends regardless of how far into the future the projections are being made. In fact, the main issue for pension funding is not population ageing per se, but its combination with changes in birth rates, the structure of employment and the practice of retirement. In a very short space of time, there has been a major restructuring of the life cycle in Britain and in most other EU member states, resulting from the truncation of employment prior to pension ages (Kohli et al, 1991; Walker, 1997). In some EU countries, such as Britain, this was a trend openly encouraged by public policy. Therefore, paradoxically, as longevity has increased, the age at which people exit from economic activity has fallen. Since the 1950s there has been an average increase in longevity throughout the EU of around ten years and a parallel decline in the age of final labour force exit of the same magnitude. The realisation that early exit created problems within employment as well as social protection (and that its benefits in terms of reducing youth unemployment were, at best, only partial) has led most EU governments to abandon or curtail its encouragement. The British government began to do so in the mid-1980s.

Therefore, demography is not the main issue for social policy and social protection in particular, but the growing insecurity of labour markets, the decline in the 'standard worker' on which most pension systems were based, and the changing nature of the family (especially the rise in divorce and the decline in fertility). Nor is demographic change the main issue for generational relations but, rather, its combination with outdated assumptions underlying social protection (such as familism) and their incompatibility with the changing socioeconomic structure.

Population ageing is a social process. Of course, we must start from the biological fact of ageing (which is itself a continuous process and is changing from age cohort to age cohort, but that is only part of the story and actually tells us little about the societal impact or the policy implications of population ageing. Here sociology is more helpful than biology: age is a social construction and social policy plays a crucial role in that process (for example, by defining the age at which people enter pension systems and, therefore, become 'old'). Since the meaning of age in different societies is determined by social processes, the impact of population ageing is subject to the influence of social policy. For example, if we look back over the last 30 years at the reasons for the growth of pensions expenditure in all OECD countries, demography played a minor role compared to policy decisions (OECD, 1988a). In other words, there is nothing inevitable about the impact of ageing on different societies, but rather it is the policy process that will determine whether or not countries age successfully.

Implications for care needs

Population ageing has widespread policy implications, which touch most aspects of economic, political and social life, but here our focus is social care. In this volume, it must be emphasised that, contrary to some Eastern portrayals of Western individualism, the family in Britain and the rest of Europe is still the major provider of personal care. The combination of longevity and changes in family structure and living arrangements are increasing the need for care on the part of older people. Indeed, what has been called the 'care gap' (Walker, 1985; Qureshi and Walker, 1989) is likely to have widened over the last ten years because the public provision of long-term care services has not kept pace with the rising need for them. The projected cost of long-term care through the first half of this century, made by Government Actuary's Department projections for the Royal Commission on Long-Term Care is £28.0 billion by 2031 and £45.3 billion by 2051. There are currently great differences in access to public domiciliary services: older people with an informal carer have lower levels of provision than those with such support. The cost of improving access for the most dependent group of older people has been estimated at £290 million currently and by year 2051 it will have risen to £900 million.

In comparison with several other EU countries, Britain is a relatively low provider of long-term care services (Table 3.1). The General Household Survey estimates that 5.7 million people provide some hours of informal care and three quarters of these care for older people. The figure is likely to be an underestimate because family members often do not see their actions as caring but as family or household tasks (Nolan et al, 1996). Also, recent research shows that cross-sectional data under-record the amount of care actually being provided (Evandrou, 2001). Women are the major providers of unpaid care, and the largest group receiving care are parents and parents-in-law.

Table 3.1: Comparison of care systems

	Total spending 1992-99 (% GDP)	Public spending (% GDP)	Aged 65+ in institutions	Aged 65+ receiving Home Help	Spending on institutions as % total public long-term care
Austria	1.4	–	4.9	24	–
Belgium	1.21	0.66	6.4	4.5	53
Denmark		2.24	7	20.3	80
Finland	1.12	0.89	5.3-7.6	14	86
France	–	0.5	6.5	6.1	59
Germany	–	0.82	6.8	9.6	48
Luxembourg	–	–	6.8	–	–
Netherlands	2.7	1.8	8.8	12	76
Sweden	2.7	2.7	8.7	11.2	–
Britain	1.3	1	5.1	16	70
Greece	0.17	–	–	–	–
Ireland	0.86	–	5	3.5	–
Italy	0.58	–	3.9	2.8	–
Portugal	0.39	–	–	–	–
Spain	0.56	–	2.9	1.6	

Source: OECD (1999, p 28)

The nature of the social contract in Britain

It is commonly believed that interpersonal relations between kin are a private matter. While legal provisions with regard to the protection of children obviously contradict this belief, no such restrictions exist with regard to relationships with older relatives. Also, it is widely accepted in the social policy and sociology of ageing, as well as more popularly, that the provision and receipt of care within families is governed by a balance of affect and reciprocity. For instance, Bengston et al, drawing on the work of Gouldner (1960), argue that:

> The implied contract of generations calls for the parents to invest a major portion of their resources throughout their adult years in the rearing of children; in old age, the caregiving is expected to be reversed. (1991, p 255)

In a similar vein, Johnson et al (1989, p 6) assert that the social contract is analogous to the "implicit contract that exists within families". In contrast, we suggest that, as far as the family is concerned, the implied individual-level contract may be a contributory factor in determining the provision of practical care or tending – but it is not a necessary condition. However, it does feature significantly in the ideological construction of the caring relationship (Walker, 1996).

In most cases, the nature of the caring relationship rests on a delicate balance between reciprocity, affection and duty (Marshall et al, 1987). However, while the quality of the caring relationship may depend on individual-level factors such as intergenerational reciprocity, its existence owes more to normative constructions. In the first place, choices about who should care for older people are based on rules that derive from stereotyped beliefs about the reciprocal 'debts' owed by children to their parents and expectations about appropriate gender roles. Secondly, even though it is clear in most instances where care is given that people do feel a personalised sense of obligation towards their parents for past help, it is equally clear that a significant minority do not share these feelings, yet still feel compelled to help by pressures external to the particular relationship (Qureshi and Walker, 1989).

This indicates that the role of ideology is central to the social reproduction of the caring relationship. Also, the lack of social policies that successfully share care between the family and the state reflects the policy objective to minimise its financial commitment in the field of social care and to sustain the primacy of the family (Walker, 1982, 1983; Caucian and Oliker, 2000). The continued absence of such policies means that unnecessary strains are placed on the caring relationships between kin as they respond to the fundamental changes in intergenerational patterns and responsibilities being brought about by sociodemographic change.

There is evidence, too, from the perspective of those on the receiving end of care or who may be so, that there is no desire to rely on extensive help from relatives. This challenges the suggestion that the family should be the most appropriate first line of support and what is left for the state to deal with are those people without families. The attempt by successive governments to create policies, which make people more dependent on relatives, goes against principles that are dear to many (Finch and Mason, 1993). In fact, redrawing the boundaries between the family and the state and adding to the responsibilities assumed to be taken on by kin comes close to bringing back the idea of "liable relatives" (Finch and Mason, 1993, p 180).

The 'right to claim' help from kin is seen as being totally out of line with how families operate:

> People reject even the idea that anyone has the right to expect assistance, let alone to demand it. The right to provide or withhold help must always remain with the potential donor, we have argued. This is a principle to which people adhere strongly, both in theory and in practice. There is a strong resistance to any suggestion that a potential recipient ever has the right to make claims. (Finch and Mason, 1993, p 180)

Finch and Mason (1993) argue that policies which rest on the assumption that relatives can be expected to assist are not in tune with real family life. Responsibilities to help relatives are accepted, sometimes at high cost to the helper. In other words, families feel an obligation towards, and assume responsibility for, the care of older relatives. This is based on a mixture of affection, reciprocity and duty, which results in ambivalence in the caring relationship. On the one hand, relatives want to help but, on the other, they may resent having to do so.

As well as worries concerning the possible abrogation of intergenerational caring responsibilities the reluctance of the state to intervene in the family to provide practical help and support probably owes something to the fact that the state is a patriarchal state, in that it is dominated both by men and by the ideology of patriarchy (Barrett, 1980). This means that the state has an implicit interest in supporting traditional – that is, gendered – patterns of caring. In practice, the state in all western societies intervenes actively in the family but it does so mainly in the form of ideology rather than by open coercion (Moroney, 1976; Donzelot, 1979). In particular, the state supports the reproduction of the gender division of domestic labour and intergenerational obligations with regard to care, and legitimises these as 'normal' or 'natural', while at the same time it promotes the myth of the private world of the family. For example, in rationing home care in Britain it is still common for the proximity of a daughter to be used as a criterion. Social security provision for women who give up paid employment to care for sick or elderly relatives excluded married women until, in 1986, the European Court outlawed this discriminatory practice.

In summary, this is not a social interactionist approach in which 'family' is constructed by the history of interactions between members that, in turn, determines the model of behaviour and expectations. Rather, it is a *structured* interactionist approach in which both ideology and policy play influential roles (we define 'policy' in broad terms as explicit as well as underlying rationales; see Walker, 1984). The state occupies a central place in the social construction of the traditional intergenerational caring relationship and, therefore, in the maintenance of the dominant role of the family, and female kin in particular, in caring for older people.

The state can influence family help both directly via coercive legislation (as in China, but rarely in the West) and indirectly by the way it organises and provides services to individuals in need and the assumptions it makes about the nature and availability of such assistance in rationing care. The state's general economic and social policies set the framework of material and social conditions within which individual families find themselves.

Recent policy responses to the growing need for long-term care

A universal policy issue at the heart of long-term care funding is how the costs are shared between the individual (and family) and the state. In Denmark and Sweden, for example, these costs are met by local authorities and funded through taxation, while in the US, all but the very poorest have to fund such care through private insurance. In Britain, funding policy has been fudged for decades and, with the rapid escalation in the provision of private residential and nursing homes since the mid-1980s and the parallel reductions in local authority budgets, this position became unsustainable in the late 1990s. The fact that thousands of older people were having to sell their houses to finance long-term care caused a public outcry in the lead-up to the 1997 General Election, and forced a response from each of the two main political parties. The response that mattered was Labour's and, soon after the election, the Labour Party established the Royal Commission on Long-Term Care.

There is no doubt that the Royal Commission's report, *With respect to old age* (1999), will be regarded as an outstanding and authoritative document by future students of social policy but, in the real world of policy and practice, the report is only as good as the government's response to it. (Having completed their deliberations in record time, Sir Stewart Sutherland and his colleagues had to wait two months longer than it took them to prepare their report for the government's response. This came, eventually, on 27 July 2000 as part of the National Health Service [NHS] Plan; see Department of Health, 2000.) The fact that the long-term care of older people was an integral part of the national plan for the NHS is important and demonstrates 'joined-up' thinking. However, sceptics might also say that this was a convenient way of deflecting attention from what was bound to be disappointing news for millions of older people and their families and most practitioners working with older people. To understand this disappointment we need to remind ourselves of what action the Royal Commission wanted to be taken, and then look at the government's proposals.

Absolutely private insurance was rejected by the commission for being unable to provide security at an acceptable cost and for its incapability of creating a universal solution. On the other hand, however, it did not suggest that all care costs should be met by the state. Its solution to the division between collective public provision and personal responsibility – the nub of all policies on long-term care – was to separate living costs, housing costs and personal care, and to argue that only the personal care element should be provided free and paid for by taxation, while the other two would be subject to means testing. The commission defined 'personal care' as "care that directly involves touching a person's body", distinguishing it from both treatment (or therapy) and 'indirect' care, such as home-help or the provision of meals. It recommended that personal care be exempt from means testing; though, of course, access to funding would have depended on the assessment of need. This would have required the restructuring of the residential care means test to cover only living and housing costs. As far as home care is concerned the Royal Commission recommended the same distinction between 'personal care' and other forms of help and support with personal care being exempt from charging. While the commission's central recommendation was by no means perfect (it would have created a massive challenge for managers of home care in particular to disentangle the different elements of care), it would have clarified what support older people could expect from the state and what they would be expected to provide for themselves, and would have injected substantial new resources into social care. If its recommendations on funding had been implemented, the total cost would have been an estimated £1.1 billion per annum. It is this rock on which the commission's report seems to have foundered.

In chapter 15 of the NHS Plan, entitled 'Dignity, security and independence in old age' it is noted that "The present system of funding [of long-term care] is confusing, complicated and anomalous" (DoH, 2000, p 126). However, the chosen route to simplification is to pare down what the state will pay to the bare minimum. Therefore the main proposal is that, from October 2001, all *nursing* care provided in nursing homes will be fully funded by the NHS. How is 'nursing' care defined? In a very restricted way: the time spent by a registered nurse in "providing, delegating or supervising care in any setting" (DoH, 2000). This is an important change, and one that will benefit an estimated 35,000 people. However, it is a very long way from what the majority of the Royal Commission wanted and which would have helped hundreds of thousands of older people. The price tag on the government's response to the commission's recommendations is £360 million per annum by 2004, a sum which is very similar to the estimated cost of the dissenters' proposals and, again, a very long way indeed from what the majority thought was necessary.

The government's justification for rejecting the majority view of the Royal Commission was purely financial. Referring to both the majority and minority reports, the NHS Plan states that the former's proposals "would absorb huge and increasing sums of money without using any of it to increase the range and quality of the care available to older people" (DoH, 2000, p 128). Yes, the sums are large; but even the worst case scenario, in terms of costs, would mean that only 1.3% of GDP would have been devoted to funding the free provision of personal care in 2051 if the commission's proposals had been accepted.

In addition to this key proposal concerning the funding of the nursing element of long-term care, the government made other policy changes in response to the Royal Commission:

- from April 2001 the value of a person's house has been disregarded from the means-testing rules for the first three months from admission to residential and nursing home care;
- the capital limits used when assessing ability to contribute to the costs of care have been restored to their 1996 value and are kept under review;
- statutory guidance will be issued to councils aimed at reducing the current variations in charges for home care;
- from April 2002 the payment of the Residential Allowance will cease for new care home residents and the resources will be transferred to local authorities;
- local authorities were made responsible for those who entered residential care before April 1993 in order to prevent people being moved against their wishes;
- a new grant will be given to local authorities to expand loan schemes to try to ensure that older people are not forced to sell their homes against their will when they go into long-term care.

The government also accepted the Royal Commission's recommendation to establish a National Care Standards Commission to regulate and improve standards of care. Also, it should be noted that the substantial increase in investment in intermediate care, an extra £900 million by 2003/4, announced in the NHS Plan, should have a big impact in promoting independence and in improving the quality of care for older people.

It would be wrong not to welcome a package of measures that will improve the quality and range of services available to older people. However, at the same time, it must be said that the government missed a golden opportunity not only to remove all the worst anomalies in long-term care funding but also to give millions of older people, now and in the future, genuine dignity, security and independence. Furthermore, by failing to implement the commission's majority recommendations, the government has reinforced the boundary between the health and social services and, in the process, introduced new uncertainties and anomalies into long-term care funding.

The key problem is the decision to publicly fund only nursing care and to define such care in an extremely narrow way. This is not to pretend that the implementation of the Royal Commission's definition of 'personal care' (that is, care that involves touching a person's body) would have been trouble free, but it is not in the same league as the problems that will be generated by the government's 'nursing' criterion. How will the distinction between 'nursing' care and 'personal' care be sustained in practice? Anyone with any experience of working with older people knows that there is a range of quasi-nursing tasks routinely provided by staff not being supervised by a registered nurse. These include helping with bathing, dressing, using the toilet, eating and drinking. In fact, the dividing line between nursing and personal care has been blurred purposely over the last two decades as governments and local managers have sought to encourage greater flexibility in responding to need. Innovations in the care of older people, such as the Neighbourhood Support Units in Sheffield, and countless other joint health and social services initiatives across the country, have been designed to combine these traditionally different approaches within a single multi-purpose worker (Walker and Warren, 1996).

The only way to separate 'nursing' from 'personal' care is to retain the arbitrary distinction between health and social services. This is what the NHS Plan appears to be encouraging with regard to long-term care funding. Yet, elsewhere in the plan, the government's often-stated commitment to breaking down this 'Berlin Wall' is clear to see, for example in the proposed creation of social care trusts combining health and social care functions. At best this indicates a complete lack of joined-up thinking. This lack of consistency will inevitably create problems for those on the ground charged with implementing these proposals. In particular, staff will have to make difficult and potentially contentious decisions, which may be challenged by family carers, on whether or not a person needs nursing care.

Before the ink even had time to dry on the NHS Plan, the Royal College of Nursing (RCN) had already pronounced the arbitrary distinction between nursing and personal care as 'unworkable'. The director of the RCN has argued that nursing care is not only provided by registered nurses, but rather, a large amount of it is delegated to health care assistants. The government's proposals, the RCN argues, would make an artificial distinction between nursing and such care assistants.

The government does not appear to have thought through the impact of its proposals on the residential and nursing home marketplace. By giving even higher subsidies to those in nursing homes they will be rewarded, in effect, for the higher dependency of their residents compared with those in residential homes. This ratchets up the perverse incentive towards dependency and against rehabilitation. It is doubtful, too, how far rehabilitation will be assisted by only a three month 'breathing space' before taking into account the value of an older person's home. And finally, the restoration of the means-test capital limit to their 1996 levels is a bit of a damp squib when so much more had been expected. Arguably the best way to help the poorest older people is not via the equity limits but by raising the personal allowance. This is currently £15.45 per week, a sum which is obviously insufficient to allow older people to retain their dignity and independence.

The NHS Plan, which is positive in many respects, is a great disappointment with regard to long-term care. It cannot provide dignity, security and independence in old age. In contrast, the Royal Commission's majority report had the potential to do precisely that.

Care and inheritance

Older people in the past left their property to their beneficiaries. These days, however, this happens less, because of the expansion in private residential care, the need for users to be able to pay for such care, and schemes that make it possible to exchange housing equity for income. In the 1980s, there was an increase in the variety and number of equity release schemes for older house owners (Hamnett, 1996). It is estimated that the number of equity extraction schemes is in the region of 10,000 per year at present. While this number is not large, the trend will depress the future growth of housing inheritance. The requirement for older people to pay their residential care costs often leads them to sell their house. In fact there is an incentive for older people to transfer their assets to their relatives before they are eaten away by care costs because about 36,000 older home owners are selling their homes to pay for care each year (Hamnett, 1996).

As the population is ageing in Britain and home ownership is growing, large numbers of older people find themselves 'house rich and income poor' (Davey, 1996). The average age of an older person starting an equity release plan is 74; half are women, widows living on their own, and only half of the respondents have children. For older people in such schemes the average gained was £35 per week, and, before joining the scheme, they had found life difficult financially (Davey, 1996). The main reason for most people joining a scheme was to boost their income and, on average, they managed to increase their income by 20%. On the whole, people seemed satisfied with the schemes, but some older people felt that they were not giving good value for money. Fifty per cent of people felt that it was important to be able to leave some assets for their families. The main worries older people have of equity release schemes are "Suspicion of schemes and concerns about value for money; fear of indebtedness; attitudes towards inheritance; and misgivings about government policy directions" (Davey, 1996, p 2).

A study that examined whether or not home ownership for older people was a benefit or a financial burden in later life, carried out by the Age Concern Institute of Gerontology (Askham et al, 1999), found that many older home owners feel angry about what they see as the policy of having to sell their home to pay for residential care, instead of being able to leave their hard earned assets to their children:

> [A]lthough not universal, there was a very strong sense of financial injustice about the prospect of having to sell their home to pay the full cost of institutional care, while those who have been tenants were seen as subsidised. (Askham et al, 1999, p 3)

To add to the confusion, the capital limit rules are widely misunderstood by both family caregivers and local authority employees, to the extent of local authorities claiming successfully the capital difference when a house was sold and changed to a smaller property. When a relative is entering a care home the financial complexity of the admission is a cause of considerable confusion for already stressed and anxious relatives (Wright, 1998). In response to the Consultation Paper from the Joseph Rowntree Foundation (2000) on charges for residential accommodation, it is made clear that the problems associated with charges are more complex than the issue of housing equity, even though the public perception is that this is the main issue.

How and why are intergenerational relations changing?

The main changes in families in this century are:

• growth in one-person households;
• decline in adult mortality;
• smaller family sizes;
• increased proportions of families spanning two, three or more generations;
• increased numbers of older people, who either live in institutions alone, or with their relatives or children (Haskey, 1996).

Research continues to show substantial intergenerational solidarity at both micro and macro-levels. At the same time increased longevity has altered the relationship between generations and, where there are intergenerational caring relationships, these have been extended and in some cases made more intense. This ageing of the older population is also resulting in a functional separation of age cohorts in retirement, with those aged 85+ being more likely than younger groups to suffer from disablement (33% are unable to go outdoors compared with 8% of the whole 65+ group), poverty and isolation. The decline in fertility means that there are fewer young labour market entrants and, as a result of early exit, fewer workers per pensioner than in previous decades. Within families there are fewer second and third generation family members to care for older relatives in need. Partly as a result of these factors, there has been increased concern among policy makers in Western society about the fiscal consequences of population ageing, and Britain is no exception to this trend.

Today children might share several decades of life with their parents as adults and have children themselves. Four-generational families are common (Lago, 2000). The Special Omnibus Survey Module (1999) found that nearly everyone in Britain has a living parent or a child; many people have both of these. Close to three quarters of the population, with the exception of those in their 50s, are part of three-generational families. Many mothers with children younger than 18 years-of-age receive help from their own mothers and half of mothers aged 50+ receive help from their eldest child, which makes intergenerational exchanges of help fairly common.

Women live longer than men, and because of this the relationship between mothers and daughters is longer and more durable than many other parent –

child relationships: one quarter of women born in 1930 still had mothers living when they reached the age of 60. Women are more likely than men to live to know their great grandchildren, perhaps even their great great grandchildren. Therefore, women are also more likely than men to be involved with family members across several generations. According to Hagestad (1985), cultural and demographic changes have depleted clearly defined expectations for intergenerational relationships and roles. Families have to create their own expectations in these relationships. Supportive services and legislation can play important roles in freeing women from excessive caregiving burdens and giving the chance for women to pay more attention to their personal life space and autonomy.

Phillipson et al (2000) argue that personal communities are more important to older people than they used to be. Old age has changed from living with kin to a norm of living alone or with partner. Friends play a large part in providing assistance and support. The role of the family is still central in older people's lives but the experience of it is different from the earlier studies of Townsend (1957) and Willmott and Young (1960) who demonstrated in their research the caring role of family members towards older people fifty years ago. The younger generation engages with older people sometimes after long periods of living separate lives, whereas before mothers had a lot of influence over the life course of the younger generation.

Again it is essential not to regard changes in generational relations as a purely cultural phenomenon or as the exercise of agency without reference to the social and political context. Once more political ideology can be seen as a critical determinant of generational relations and their future prospects.

Here we turn to the macro-level social contract on which modern welfare states are based: there is a generalised obligation on those who are young and fit enough to be economically active to make provision for those too young or too old to join them in wealth creation. In turn these workers were led to expect that future generations of producers would reciprocate their sacrifice and ensure their wellbeing in times of need. Therefore in the welfare state, the ethical principles of intergenerational solidarity were embodied in social policy, but, in addition, under the guidance of Keynesian theory and practice, they were regarded as sound economics as well. This was because Keynes allocated a key role to the public sector not only in attempting to flatten out economic booms and slumps, but also in maintaining economic efficiency by keeping wage costs low by spreading risks throughout the community and across generations. Both Beveridge and Bismarck favoured this intergenerational solidarity. Sometimes commentators in Asia regard Western societies as too individualistic. This may be true of some Western societies but *not* of those in the EU – the intergenerational contract could not have been born in an individualistic society.

In Britain and other European welfare states the social contract is primarily a public pensions contract through which resources are transferred between the generations via taxation and social spending. In fact, most welfare states originated in pension provision for older people and, in all EU and OECD countries today, they are the main beneficiaries of social expenditure. Moreover, most Western public pension systems are to some extent pay-as-you-go, wherein the current employed generations pay some or all of the pensions of the retired. In Scandinavian countries, social care provision also forms part of the social contract between generations and it has an important gender dimension in enabling women to enter employment without having to carry out excessive domestic caring responsibilities.

Although public transfers are only one of the four 'pillars' on which retirement income is founded (Reday-Mulvey, 1990) they are the largest one in the majority of EU and OECD countries. The proportion of the gross income of retired households deriving from social security (insurance and social assistance) ranges from over 80% in Sweden and Germany to around 50% in Canada and the US. Of course the social contract on which these transfers are based is not like any normal contract in that it is unwritten and is imposed by the state on those in employment rather than being freely negotiated and is heavily sanctioned by the work ethic. Therefore there is not a direct exchange between the generations involved, the relationship between them is operated by the state. The essence of this contract was clearly expressed by one of the main architects of the postwar welfare state:

> Social security must be achieved by cooperation between the State and the individual. The State should offer security in return for service and contribution. (Beveridge, 1942, p 6)

When the first pension schemes were introduced in the late 19th century, they benefited only those who had the good fortune to survive beyond average life expectancy. The 20th century has seen not only growth in the numbers of older people in the population of Western societies but also a rising proportion of those eligible for pensions being able to collect them and then subsequently to go on doing so for longer periods (though there remain significant differences in mortality rates between social classes). It is this sociodemographic revolution, coupled with low growth in the 1980s and early 1990s, that has prompted debate about the future costs of pensions in most Western countries. In some quarters, population ageing has been greeted with outspoken pessimism and alarm.

Evidence from a 1992 survey of public opinion in all 12 of the then EC countries shows that the social contract between generations is remarkably resilient, despite current economic conditions. Across the EU as a whole some four out of five of the general public supported the idea of an intergenerational pensions contract (in Denmark it was 90%). There was a slight tendency for those aged 15-24 and 25-34, across the EU as a whole, not to be as strong in their agreement as the older age groups. However, these younger age groups were more likely than the older groups to agree slightly, so the overall consensus on the importance of intergenerational solidarity was maintained (Walker, 1993).

At the same time it must be said that we detected quite a high level of pessimism among the general public about how far the pensions contract will be honoured in the future. Therefore, when asked whether people will get *less* pension for their contributions in the future just over one half of the public in the EU said 'yes'. Perhaps this is not surprising, given the pessimistic nature of the debate about population ageing in most EU countries. Nonetheless it points to considerable doubts about whether the pensions contract will be maintained in its current form (the pessimists comprised more than three quarters in France and three fifths in Belgium, Denmark and the Netherlands). People were also pessimistic about the ability of the welfare state to continue to grow and be able to take care of older people better than now. One half of the EU's general public were pessimistic about the future of the welfare state and, by 1999, when the question was repeated, this proportion had increased even further (Walker, 1999).

Attitudes towards the care of older people

British public opinion with regard to long-term care echoes this pessimism, particularly among young people. The Royal Commission on Long-Term Care looked at the attitudes towards long-term care of young people aged 18-29. Young people's knowledge of issues around the provision of long-term care is not in-depth or up-to-date, and they tend to be more concerned about the service provision for their older relatives than for themselves in later years. In addition, young people's awareness of funding issues for long-term care is limited. One of the major differences between the younger generation and older people was the former's enthusiasm for personal responsibility and acceptance that private provision will be almost inevitable, because of the erosion of state provision over the years. They were less concerned with social justice, but they were keen to see state provision as a minimum standard for people who cannot look after themselves. Younger people's expectations of the state as a care provider were low; they believe that the provision of care will be their responsibility when the time comes, whether they like it or not.

The perceptions of residential care facilities among most young people were very negative, but it was agreed that it is necessary and appropriate to provide residential care to some older people. In-house care was seen in terms of informal care, which was provided by the family, and it was understood as a way of providing the best quality of life for older people. Young people felt that families have an obligation to help older people stay at home, this was particularly true of young Asians, emphasising the extended family's role in caring for older people:

> They feel that current care services are not delivered to a high enough standard. They feel there should be a greater range of services to enable people to get in-home care. They want more flexible and targeted services, designed to meet different client needs, and that are sensitive to different

cultures. However, most do not appreciate the cost implications of meeting these demands. (Bunting et al, 1999, p 312)

There was an agreement among the young people about the financing of the current system not being sustainable and the fact that new ways of financing have to be found. There was however no consensus on what would be the best way forward in terms of paying for long-term care.

The impact of age on people's attitudes towards provision for older people was looked at by the Royal Commission which was based mainly on the British Social Attitudes Survey (BSA) datasets. Support was overwhelmingly for the government to provide a decent standard of living for older people. Even though, more people were saying 'probably' instead of 'definitely', as they did a decade ago, which might be due to the growing public awareness of what the state might not be able to afford to provide a decent standard of living in the face of an ageing population. Fifty-five per cent of people thought that 'age should make no difference' to the services provided in health care. The views of 18 to 29-year-olds were indistinguishable from other respondents as a whole. There is not much difference in attitudes between age groups when it comes to extra spending on health but, understandably, a different picture emerges about extra spending on pensions. People aged 65+ were three times more likely to advocate more spending on pensions than people aged 18-29, who opted for the status quo. Many people were aware of the effects of ageing population and declining proportion of people contributing to the welfare state through income tax, which could mean that the resources to fund care provisions might not be there in the future. It was suggested that the younger generation might have to think of financing their own care in their old age. However, for the people coming to their retirement now, care should be provided, because they had not been warned of the need to provide largely for themselves, since they were encouraged to think that care would be provided from the taxes they paid over their working lives.

It was widely thought that the care of older people must be a safety net instead of a universal benefit: 66% of respondents supported some form of means testing in care provision. However, the National Survey on the Care of Elderly People (Parker and Clarke, 1998), which reproduced some questions of the BSA, found a strong commitment to the idea of the government taking responsibility for the care of older people. It was felt, by the majority of respondents, that the responsibility of the care of all older people, not just the ones who could not afford the cost of care, was the responsibility of the state.

The great majority of respondents felt that the state should have primary responsibility for the provision of care for elderly people. Almost all (89%) agreed that "the state should be responsible for providing care for elderly people" (Jarvis, 1999, p 238).

Ideology and policy: the new social contract

To some extent, public opinion reflects the ideological climate in a particular country. It was not mere coincidence that the countries that moved furthest and fastest in the 1980s to alter the terms of the social contract were those under neoliberal economic management – be it Reaganomics in the US, Thatcherism in Britain, or Rogernomics in New Zealand. The restructuring of pension provision in Britain cannot be attributed to the need to curb the generosity of payments to pensioners. In comparison with other EU and OECD countries, British pensioners fare poorly in terms of public pension replacement ratios (pensions as a proportion of earnings in the year before retirement for workers with average wages in manufacturing) and poverty (Walker et al, 1993).

Nor can the restructuring of pensions be attributed to any overt concern about justice between generations. The issue of 'intergenerational equity' did surface in the mid-1980s but only very briefly (and in far less sensational terms than in the US). In fact, there is no objective basis for open generational conflict over resources in Britain. There is no empirical evidence of any net transfer of state spending from younger to older people. In other words, there is no foundation for the contention, dramatically expressed by Thomson (1989, p 36) that the 'welfare generation' has 'captured' the welfare state and steered it from being a youth-oriented state to one directed towards older people. The British welfare state has been neutral in distributional terms between children and older people (Johnson and Falkingham, 1988). Looking over the longer term it is only the cohort born in the early years of this century that can be described as net gainers from the intergenerational contract (Hills, 1996). Any changes in the age cohort distribution of welfare state spending are a reflection of underlying movements in demographic structure rather than being the result of a takeover by so-called 'greedy elders'. This is largely true in all OECD countries because the projected rise in social expenditure in all of them is less than the rise in the proportions of older people in their populations.

Changes to the social contract in Britain can be attributed to two factors. In the first place, there is the longstanding economic pessimism concerning public expenditure on the welfare state. This seemingly innate pessimism derives from the 'public burden' model of welfare, which lies at the heart of economic assumptions concerning the respective economic contributions of the public and private sectors, and particularly the contention that the public is an unproductive burden on the private. This is of great importance to pensions and older people because the concept of old age stemming from such theories is one of homogeneity, economic dependence and lack of productivity. Therefore older people are marginalised economically, even though they may be performing vital roles in the informal economy. The pensions they receive from the state are regarded economically as a burden.

Secondly, ideological change seriously undermined the moral, social and economic foundations of the welfare state as envisaged by Keynes and Beveridge.

In Britain (and countries such as Australia, Canada and New Zealand), monetarist economics – with its in-built opposition to public expenditure on welfare and restricted, supply-side only view of the costs of employers' social security contributions – has been more important than demography in explaining policies aimed at installing a new social contract. The rate of GDP growth per annum in Britain required to finance projected increases in social expenditure due to demographic factors is only 0.16%, for Sweden 0.14%, and for the US 0.84% (OECD, 1988b, p 39). Therefore, rather than the main pressure deriving from demographic change, it is ideological shifts, particularly in economic orthodoxy, which have altered assumptions about the role of the state with regard to welfare and encouraged some countries to take what looks like, at best, premature action on the social contract. Britain provides a clear example of this triumph of ideology over both conventional morality, with regard to welfare, and demographic reality in the restructuring of its pension provision to reduce the role of public pensions and increase that of publicly subsidised private pensions (Walker, 1990). In other words, the alignment of ethical and economic principles in the intergenerational pension contract, forged in the immediate postwar period, has been put in jeopardy by the introduction of a new economic order.

The conjunction of these two factors in Britain and a few other Western countries during the 1980s and 1990s suggests that concern about population ageing was artificially amplified as an economic/demographic imperative intended primarily to legitimate policies aimed at restructuring the welfare state. The dual social functions performed by this amplification process are, on the one hand, to encourage gratitude and political acquiescence on the part of older people and, on the other, to prompt younger adults to provide for their old age in the private market. In addition it diverts attention from the real ideological imperative behind policy.

Conclusion

It is in the policy arena rather than the attitudes of younger generations that we find the main threat to the intergenerational solidarity underlying the British and other Western welfare states. In describing pensions as a burden on the economy, policy makers might encourage the popular view that older people are themselves a burden which, in turn, may weaken the resolve of younger generations to support older ones. Therefore, the very process of revising the social contract may itself create the conditions for intergenerational conflicts, especially if policy makers portray older people as economic burdens. Similarly, at the interpersonal level, the increasing policy emphasis on individual responsibility and self-reliance and the failure to provide sufficient resources to support older people and families may undermine caring relationships within families by over-burdening them with unreasonable pressures and expectations. A society without intergenerational solidarity is unimaginable, but policy makers must wake up to the potentially negative impact of their actions and begin to promote solidarity rather than undermining it.

References

Askham, J., Nelson, H., Tinker, A. and Hancock, R. (1999) 'Older owner-occupiers' perceptions of home ownership', Joseph Rowntree Foundation (www.jrf.org.uk/knowledge/responses/docs/residentialaccommodation.htm).

Barrett, M. (1980) *Women's oppression today*, London: Verso.

Bebbington, A.C. (1991) 'The expectation of life without disability in England and Wales, 1976-1988', *Population Trends*, vol 66, pp 26-29.

Bengston, V., Marti, G. and Roberts, R. (1991) 'Age group relations: generational equity and inequity', in K. Rillemer and K. McCartney (eds) *Parent–child relations across the lifespan*, Hillsdale, NJ: Lawrence Erlbaum, pp 253-278.

Beveridge, W. (1942) *Social insurance and allied services*, London: HMSO.

Bunting, M., Meadon, K. and Stewart, S. (1999) 'Young people's perspectives on long term care with respect to old age' in Royal Commission on Long-Term Care, *With respect to old age: Long term care – Rights and responsibilities*, Cm 4192, London: The Stationery Office, pp 305-19.

Caucian, F. and Oliker, S. (2000) *Caring and gender*, Thousand Oaks, CA: Pine Forge Press.

Davey, J. (1996) *Equity release for older home owners*, Joseph Rowntree Foundation (www.jrf.org.uk/knowledge/findings/housing/h188.htm).

DoH (Department of Health) (1992) *The health of elderly people – An epidemiological overview*, London: HMSO.

DoH (2000) *The NHS Plan*, Cm 4818, London: The Stationery Office.

Donzelot, J. (1979) *The policing of families*, London: Hutchinson.

Dunnell, K. (1995) 'Are we healthier?', *Population Trends*, vol 82, pp 8-12.

Esping-Andersen, G. (1996) *Welfare states at the end of the century*, Paris: OECD (mimeo).

Evandrou, M. (2001) *ESRC 'Growing Older' project on family, work and quality of life: Changing economic and social roles*, University of Sheffield (www.shef.ac.uk/uni/projects/gop).

Finch, J. and Mason, J. (1993) *Negotiating family responsibilities*, London: Routledge.

Gouldner, A.W. (1960) 'The norm of reciprocity', *American Sociological Review*, vol 25, pp 161-78.

Hagestead, G. (1985) 'Older women in intergenerational relations', in M.R. Haung, A.B. Ford and M. Sheafer (eds) *The physical and mental health of aged women*, New York: Springer.

Hamnett, C. (1996) 'Housing inheritance in Britain: its scale, size and future', in A. Walker (ed) *The New Generational Contract: Intergenerational relations, old age and welfare*, London: UCL Press, pp 135-58.

Haskey, J. (1996) 'Population review: (6) Families and households in Great Britain', *Population Statistics*, (*Population Trends* 85), ONS, Autumn.

Hills, J. (1996) 'Does Britain have a welfare generation?', in A. Walker (ed) *The new generational contract: Intergenerational relations, old age and welfare*, London: UCL Press, pp 56-80.

Jarvis, L. (1999) 'The impact of age on people's attitudes towards provision for older people in *With respect to old age*', in Royal Commission on Long-Term Care, *With respect to old age: Long term care – Rights and responsibilities*, Cm 4192, London: The Stationery Office, pp 213-36.

Johnson, P. and Falkingham, J. (1988) *Intergenerational transfers and public expenditure on the elderly in modern Britain*, London: Centre for Economic Policy Research.

Johnson, P., Conrad, C. and Thomson, D. (eds) (1989) *Workers versus pensioners: Intergenerational justice in an ageing world*, Manchester: Manchester University Press, in association with the Centre for Economic Policy Research.

Joseph Rowntree Foundation (2000) 'Responses to government consultation: Charges for residential accommodation' (www.jrf.org.uk/knowledge/responses/docs/residentialaccommodation.asp).

Kohli, M., Rein, M., Guillemard, A.M. and van Gunsteren, H. (eds) (1991) *Time for retirement*, Cambridge: Cambridge University Press.

Lago, D. (2000) *Older women: Key intergenerational figures* (agexted.cas.psu.edu/docs/21600477.html).

Mannheim, K. (1952) *The problem of generations: Essays on the sociology of knowledge*, London: Routledge & Kegan Paul.

Moroney, R.M. (1976) *The family and the state*, London: Longman.

Nolan, M., Grant, G. and Keady, J. (1996) *Understanding family care*, Buckingham: Open University Press.

OECD (1988a) *The future of public pensions*, Paris: OECD.

OECD (1988b) *Ageing populations: The social policy implications*, Paris: OECD.

OECD (1999) *Ageing and care for frail elderly persons: An overview of international perspectives*, Paris: OECD.

Parker, G. and Clarke, H. (1998) 'Paying for long-term care in the UK: policy, theory and evidence', in P. Taylor-Gooby (ed) *Choice and public policy: The limits to welfare markets*, Basingstoke: Macmillan Press, pp 24-41.

Phillipson, C., Bernard, M., Phillips, J. and Ogg, J. (2000) 'The family and community life of older people', in *Social networks and social support in three urban areas* (www.brookes.ac.uk/schools/social/population-and-household-change/9_philip.html).

Qureshi, H. and Walker, A. (1998) *The caring relationship*, Houndmillls: Macmilllan.

Reday-Mulvey, G. (1990) 'Work and retirement: future prospects for the baby boom generation', *Geneva Papers*, vol 55, pp 100-13.

Royal Commission on Long-Term Care (1999) *With respect to old age: Long term care – Rights and responsibilities*, Cm 4192, London: The Stationery Office.

Social Trends (1995) *The Central Statistical Office UK* (CD-ROM).

Special Omnibus Survey Module (1999) *National dwelling and household survey, and survey of English housing*, DETR; Labour Force Survey, ONS.

Tallis, R. (1992) 'Rehabilitation of the elderly in the 21st century', *Journal of the Royal College of Physicians of London*, vol 26, no 4, pp 413-22.

Thomson, D. (1989) 'The welfare state and generation conflict: winners and losers', in P. Johnson, C. Conrad and D. Thomson (eds) *Workers versus pensioners: Intergenerational justice in an ageing world*, Manchester: Manchester University Press, in association with the Centre for Economic Policy Research, pp 33-56.

Townsend, P. (1957) *The family life of old people*, London: Penguin.

Walker, A. (1999) *Attitudes to population ageing in Europe* (www.sheffield.ac.uk/uni/academic/R-Z/socst/staff/a_walker.htm).

Walker, A. (1997) *Combating age barriers*, Luxembourg: Office for the Official Publications of the European Communities.

Walker, A. (ed) (1996) *The new generational contract: Intergenerational relations, old age and welfare*, London: UCL Press.

Walker, A. (1993) *Age and attitudes*, Brussels: Commission of European Communities.

Walker, A. (1990) 'The economic 'burden' of ageing and the prospect of intergenerational conflict', *Ageing and Society*, vol 10, no 4, pp 377-96.

Walker, A. (1985) *The care gap*, London: Government Information Service.

Walker, A. (1984) *Social planning*, Oxford: Blackwell.

Walker, A. (1983) 'Care for elderly people: a conflict between women and the state', in J. Finch and D. Groves (eds) *A labour of love*, London: Routledge, pp 106-28.

Walker, A. (ed) (1982) *Community care*, Oxford: Blackwell.

Walker, A. and Warren, L. (1996) *Developing services for older people*, Buckingham: Open University Press.

Walker, A., Guillemard, A.M. and Alber, J. (1993) *Older people in Europe, social and economic policies*, Brussels: Commission of European Communities.

Willmott, P. and Young, M. (1960) *Family and class in a London suburb*, London: Routledge and Kegan Paul.

Wordsworth, S., Donaldson, C. and Scott, A. (1996) *Can we afford the NHS?*, London: IPPR.

Wright, F. (1998) *Continuing to care: The effect of spouses and children of an older person's admission to a care home*, Joseph Rowntree Foundation (www.jrf.org.uk/ knowledge/responses/docs/residentialaccommodation.htm).

FOUR

Ageing and intergenerational relations in Japan

Misa Izuhara[1]

Introduction

Ageing of the population has affected many industrial societies, upsetting the existing balance of financial, material and instrumental resources across generations. The remarkable speed of societal ageing in Japan also poses a considerable challenge to the family and the state partly due to the increasing need for nursing care. This chapter explores, in the context of postwar demographics and socioeconomic and policy changes, the changing patterns of intergenerational relations, and in particular, the reciprocal dimension of the exchange of goods and services between ageing parents and their adult children.

Given the specific cultural norms and traditions, this chapter first examines how intergenerational relations have been perceived in Japan, and how they are transforming with particular reference to living arrangements, co-residence in particular, and the provision of nursing care. The wider issues linked to the development of social policy is then discussed. How the introduction of *koteki kaigo hoken* – long-term care insurance (LTCI) – in April 2000 alters the existing arrangements on care delivery is a central concern of this chapter. Finally, one particular exchange tradition between the provision of nursing care and inheritance within the family is examined. Contemporary factors such as people's value shift towards independence and individualism, increasing rates of female labour market participation and the postwar development of social policy have started to alter the conventional 'generational contract'. Gender issues are also explored throughout this chapter.

Ageing Japanese society

At the beginning of the 21st century, Japan is the fastest ageing society in the world. It has taken only 25 years for Japan to double its rates of societal ageing. Japan earned the UN's definition of an 'ageing society' (people 65+ exceeding 7% of its total population) in 1970; by 1996 the rate had reached 14.5%, entering the UN's definition of an 'aged society'. The speed is indeed phenomenal if we compare how long the same process has taken in other countries: for example, 45 years for Britain (1930-75), 85 years for Sweden (1890-1975), and 115 years for France (1865-1980) (US Census Bureau, 2001). Since 1950, fertility has decreased very sharply, and now Japan has one of the lowest birth rates in the world (1.36 in 2000[2]) (Figure 4.1). Having a smaller family has become a trend, but this is also partly due to general decline in marriage rates since births to unmarried mothers remain uncommon in Japan. In 1995, 9.07% of men and 5.28% of women at the age of 50 were never married. The average age of first marriage for men has increased from 26.2 in 1950 to 30.5 in 1995, and for women from 23.6 to 27.2, which also means a shorter reproductive period. In particular, marriage rates of younger women have started to decline sharply over the last decade. Fifty-four per cent of women aged 25-29 were single in 2000, an increase from 30% in 1985 (Management and Coordination Agency, 2000). The low birth rate, combined with reductions in infant and maternal mortality, and an increase in life expectancy (77.64 years for men and 84.62 for women in 2000) has brought about a very sharp increase in the number and proportion of the older population. It is projected that one in four people in Japan will be 65+ by 2025 (Ministry of Health and Welfare, 1999) (Figure 4.2). Indeed, the rapidly ageing society, with the remarkable increase in the old-old age groups, poses great challenges for many areas of social policy.

Policy makers fear that an ageing society will break down the existing balance

Figure 4.1: Decline in fertility rates in Japan[a]

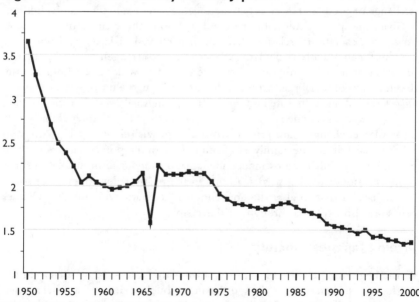

[a] The significantly low birth rate in 1966 was due to superstitious reasons – the year corresponded to *Hinoe-uma* [fire horse], considered bad luck for women born in that year.

Source: Ministry of Health and Welfare (1950-2000)

Figure 4.2: Ageing rates of society in Japan (%): 1950-2000 actual and 2005-25 projection

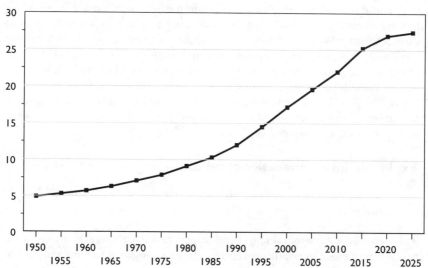

Source: Management and Coordination Agency (1950-2000); National Institute of Population and Social Security Research (1997)

between the 'productive' age groups and the 'dependent' population[3] – fewer people paying taxes and more drawing pensions as well as health and welfare costs. The shrinkage of the 'productive' population is, however, not only a result of the low birth rates and an ageing of the population in Japan. Other reasons include Japan's strict immigration policy, which does not allow an expansion of young migrant workers, and the increasing number of younger people spending longer years in higher education. The ratio of those who went to higher education after upper secondary school (15- to 17-year-olds) has increased from 36.9% in 1990 to 45.2% in 1995. The struggle to balance the productive–dependency ratios has been further accentuated by the prolonged recession in the *Heisei* period (1989 to present) with the unemployment rate having reached a record high 5.5% by the end of 2001. Risk and uncertainty in employment have indeed been increasing. For the younger generations, however, being unemployed does not appear to carry the same stigma as it once did, and, according to *The Economist*, "about half of university graduates actually prefer temporary and part-time work to full-time employment or graduate studies" (23 December 2000, p 11). Moreover, this recent phenomenon implies that, despite the prolonged recession, many Japanese 'middle-class' parents are still affluent enough to support their children at home well into young adulthood. In fact, the Japanese virtue of filial piety may therefore be operating in reverse at the beginning of the 21st century.

In this context, the 1990s saw the beginning of new changes in the social policy agenda: a combination of further cuts in social expenditure and increases in financial resources through various means has become inevitable in response to the increasing cost burden of the ageing society. In relation to long-term care, following Western trends, the emphasis to provide health and welfare services for frail older people has shifted from expensive institutional care towards cost-effective home care options through a series of Gold Plans[4]. Under the national health insurance schemes, user fees were introduced to older patients (aged 70+) for their health services in 1999. More recently, the government has reformed the social security system through the introduction of the long-term care insurance in April 2000.

Exploring intergenerational relations

> Relations between generations have been the source of both extraordinary solidarity and major conflict. (Walker, 1996, p 1)

This debate can be applicable to both micro- and macro-level relations. Due to the recent trend in population ageing, the issue of generational equity as the source of conflict forms one of the major debates in welfare states (see, for example, Hills, 1996; Becker, 2000). Variations in cohort size (for example, baby boomers), changes in economic performance, and shifts in policy and political direction over time are likely to generate inequalities among 'generations'. There also exists a highly 'gendered' conflict within the family as well as in society. In Japan, this partly originates from the traditional patriarchal family system where the roles and responsibilities of family members were clearly set. The role of women in the family such as a care provider has been indeed socially and politically constructed, and can not be explained without reference to macro-structural determination (for example, the relationship of the family with the state as well as the labour market). However, the focus of this chapter is at the more micro-level relations between generations, and 'family solidarity' is represented by the well-maintained structural context of co-residence within which the exchange of instrumental, material, and financial resources between family members takes place.

The pattern of support exchanges between generations in the family may be more demanding and frequent in Japan than it is in Western societies. Traditional Japanese culture seems to have more scope for structuring predictable and fair exchanges between parents and children with long-established values of 'individualism' and independence (Kendig, 1989). Indeed, the role of the family as a welfare provider has been more explicitly defined in the laws and the welfare state. This is not only a moral obligation influenced by traditional values and ideologies, but the family was also legally obliged to provide welfare to other members. It was not until the 1970s, at the end of a period of rapid economic growth, that Japanese social welfare legislation seemed to acknowledge the end of their legal obligation to provide welfare. In the same decade, however, in response to the recession, the role of the family was politically redefined in the new form of *Nihon-gata fukushi* – the Japanese-style welfare state – emphasising "a traditional Japanese spirit of self-respect, self-reliance and mutual assistance" (from Prime Minister Ohira's speech at the Japanese National Diet, January 1979).

Family support, household structure and social change

The role and structure of intergenerational relations have various dimensions. The generations exchange material, instrumental and financial resources, often classified as economic support, personal care, practical support, emotional and moral support, or accommodation (see, for example, Finch, 1989; Lawton et al, 1994). One form of intergenerational relationship that is notably strong in Japan is represented structurally by accommodation, or living arrangements. One of the most conspicuous differences between the lives of older people in Western societies and those in Japan has been the Japanese preference for extended-family living arrangements. The vast majority of people used to spend their entire life living with the extended family, and one half of older people still live with their adult children today (Ministry of Health and Welfare, 2000). Although 'intimacy at a distance' (Rosenmayr and Koeckeis, 1963) can effectively deliver certain types of family support, co-residence certainly provides a perfect structural context for exchanging family support, reinforces their responsibilities, and sometimes makes asset transfer easier over the generations. It is inevitable that the burden of nursing care falls first on the family members, especially on female members, when the generations share accommodation.

Postwar industrialisation and Westernisation transformed household structure. The geographical distance between generations, created by high educational and occupational mobility, upward social mobility of the younger generation, or even lifestyle change, increased the trend towards family nuclearisation. Many scholars previously believed, however, that family nuclearisation would advance more quickly in Japan than has actually been the case (Morioka, 1973). Elderly-only households have been gradually increasing for the last two decades. Among all the households with older members, both single-elderly and elderly-couple households increased from 11.3% to 17.5%, and from 16.7% to 25.2%, respectively, between 1983 and 1998 (Management and Coordination Agency, 1998). Co-residence may have been viewed as a mode of survival in the past, since older people who live independently are generally wealthier (Hayashi et al, 1988). Therefore, the current expansion of elderly-only households can be explained by greater financial independence of older people gained through increased levels of pensions, savings, and other assets. A value shift may be another possible explanation. It has been argued that the steady decline of co-residence is a temporary arrangement or possibly a mere postponement until life-course events such as retirement, widowhood or illness occur (Hashimoto, 1993). Some older people however started to value independent living, or alternatively express their preference for living close to their children without sharing accommodation (Izuhara, 2000). Combined with factors such as the increasing rates of female participation in the labour force, the decrease in co-residence has impacted upon the transformation of the conventional forms and levels of family support exchange.

The government may have viewed this pattern of household structure – the extended-family living arrangement – as a unique asset; therefore, housing-related policies and initiatives have been introduced to reflect and reinforce intergenerational solidarity. Since the 1980s, both the Ministry of Construction and the Ministry of Health and Welfare have begun to focus on housing policies directed at extended family living, which seems to be designed to preserve the traditional system of family support. For instance, a new type of housing for five-person three-generation families called *4LLDK* – that is, four bedrooms, two living rooms, a dining-kitchen and a bathroom – was introduced into public housing. The private sector has also started to promote *ni-setai jutaku* [two-household housing]. This new type of housing is designed to reduce the common tension between the generations, and between mother-in-laws and daughter-in-laws in particular, caused by the close proximity of conventional co-residence. It allows the creation of two separate households with separate amenities and facilities, but all under one roof. In addition, the Government Housing Loan Corporation has introduced the 'two-generation housing loan', a loan inheritance system spanning generations. Further incentives to live intergenerationally are also encouraged through tax breaks. Furthermore, the importance of intergenerational relations appears to be strengthened through equity extraction schemes such as a reverse mortgage scheme (using home ownership to generate income for old age), requiring older homeowners a guarantor (not always, but often children), when they sign up to the scheme. Those policies help families maintain the traditional support mechanism.

Functional support – or, more precisely, providing nursing care to older parents(-in-law) – is another notable dimension of Japanese family relations. Characteristic of this has been helping each other in the family with daily tasks, especially older people receiving high levels of support from their adult children. Postwar socioeconomic and structural change, however, led to behavioural change which in turn has reshaped expectations concerning intergenerational relations (Kendig, 1989). As Marshall et al argued, "the nature of the caring relationship rests on a delicate balance between reciprocity, affection and duty" (1987; also quoted in Walker, 1996, p 27). With other competing tasks, the younger generation may now view family support more as a 'burden' than as a 'natural obligation of a child' or 'good custom'. In fact, the value shift which Japanese youth exhibit towards 'individualism' may suggest a breakdown of this traditional practice. According to a survey conducted by the Office of the Prime Minister (1994), only 23% of Japanese youth aged between 18 and 24 years-of-age were 'positively' thinking of supporting their parents in their old age, in contrast to 63% of their US and 68% of their Korean counterparts. Having different family values from the younger generation, some older people feel more pronounced generational discontinuities. Despite the traditional solidarity between the generations, the marriage bond between younger couples seems to be superseding the vertical bond or obligations between older parents and their adult children (Izuhara, 2000). Consequently, resisting the idea of relying on their adult children and becoming a burden to them is a common wish of older people in recent years.

Reciprocal arrangements are often key to family support. The norm of reciprocity governs how individuals accept and provide social support, involving rights and responsibilities, and credits and debts (see, for example, Akiyama et al, 1997). In Japan, for instance, the debt children feel towards their parents' sacrifices throughout their upbringing has to be reciprocated by caring for their parents in old age. For parents, therefore, having raised children earlier in life can serve as a credit for the receipt of support from them in their old age (Hashimoto and Kendig, 1992). Indeed, under traditional arrangements, it was the duty of the eldest son as the successor of the household to provide care for their ageing parents (although practical care was often provided by his wife).

There are some exchange rules applied to family members. Between generations, it is possible for the exchange to be one-way over the long term, if it is somehow reciprocated in the end. For example, parents may be net 'providers' at a particular point in time due to a reasonable expectation that they may be net 'receivers' at a later date. In fact, due to the affluence brought to postwar families, parents supporting their adult children indefinitely is not such an unusual practice, since support often flows from the wealthier generation to the poorer one, which evens out inequalities. Moreover, compared with the US family system prescribing 'symmetrical reciprocity' as an exchange rule, the exchange of different kinds of resources, such as money and affection, is quite common in Japanese families (although 'symmetrical reciprocity' is the norm between non-family members) (Akiyama et al, 1997). Finally, the 'generational contract' of family reciprocity can be a continuous chain of obligations over generations rather than one particular parent–child relationship. Research into Japanese migrant women growing older in British society suggests that the geographic distance prevented the majority providing care for their parents, and therefore their 'unfulfilled' feelings seem to reinforce their own attitudes towards not expecting support from their children (Izuhara, 1999). Although this is an extreme case constrained by cross-national migration, the same exchange rules may be applicable to those generations geographically separated within the same country.

Reinventing a social contract: the introduction of Long-Term Care Insurance

Given the characteristics of the family role and their implicit obligations, a remarkable imbalance is found among services and benefits in the development of welfare programmes. Its development was often regarded as lagging behind the significant economic achievement of the postwar period. Criticism was indeed found in both Western and Japanese literature that Japan had gained postwar economic success partly at the sacrifice of welfare (see for example,

Figure 4.3: Social security expenditure as percentage of GDP

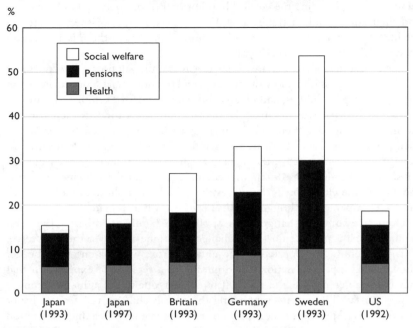

Source: National Institute of Population and Social Security Research (2000) (www.jpss.go.jp)

Nakagawa, 1979; Lee, 1987; Rudd, 1994). Despite the greater economic growth rates of the late 1980s, Japan's social security expenditure[5] has been low compared with more mature European welfare states when measured as a proportion of GDP (Figure 4.3). For example, the percentage devoted to social security expenditure in 1997 was 17.8%, approximately equivalent to the British rates in 1980 and the Swedish rates in the 1960s (Ministry of Health and Welfare, 1999). The low percentages were due in part to the relatively young population in the past. However, the next few decades will likely foresee a rapid increase in the level of expenditure.

Others argue that the government's emphasis on traditional family values has held back the development of some areas of welfare programmes. In other words, the structure and nature of the Japanese welfare state have reflected and determined the role of the family, especially that of female members, in the delivery of welfare. Apart from two major items of public expenditure – public pension schemes (52.4% of the total expenditure in 1997) and national health insurance (36.5%), other areas of welfare such as social service provision (11.1%) have been considerably underdeveloped (Figure 4.4). For example, although the number of home-helps was expected to triple over the last decade, according to figures set out under the Gold Plan[6], the target number was still equivalent to only approximately one fifth the number in Denmark. The rapidly ageing society, however, entails increasing costs of social services in response to increasing

Figure 4.4: Distribution of public expenditure in Japan (billion yen)

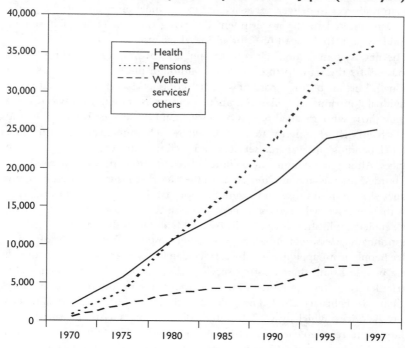

Source: National Institute of Population and Social Security Research (2000) (www.jpss.go.jp)

numbers of the old–old age groups. The target provision as well as an absence of services in some areas of welfare may have served as driving forces to create inequalities and new social divisions in the family, the labour market and society as a whole. This section analyses a new policy direction concerning the increasing care needs and subsequent cost burdens on individuals, the family and the state in the ageing society. The challenge to maximise available financial and human resources and reducing inequalities is examined in relation to the transforming relationships among various parties involved in the care provision in the society.

The current policy debates in this arena concern the introduction of Long-Term Care Insurance (LTCI) in April 2000, following the German model. This is the fifth national insurance scheme following health insurance, pension insurance, workers' compensation insurance, and unemployment insurance (see Chapter Two of this volume; for the planning process, see, for example, Masuda, 2001). The early impact of the scheme upon care relationships and arrangements is indeed an interesting point for investigation.

From the start, this hastily implemented scheme (the law was passed in December 1997 and implemented in April 2000) has caused chaos to the public, due to its fragmentation and uncertainty concerning the balance between contributions and service provision, the assessment procedure, and the lack of human resources to deliver necessary services. Uncertainty among the public has even resulted in the government deferring the collection of insurance premiums from those aged 65+ for an initial six months.

The new system made it clear to the public that nursing care is no longer 'allocated' by the state to those in need (although public provision has been residual), but has become part of a 'social contract' based upon a system of individual contributions. The insurance resources are raised from two distinct parties: those who are aged 65+ (Category I) and those aged between 40 and 64 (Category II)[7]. Premiums are determined by each municipality, and therefore differ depending on available services and facilities, and the demand for care services. Although premiums are income-related (there are measures to moderate the burden for low-income individuals), the fact that insurance premiums are deducted even from those on meagre pensions has been a source for criticism, as is the controversial need-assessment procedure. The combination of filling out detailed application forms, visits by qualified staff and a computer-assisted questionnaire assessment are among the other obstacles that may put off some older people from applying for the services, and may even result, therefore, in some people losing their existing services (Ito, 2000). The assessments also restrict levels of service granted to users as well as the maximum costs available to them. In February 2002, 2.83 million of those aged 65+ were qualified to receive services, which was 12.3% of all older insurers. Among them, 1.63 million were receiving services at home and another 670,000 in institutional settings, which meant 640,000 older people were qualified but not receiving services (although this figure also includes those in hospital). According to the survey, of 1,263 service users who compared their service amounts before and after the introduction of LTCI, 67.5% of the respondents reported that their services had increased, while 17.7% experienced a reduction (Yabe, 2002).

Affordability has become another major issue. Even once older people are qualified to receive services, they must now pay a 10% user fee for each service received. While this benefits middle to high-income older people, who in the past purchased services fully out of their own pockets, such user fees are however likely to dissuade many low-income people from receiving services they are qualified to receive. The increased financial burden on individuals from both insurance premiums and user fees may lead some older people to limit their take-up of services and under-practice their 'rights' obtained through the new social contract. The take-up rates vary slightly depending on categories of care-needs, but, on average, older people used only 41.2% of the maximum costs/services limit available to them (Yabe, 2002). Those in the lowest need category of 'assistance required' tend to utilise their share the most (49.5%). This is partly because the services which they require are on average a much lower cost and are therefore more affordable compared with those in greater need. The survey of 1,361 municipalities also confirmed this: 67.4% of the sample municipalities observed the tendency of older people to ration their 'qualified' services due to the financial burden (Hiraoka, 2002). The same survey, however, reported that people were not necessarily moving away from receiving more expensive services but towards less costly options (54.4%). There is a danger that their choice may be driven by affordability rather than by what is appropriate or necessary. Overall, like the typical criticism found in the nature of welfare states, this scheme mainly tends to benefit middle to high-income individuals and families, which helps to widen the gap between high and low-income households.

Apart from establishing the notion of a 'social contract' involving rights and responsibilities, a market-oriented approach in care delivery has been also introduced. This is a shift away from the existing division of care delivery in the postwar period since home care had been provided informally by family members with limited (means-tested) services by municipalities while institutional care had been predominantly provided by municipalities and non-profit organisations called *shakai fukushi hojin* [social welfare corporation, quango]. The role of *shakai fukushi hojin* as sub-contractors of the public sector has mainly been to provide institutional care. The difference between *shakai fukushi hojin* and voluntary organisations in Britain is the restriction of the former to provide services only, the type and range being defined by law. *Shakai fukushi hojin* requires an approval by the government to operate homes for older people, and in return receives great tax incentives. In order to fill the gap, locally based groups and organisations have emerged and have started providing welfare services such as meal delivery and home-help beyond the formally defined categories over the last 30 years. One of the aims of the LTCI is therefore to develop the role of such (both non-profit and for-profit) service providers. In theory, an expansion of service providers would not only result in greater competition among providers, and therefore a reduction of prices, but would also result in an increase in the amount and quality of services.

The principles of a market approach include free entry to the market, competition among providers, greater consumer choice (instead of allocation), and a contractual relationship between consumer and provider. Given the restrictions under the system, however, the current system can instead be described as a 'quasi-market' (Le Grand and Bartlett, 1993; Hiraoka, 2002). Financial resources are raised mainly through insurance premiums and public funds; non-profit (and for-profit) organisations are encouraged to provide services; and the governments intervene and regulate the market (for example, only approved organisations can provide services). There is little evidence to suggest whether or not greater competition among providers has resulted in reducing the cost of services or increasing efficiency. In addition, whether or not consumer choice is practiced is also questionable, since older clients can only choose services from approved providers and care managers are the ones who package services from the available resources in the area. However, people who reside in larger cities inevitably exercise greater choices (Hiraoka, 2002).

Like community-care policies in Britain, LTCI was introduced to strengthen home care services. The changing balance between institutional care and home care is one of the key indicators to assess the successful implementation of the insurance scheme. According to analysis conducted by Hirano (2002) based on a computer assessment package, there are wide regional variations and characteristics. On average, the ratio of older people who receive services at institutions to those at home is currently 1:2 (32.3%:67.7%). However, this ratio is reversed when the costs of services are examined (63.7%:36.3%, respectively) since the price of institutional care is usually higher than that of home care, and also a budget ceiling is applied for individuals to receive home care. One of the concerns about the scheme is the uneven distribution of care facilities across the country, resulting in a shortage of such facilities, both public and private, in some regions, especially in rural areas. On the other hand, due to the scarce resources of home care in prefectures such as Iwate (northern, rural), the ratio of people receiving care in institutions is higher than in other regions.

The stagnated growth in home-help services can be explained by the low profitability of the business, as well as the difficulty in recruiting human resources. Compared with the provision of institutional care which is often more profitable (for example, *tokubetsu yogo rojin home* [nursing homes] receive average profits of ¥3,012,000 per month[8]), organisations which specialise in providing home-help services were on average ¥99,000 (£495) per month in the red (*Asahi Shimbun*, 13 May 2002, p 1). The fee schedule (*hoshu tanka*) for home-help services is currently under revision and likely to be increased in April 2003.

Moreover, one of the major problems holding back widespread promotion of the scheme is the shortage of care providers. The new scheme requires effective organisation of the potential human resources in the labour-short Japanese economy, especially in such a service-intensive industry. Due to their current poor and unstable working conditions and low wages, the industry tends to attract the 'residual' labour force of households (often wives who have a principle breadwinner). Japan is, therefore, likely to face the same problems as other mature welfare states such as Sweden, where social services are provided by foreign workers from neighbouring countries. The current immigration policy, however, restricts Japan from taking this option. This is likely to lead to the creation of a new gender-biased labour market, since the majority of care workers, both in the public and private sectors, are women. Indeed, this system works hand-in-hand with the existing 'family-as-a-unit' social security systems. Discriminatory taxation treatment of two income households, for example, discourages the second earner (often wives) from taking a full-time job which pays more than ¥1.3 million (£6,500) annually. In addition, pension schemes favouring housewives help retain married women as part-time and casual labour force. In fact, according to a national survey conducted by the Japan Labour Research Institute in 1999, 96.7% of home-helps were reported to be women, and almost half were working part-time.

Reducing the number of older people who are 'socially hospitalised'[9] is one of the aims of the LTCI due to the increasing costs of health care. Hospitals are now divided into various types, and, in order to keep down their costs, 'long-term care oriented' hospitals have more nurses and care staff and less medical doctors compared with ordinary hospitals. Indeed, at the same time, an adequate supply of nursing homes and the adaptation of individual dwellings would also be required. A new type of nursing home – *shin-gata tokuyo* – is planned to respond to such emerging needs. The idea behind the project is similar to the British approach of separating the costs of accommodation and nursing care – accommodation costs will be charged to new residents according to their means.

Overall, a new relationship has been formed between service users and various providers since the new scheme began to contract out the service provision to private and non-profit organisations. Such contractual relationships have commodified welfare services that were once provided by the state and family free of charge. At the same time, however, the potential shortcomings of the scheme may reinforce conventional family support rather than liberating or formalising female care workers in the 'post-bubble' welfare state.

The generational contract between care and inheritance

Under the *Meiji* Civil Code in pre-war Japan, one-son succession was the norm, reflecting *ie*, the patrilineal stem-family system. It was the duty of the eldest son, as the designated successor to the household, to perpetuate the family collectively, as family name, assets (including the tomb and Buddhist altar), social status of the family, and occupation were usually inherited by the son. A strict exchange rule formed the 'generational contract', as the eldest son was expected to provide care to his ageing parents within an extended-family living arrangement (although the daughter-in-law actually provided the practical care) and in return, inherit the entire family wealth. Surprisingly, this system has survived in some families of rural communities in contemporary Japan. Although some traditional family elements remained deeply embedded in the social structure of Japanese people, postwar socioeconomic and legal changes inevitably brought new ideology, functions, and relations into the family. As a part of the postwar democratisation process, *ie* ideology and practices were officially renounced, and the concept removed from the new constitution in 1946, the new civil code in 1947, and the Family and Inheritance Law in 1948. The definition of the family shifted legally from the extended family of the paternal lineage to a nuclear family under the postwar civil code. Even though adult children still had a legal responsibility to their older parents in terms of need, it was of lesser importance than responsibility to their spouse and children. Consequently, the previously defined 'generational contract' became ambiguous and fragmented with different boundaries, expectations and obligations among family members (see Izuhara, 2002).

Home ownership and inheritance

The particular exchange concerned here involves family wealth in the form of dwellings, given the fact that levels of home ownership among older people in Japan are high – 85.2% in 1998[10]. Since ownership of property usually forms the largest share of household assets, home ownership plays an important role in the accumulation of family wealth over generations (see, for example, Forrest and Murie, 1995; Hirayama and Hayakawa, 1995). In the context of family reciprocity, real estate assets become a crucial commodity for older people to own when negotiating the 'generational contract' with younger family members.

In recent years, the increase in home ownership and a decline in fertility rates may suggest that the younger generation is more likely to inherit family wealth from their parents. However, prolonged longevity in recent decades means that two generations exist, often independently, for a longer period of time, consequently leading to a delay in the intergenerational transfer of family wealth. The timing of inheritance can be crucial considering the advantage that inheritance may offer the younger generations to enter the home-ownership sector, or help them accumulate housing wealth. In postwar Japan, however, the transfer of assets, home ownership in particular, does not usually skip widowed wives, unlike the pre-war patriarchal succession system. The survey conducted by the Tokyo Women's Foundation (1997) indicated a marked shift for inheritance at the age of 50. If an intergenerational transfer occurs in the later stage of children's life-courses, they may have an established household with a mortgaged house by the time they inherit the family assets. Furthermore, the prolonged third age and widowhood (often of women) create uncertainty surrounding how much wealth older people consume before they pass away. Since household assets including home ownership can be used to finance the costs of care in old age, the development of various equity extraction schemes will possibly reduce the housing equity available for inheritance in the future.

An alternative to relying on family support for ageing parents is moving to more suitable housing to receive adequate support services while maintaining (a certain degree of) independent living. Older people who decide to take up this option are likely to break the conventional 'contract' with their children since it often involved the sale of their 'family residence'. If older people are reluctant to move to supportive housing or trade down their property due to their attachment to such 'family residence', a reverse mortgage scheme may provide a compromise. In Japan, only 15 local authorities were operating such schemes in 2000, mostly in association with private financial institutions; however, the take-up rates are still very low. Many restrictions apply to older homeowners such as the borrowing limit against their property values and purpose-oriented monthly spending limits. At the death of borrowers, beneficiaries (often their children) are more likely to pay off the debts from their own savings or loans rather than raising funds from the sales of an inherited house. The importance of family wealth and intergenerational transfers is determined by the fact that a guarantor (often adult children) is required for older homeowners to sign up to the scheme. This explains the characteristic of current borrowers being those without children. Such institutional constraints help families maintain the 'generational contract'.

Inequalities among siblings and between genders

As an initial effort in postwar democratisation, a shift was made to define children's equal rights on inheritance regardless of their gender and birth order. However, inequalities among siblings and between genders continue to exist in contemporary Japan. Despite the legal definition of equal inheritance rights among children, the larger the family size (number of siblings), the lower the chances that every child will inherit equally. Sons, especially, the eldest son with more than one sibling, are still in a stronger position to inherit family property intact while daughters tend to receive cash gifts (see for example, Noguchi et al, 1988). Other characteristics of beneficiaries include *married* children (again, sons more so than daughters) who live with their parents (Kokumin Seikatsu Center, 1996), and children who experience less geographic mobility. To illustrate this point, a survey conducted by the Economic Policy Institute showed that 26% of older respondents wanted to leave their property to the eldest son; 25.3% equally among their children; and 15.9% to a co-resident child (Noguchi et al, 1988). In the same survey, 17.5% of the respondents wanted to leave it to whichever child provided nursing care for them. The imbalance in shares of inheritance among adult children can be inevitable considering the nature of property that is difficult to divide unless exchanging it to cash. In Japan, sole inheritance of property has been preferred in association with a traditional role of home ownership ('family residence') as a crucial means to maintain family continuity through wealth accumulation in the form of dwellings.

Inequalities between siblings and genders are also evident in the practice of exchange. In fact, the generational contract in Japan does not always represent a straightforward exchange of goods (family home) and services (nursing care) in a specific relationship between two individuals in the family. The Japanese contract may be viewed as a 'joint contract' between several parties in the extended family. The gender fragmentation and imbalance in the exchange certainly exists on an individual basis, since sons are more likely beneficiaries of property, while care provision tends to be a duty of female family members[11]. However, if a wife provides care for her parents-in-law, and her husband inherits family wealth, their rights and responsibilities as a household are reciprocated across generations. The major issue still remains since this exchange arrangement reinforces the gender roles and positions in the family and society. Moreover, women also continue to be disadvantaged in individual asset formation within the family. The stronger position of sons in inheritance is inevitable due to their higher chances to co-reside with their parents. In recent years, however, with changing family traditions and social norms, older people are not restricted to such traditional arrangements. Many older people, especially mothers, have closer ties with their daughters and express their preference to live with their daughter's family without many of the traditional obligations (Izuhara, 2000). This new pattern of co-residence will also impact upon the patterns of inheritance.

Changing nature and patterns of the 'generational contract'

Finally, increased levels of financial independence by older people through home ownership, savings and social security influence the nature and patterns of the 'generational contract'. Partly due to the postwar development of social security such as pensions, the majority of Japanese people are planning to support themselves financially in their old age with their own resources (Figure 4.5). Apart from pensions (83.5%), the most commonly mentioned sources of income in old age have been savings (50.7%), retirement allowances (32.2%) and insurance premiums (31.7%) (Noguchi et al, 1988). The balance will probably change with the increasing precariousness in both public and occupational welfare in the 'post-bubble' era. On the other hand, to mention children as an income source in old age is rare (6.6% of the respondents in the same survey). Even though older people have become more independent financially, support required in their nursing care can be a separate issue, and this has been the area largely left to family responsibilities before the implementation of LTCI. Different views have been expressed between genders

Figure 4.5: Views of people aged 60+ towards old age (%)

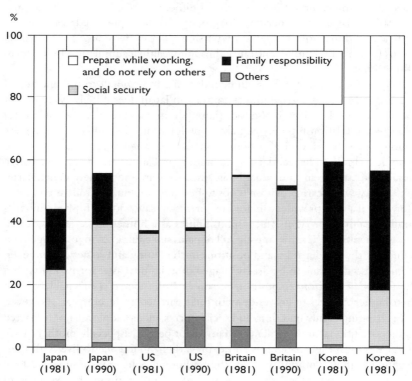

Source: Management and Coordination Agency (1992)

and across generations regarding the responsibility of care provision. Married men typically expect to receive old-age care from their wife (66.2%), while women frequently mentioned residential or nursing home care (37%), partly reflecting the higher likelihood of women becoming widowed, according to the survey conducted by the Economic PR Center (*Yomiuri Shinbun*, 13 September 1997). Across generations, 63.4% of older males expected their family to look after them, while only 29.3% of males and 9.1% of females in the 'baby-boomer' cohort shared this expectation (Kokumin Seikatsu Center, 1996). Moreover, 'individualism' as opposed to 'family-orientation' appears to be dominant among the younger generation: 41.6% of middle-aged respondents would like their parents to consume their wealth for themselves, instead of leaving it to their children (Tokyo Women's Foundation, 1998).

Furthermore, some parents adopt strategic bequest motives and plan to leave their assets in exchange for nursing care from their children in recent years. A series of surveys on 'saving and bequest motives of older people' has been conducted to measure the patterns, strength and characteristics of the family model or the 'generational contract' in Japan. Despite the romanticised values of family-orientation, Horioka et al (1998, 2000) claimed that the selfish 'life-cycle model', rather than 'altruism' or 'dynasty model', is the dominant model of household saving behaviour. Only 25.7% of Japanese respondents wanted to make efforts to leave a bequest to their children in the 1996 survey (Horioka et al, 1998). The majority of individuals either did not plan to leave any bequest, or planned to leave a bequest only if their children looked after them in their old age. Any other bequests were either accidental or unintended.

Conclusion

The ageing of its society has brought many issues to Japan. The increasing ratio of 'dependant' population has started to upset the existing balance of financial, material and instrumental resources across generations. An ageing society also means increasing numbers of old-old age groups, with increased needs and greater costs for welfare provision. In this context, the question remains whether intergenerational relations can maintain the conventional support mechanism.

The family has been, and still is, the central source of support provision. The traditional household structure – co-residence – has effectively assisted the retention of traditional norms and practices surrounding family reciprocity. The number of elderly-only households has however been increasing despite recent policy responses attempting to preserve this traditional living arrangement. Many contemporary factors – such as increased labour force participation by women, changing family values and traditions, and financial independence of older people gained through savings and social security – have been transforming both the capacity for family support and the willingness of family members to carry it out. Due to increased longevity, family carers have also been ageing, and periods of care have often become prolonged. In this context, the long-term care insurance scheme was introduced to raise financial resources to cope with the growing care needs in ageing society and fill the gap vacated by the traditional family. Although it may be too early to assess its real impact on the existing care arrangement, this newly invented 'social contract' will help form a new relationship between service users and providers, and the household and women in a changing society.

Finally, does exchanging nursing care and inheritance in contemporary Japanese families remain part of the 'generational contract'? Perhaps the rights and obligations of the eldest son (and his wife) towards his parents have become less important in contemporary families. Gender issues still remain, however, since the burden of care continues to fall disproportionately on female members, who are still disadvantaged both in terms of individual asset formation and inheritance in the family. Some changes to existing arrangements have been observed. Whether it is because the perceptions, values and attitudes of older people themselves are moving towards independent living, or their options are constrained by the structural inequality of the support relationship, is still open to discussion. Some evidence suggests that older people have started to make a pragmatic decision to utilise their wealth to purchase support services or to move to supportive housing in their old age, thereby breaking the conventional 'contract' with their children.

Notes

[1] This chapter draws on research from 'The generational contract between care and inheritance: Anglo-Japanese perspectives', supported by a small grant from the Nuffield Foundation in 2000.

[2] The population replacement rate (the number of children necessary to maintain the same population size) is 2.08 live births per woman. In Japan, the rate dipped below this figure in the mid-1970s.

[3] The burden of dependency in a population is defined as the ratio of the number of dependent children (aged 15 and younger) and retired persons (65+) to the numbers in 'productive' age groups (aged 16-64). Since the productive age groups include people outside paid employment (such as full-time students and housewives), but do not count older people still engaged in paid work, the ratio can be misleading.

[4] The first Gold Plan was promulgated in 1989 with a total expenditure of over six trillion yen for the provision of welfare services for the following ten years. The Gold Plan was amended to a higher level, called the New Gold Plan in 1994 and then the Gold Plan 21 in 2001, with more realistic and feasible targets concerning service provision.

[5] Following the International Labour Organisation, social security expenditure includes public social insurance, health care and social services, and social assistance.

[6] According to this plan, the number of home-helps was to be increased from 31,405 (1989 figure) to 100,000 before the year 2000. The New Gold Plan revised the target rates to 170,000, and the number of home-helps was 137,000 in 1997 (Ministry of Health and Welfare, 1999).

[7] Category I consists of those aged 65+ who receive a monthly public pension above ¥15,000 (£75). Their premium, deducted from their pensions, is currently based on ¥3,000 (£15) per month (divided into five income groups). Category II applies to those aged 40-64 who are members of health insurance schemes. Depending on their employment/dependency status, the premium is added to their health insurance premiums.

[8] Since £1 = ¥200, this monthly profit figure is equivalent £15,060.

[9] 'Social hospitalisation', where older people stay in hospitals for lengthy periods without critical medical conditions, has been a phenomenon found among Japanese older people. It is due, in part, to the structure of co-payments under the medical insurance, the underdeveloped home care services, and inadequate housing provision and adaptation. The average length of stay in hospitals and other inpatient institutions is appreciably longer in Japan than in other industrial societies (that is, 79 days in 1990 for people aged 65+).

[10] However, home ownership rates were lower among elderly-only households: 84.9% of elderly-couple households and 65.3% of single-elderly households owned a house in 1998 (Management and Coordination Agency, 1998).

[11] For example, approximately 85% of carers for bedridden older people were female: approximately one third of them were *yome* [daughters-in-law]; 28% were a spouse (mainly wife); and 20% adult children (daughters) (Ministry of Health and Welfare, 1992).

References

Akiyama, H., Antonucci, T.C. and Campbell, R. (1997) 'Exchange and reciprocity among two generations of Japanese and American women', in J. Sokolovsky (ed) *The cultural context of aging: Worldwide perspectives* (2nd edn), London: Bergin & Garvey, pp 163-78.

Becker, H. (2000) 'Discontinuous change and generational contracts', in S. Arber and C. Attias-Donfut (eds) *The myth of generational conflict: The family and state in ageing societies*, London: Routledge, pp 114-32.

Finch, J. (1989) *Family obligations and social change*, Cambridge: Polity Press.

Forrest, R. and Murie, A. (eds) (1995) *Housing and family wealth: Comparative international perspectives*, London: Routledge.

Hashimoto, A. (1993) 'Family relations in later life: a cross-cultural perspective', *Generations*, Winter, pp 24-6.

Hashimoto, A. and Kendig, H.L. (1992) 'Aging in international perspective', in H. Kendig, A. Hashimoto and L.C. Coppard (eds) *Family support for the elderly: The international experience*, Oxford: Oxford University Press.

Hayashi, F., Ando, A. and Ferris, R. (1988) 'Life cycle and bequest savings: a study of Japanese and US households based on data from the 1984 NSFIE and the 1983 survey of consumer finances', *Journal of the Japanese and International Economies*, vol 2, no 4, December, pp 450-91.

Hills, J. (1996) 'Does Britain have a welfare generation?', in A. Walker (ed) *The new generational contract: Intergenerational relations, old age and welfare*, London: UCL Press, pp 56-80.

Hirano, T. (2002) 'Jichitai seisaku hyoka shien to kaigo hoken jigyo jisseki no jisseki hyoka' ['Supporting municipal policy evaluation and evaluating the impact of Long-Term Care Insurance'], in *Kiso jichitai ni okeru kaigo hoken seido no koritsu-teki unyo to seisaku sentaku no hyoka kijun ni kansuru hikaku kenkyu sogo hokoku-sho*, Report for the Ministry of Health, Labour and Welfare Research Grant, pp 56-76.

Hiraoka, K. (2002) 'Kaigo service chijo no jokyo' ['The current state of the care service market'], in *Kaigo service kyokyu system no sai-hensei no seika ni kansuru hyoka kenkyu*, Report for the Ministry of Health, Labour and Welfare Research Grant.

Hirayama, Y. and Hayakawa, K. (1995) 'Home ownership and family wealth in Japan', in R. Forrest and A. Murie (eds) *Housing and family wealth: Comparative international perspectives*, London: Routledge, pp 215-30.

Horioka, C.Y., Fujisaki, H., Watanabe, W. and Ishibashi, N. (1998) 'Chochiku Doki/Isan Doki no Nichibei Hikaku' ['A US–Japan comparison of saving and bequest motives'], in C.Y. Horioka and K. Hamada (eds) *Nichibei kakei no chochiku kodo* [*The saving behaviour of US and Japanese households*], Tokyo: Nihon Hyoronsha, pp 71-111.

Horioka, C.Y., Fujisaki, H., Watanabe, W. and Kouno, T. (2000) 'Are Americans more altruistic than the Japanese?: a US–Japan comparison of saving and bequest motives', *International Economic Journal*, vol 14, no 1, pp 1-31.

Ito, S. (2000) *Kensho: Kaigo hoken* [*Examining Long-Term Care Insurance*], Tokyo: Aoki Shoten.

Izuhara, M. (1999) 'Ageing in British society: perspectives of Japanese women', Paper presented to the conference on Migrant Families and Human Capital Formation, University of Leiden, Netherlands, 19-21 November.

Izuhara, M. (2000) *Family change and housing in postwar Japanese society: The experiences of older women*, Aldershot: Ashgate.

Izuhara, M. (2002) 'Care and inheritance: Japanese and English perspectives on the "generational contract"', *Ageing and Society*, vol 22, no 1, pp 61-77.

Kendig, H. (1989) *Social change and family dependency in old age: Perceptions of Japanese women in middle age*, Tokyo: Nihon University, Population Research Institute.

Kokumin Seikatsu Center (1996) *Kodomo to roshin heno sekinin to jibun no rogo* [*Responsibilities towards children and ageing parents, and own old age*], Tokyo: Kokumin Seikatsu Center.

Lawton, L., Silverstein, M. and Bengtson, V. (1994) 'Solidarity between generations in families', in V. Bengtson and R. Harootyan (eds) *Intergenerational linkages: Hidden connections in American society*, New York, NY: Springer Publishing Company.

Le Grand, J. and Bartlett, W. (eds) (1993) *Quasi-markets and social policy*, Basingstoke: Macmillan.

Lee, H.-K. (1987) 'The Japanese welfare state in transition', in R. Friedmann, N. Gilbert and M. Sherer (eds) *Modern welfare states: A comparative view of trends and prospects*, Brighton: Wheatsheaf Books, pp 243-63.

Management and Coordination Agency (1992) *Life and views of older people*, Tokyo: Bureau of Statistics.

Management and Coordination Agency (1998) *Jutaku tokei chosa* [*Housing survey of Japan*], Tokyo: Bureau of Statistics.

Management and Coordination Agency (2000) *Kokusei Chosa* [*Population census of Japan*], Tokyo: Bureau of statistics.

Marshall, V., Rosenthal, C. and Dacink, J. (1987) 'Older parents' expectations for filial support', *Social Justice Research*, vol 1, no 4, pp 405-24.

Masuda, M. (2001) 'Kaigo hoken seido no seisaku keisei katei no tokucho to kadai: kanryo soshiki ni okeru seisaku keisei katei no jirei' ['Characteristics and issues of the policy-making process for the Long-Term Care Insurance system: a case in the Japanese bureaucracy'], *The Quarterly of Social Security Research*, vol 37, no 1, pp 44-58.

Ministry of Health and Welfare (1999) *Kosei hakusho* [*White paper on health and welfare*], Tokyo: Ministry of Health and Welfare.

Ministry of Health and Welfare (2000) *Kokumin Seikatsu Kiso Chosa* [*Basic Survey on the Life of People in Japan*], Tokyo: Ministry of Health and Welfare.

Morioka, K. (1973) *Kazoku shuki-ron* [*Family life-cycle*], Tokyo: Baifukan.

Nakagawa,Y. (1979) 'Japan, the welfare super-power', *Journal of Japanese Studies*, vol 5, no 1, pp 5-51.

National Institute of Population and Social Security Research (1997) *Nihon no shorai suikei jinko* [*Population projection in Japan*].

Noguchi,Y., Uemura, K., Kitoh,Y. and Midohoka, K. (1988) *Sozoku no jittai to eikyou ni kansuru chosa kenkyu* [*Study on facts and effects of inheritance*], Keizai Sesaku Kenkyu-sho.

Office of the Prime Minister (1994) *Sekai no seinen tono hikaku kara mita nihon no seinen* [*Japanese youth in comparison with youth around the world*],Tokyo: Office of the Prime Minister.

Rosenmayr, L. and Koeckeis, E. (1963) 'Propositions for a sociological theory of ageing and the family', *International Social Science Journal*, vol 15, pp 410-26.

Rudd, C. (1994) 'Japan's welfare mix', *The Japan Foundation Newsletter*, vol 22, no 3, pp 14-17.

Tokyo Women's Foundation (1997) *Tsuma to Otto no Zaisan* [*Assets of wife and husband*], Tokyo.

Tokyo Women's Foundation (1998) *Zaisan, kyodosei, gender* [*Assets, partnership and gender*], Tokyo.

US Census Bureau (2001) *An aging world: 2001, international population report*, Washington (DC): US Government Printing Office.

Walker, A. (ed) (1996) *The New Generational Contract: Intergenerational relations, old age and welfare*, London: UCL Press.

Yabe, M. (2002) *Kaigo hoken no jisshi jokyo to kongo no kadai ni tsuite* [*Current situation and future issues of long-term care insurance*], Zenkoku kaigo hoken tantou kachou kaigi shiryou, 4 June.

FIVE

Domestic violence, research and social policy in Britain

Ellen Malos

Introduction

The beginnings of change: a hidden issue becomes visible

Violence against women, and domestic violence in particular, became a public issue in Britain during the last quarter of the 19th century. Influenced by the feminist movement of the time, legal changes gave women the right to protection against the severest forms of assault by their husbands, including the right to apply for legal separation and to keep their own earnings, if separated (Cobbe, 1978; Dobash and Dobash, 1980; Mulvey Roberts and Mizuta, 1994). (It was not until later that married women living with their husbands gained full property rights.) The subject then lapsed from the political agenda until 100 years or so later, and only became a public issue again in the last 30 years of the 20th century.

Despite some changes in opinion reflected in 20th-century case law, attitudes to violent and coercive behaviour by men towards their wives and partners in the second half of the 20th century were still heavily influenced by beliefs about the rights of men in the family and the privacy of the household similar to those in the late 18th century (Dobash and Dobash, 1980, 1992; Pahl, 1985; Hague and Malos, 1993, 1998). The persistence of traditional attitudes towards gender hierarchy in the family, and the newer psychological approaches which located 'personal' problems in an individual or family matrix, combined to minimise and obscure violence against women in general, including domestic violence, as a social phenomenon (Dobash and Dobash, 1980, 1992; Hague and Malos, 1993, 1998).

In addition, there was a belief that the postwar welfare state had eradicated poverty, and therefore significantly reduced what were thought to be the major social causes of violent and 'deviant' behaviour. Instances of social problems, including violence in society and in the family (including child abuse and domestic violence), were subsumed under the heading of 'deviance' by sociologists and criminologists and were normally viewed by social welfare agencies as a consequence of pathological individual psychology or of 'family dysfunction' (Parton, 1985; Hague and Malos, 1993, 1998).

In Britain, the beginnings of a break with such attitudes came in the 1970s through a combination of processes, the most important of which was the advent of the Women's Liberation Movement. Some key factors here were the growing realisation that equality between the sexes was an ideal which had not been realised, either in the 'public' realm of the labour market, the law and politics, or in the 'private' sphere of family life and personal relationships. One key change was the questioning of the very division between the public and the private with the assertion that 'the personal is political' and the beginnings of an analysis of gendered power relationships as common to both spheres.

The movement against domestic violence, and the particular shape it took in Britain, should be viewed in this context. It also needs to be seen in relation to a number of social and legal developments, among them being changes in the divorce laws; a lessening of stigma in relation to divorce, cohabitation and the birth of children outside marriage; and also developments in social security and the labour market. Together these made it possible for women to survive outside of marriage, even with children.

The development of awareness of the prevalence of domestic violence came from women themselves 'speaking out' about their experiences. This ran parallel with the movement against rape, and women survivors revealing sexual abuse by fathers and family members or friends when they were children, which helped to give rise to current awareness about child sexual abuse. Women seeking help to escape from violent relationships, or to put an end to the abuse, triggered the growth of the refuge movement – Women's Aid – and led to the formation of four national Women's Aid federations for England, Wales, Scotland and Northern Ireland (Pizzey, 1974; Pahl, 1985; Rose, 1985; Hague and Malos, 1993, 1998).

Developing alliances, legal and social policy changes, and the beginnings of research

By the later 1970s, alliances had been made between the refuge movement and other campaign and pressure groups, most notably those campaigning against homelessness. This resulted in the recognition in the homelessness legislation of 1977 that women leaving home because of domestic violence were, in law, homeless and, if they had children, were prioritised for the allocation of public, rented housing. Alliances with members of parliament also led to Private Member's Bills introducing a range of civil injunctions against a violent partner, which were not, as before, dependent on marital status and the commencement of divorce proceedings.

The key developments relating to domestic violence against women, therefore, included the growth, from the mid-1970s, of the Women's Aid movement and the growing visibility of the issue of domestic violence, resulting from public and media campaigns by the movement (Dobash and Dobash, 1992; Hague et al, 1996).

Research on domestic violence has developed in concert with the growth of the movement against domestic violence and against violence with regard to women in general. It has both influenced and been influenced by the responses of public agencies and public policy towards such violence. I wish now to document the development of the relationship between the emergence of domestic violence as a social issue in Britain and the interlinked development of domestic violence research.

The state of knowledge on the nature and level of domestic violence in Britain

Incidence, prevalence and impact of domestic violence

The character and the strengths and weaknesses of the state of knowledge on domestic violence in Britain reflects both the history and the nature of the relationship between the movement and policy makers at both national and local level. It has also been affected by the nature of opportunities for research funding on such issues and by the lack of a national statistical research centre with the capacity (or commitment) to mount large-scale studies on the incidence and prevalence of violence against women, including domestic violence. These factors help to explain why Britain, which saw the birth of the most recent movement against domestic violence (Dobash and Dobash, 1980, 1992; Coote and Campbell, 1982; Rose, 1985; Hague and Malos, 1993, 1998), has no comprehensive statistical survey of the incidence and/or prevalence either of domestic violence, or violence against women in general[1]. It appears that Britain has been overtaken in this respect by a number of European countries, where both the movement and the policy response are far less developed. For example, a national survey on women, looking at both labour market issues and violence, has recently taken place in France (ENVEFF, 2001), and in Italy a number of large-scale regional surveys are being conducted (Prato Conference, 2001; see also Hagemann-White, 2001).

This is not to ignore the importance of the investigation into the incidence of domestic assaults in recent British Crime Surveys. However, the British Crime Survey does not take in the full range of domestic violence (including psychological violence and financial coercion) which derives from the still unequal power between men and women both in society and in their intimate relationships. Sylvia Walby, a professor at the University of Leeds, has developed a module based on the Statistics Canada model, incorporating domestic violence in a broader context as well as other forms of violence against women, for inclusion in the British Crime Survey (Statistics Canada, 1993; Walby, 1999; Hague et al, 2001). Unfortunately for the purposes of this volume, information from this survey is not yet available. In addition a useful booklet summarising statistical and other information on interpersonal violence has been published by the Economic and Social Research Council Violence Research Programme (Stanko et al, 2002).

There has been no national study of the proportion of women who have experienced violence in relationships over any period of time, be it a limited period (similar to the French survey) or over longer periods. However, there have been a number of localised or small-scale studies taking a broad definition of domestic violence (Dobash and Dobash, 1980; Women's Aid Federation, 1992; Mooney, 1994; Dominy and Radford, 1996; Stanko et al, 1998). These suggest that between one quarter and one third of women experience violent and/or systematically coercive relationships. Other studies of the prevalence of a range of abusive behaviours suggest that violence towards the female partner occurs in between 30-50% of male–female relationships[2] (Ball, 1995; Kelly, 1996). In addition, a recent national 'snapshot' census of referrals to agencies revealed that a large number of women seek help from agencies despite the known low rate of reporting, indicating the serious nature of the problem and the necessity for action (Stanko, 2002; see also McGibbon et al, 1989).

Currently, however, the British Crime Surveys are the only large-scale statistical study of the subject in Britain. Although they include questions concerning domestic violence and means of measuring physical assault, they do not concern themselves with other common types of coercive and violent behaviour that comprise domestic violence in its fullest sense. According to successive British Crime Surveys, domestic violence – in the form of actual physical assault – was the most rapidly increasing violent crime over a number of years between 1981 and 1993. Recently, rates appear to have decreased, although numbers reported to the 2000 survey were, nevertheless, almost double those reported in 1981[3]. Figures extrapolated from the survey (Mirlees–Black, 1995) suggested that one in ten women who have lived with a male partner experienced physical assault from their partners at some time. About one third of these assaults occur after separation.

The 1996 survey received wide media publicity because it included a self-report questionnaire, which shows an apparently equal incidence of 'assault' by men and women who are current or former partners (Mirlees–Black, 1995; Home Office, 1999). However, there was less publicity for the finding that women were twice as likely as men to be injured and to have been assaulted three or more times[4]. Financial issues often increased the frequency of assault, and it was more commonly used against young women aged 16-24, women without employment, and women with children. Like other research that takes in a wider definition of violence (such as Mooney, 1994) the British Crime Surveys suggest that even physical violence against women in personal relationships is most likely to go unreported. This survey has since been repeated, but the results have not yet been published at the time of writing.

Violence, then, is not just physical assault, although that can be extremely serious and, of course, includes murder – 40-45% of homicides against women are by a husband, partner or former partner, compared with 7% of homicides against men (Home Office, Annual). However it is important to realise that violence may involve many other forms of coercive behaviour, including sexual abuse or rape, and can include psychological abuse of various kinds, including virtual imprisonment and physical deprivation because of abuse of financial power. Children often witness abuse and can be involved in it, either as the targets of abuse or being forced to participate in various ways in the abuse of their mother (Malos and Hague, 1993, 1997; Hester et al, 2000; Mullender et al, 2002: forthcoming).

It is also important to understand that the persistent nature of such abuse cannot always be escaped by leaving the violent partner. Indeed, leaving may exacerbate the problem unless there are a variety of supporting interventions in place. When women try to end the relationship, this often leads to homelessness and isolation because personal ties and networks are also broken. Ending the relationship can also be very dangerous, since women are more likely to be murdered after separation (Hester et al, 2000).

Domestic violence: problems of naming and defining

Partly because of the way the problem of violence against women within marital and intimate relationships was hidden within the 'private world' of the family, a number of different terms for domestic violence have been used that vary both within and between countries. In the British legal and policy sphere it was called 'domestic violence' to the extent that it was recognised at all. In the US, it was subsumed under 'family violence' and both terms are still used in both countries. When it was rediscovered as a separate issue in Britain, the women were known as 'battered wives' or 'battered women' by analogy with the then newly coined 'battered baby syndrome' (see, for example, Pizzey, 1974). Many women who experienced such violence found the term 'battered women' both demeaning and misleading and it is no longer commonly used in Britain, though it is still in use in the US. Other terms used are 'domestic abuse', 'women abuse' or 'violence towards women from known men'. All of these terms are problematic in relation to defining the experience and forming a sufficiently clear descriptive basis for action against the complex set of practices it encompasses[5].

However, in a policy and legal context in Britain, 'domestic violence' is the term most often used and given force in law. It has also been redefined in practice so that some of the problems of definition meaning have been reduced. For example, it is widely recognised that 'domestic violence' is most usually directed by men towards women in a close personal relationship (Dobash and Dobash, 1980, 1992; Mooney, 1994; Home Office, 1995; Women's Unit, 1999). It is therefore the term used here, and, where necessary, is supplemented by other clarifying terms.

There are also many problems with the definition of 'violence'. However, within this chapter, 'violence' means any abusive or violent behaviour – whether physical or non-physical – which is used by one person to control or dominate another with whom they have, or have had, a close personal relationship (Hester et al, 2000). This chapter also focuses mainly on violence directed by men at their female partners.

Moving from the margins: the developing links between activism, research and policy

Despite the absence of large-scale statistical studies of the incidence and prevalence of domestic violence, there is a significant and growing body of research on the subject in Britain. This is strongest and most developed in a wide range of critical research on policy and practice.

The 1970s to the 1980s: research on domestic violence in Britain

The development of the refuge movement and the need to demonstrate the serious nature of domestic violence led to the beginnings of research. Initially, this was on a very small scale and usually undertaken by Women's Aid activists and/or by campaigners challenging violence against women in general, in order to establish the existence and nature of domestic violence. Much of the information was drawn from the accounts of women who had experienced domestic violence, thereby making them "heroes of their own lives" (Gordon, 1989). It was often used to demonstrate to local statutory agencies or to the government, the need for safe accommodation (refuges and resettlement into permanent housing) and for protection by police, as well as civil and criminal law.

Very little of this early research was published formally. However, one important exception was Dobash and Dobash's *Violence against wives* (1980), first published in the US in 1978 and two years later in Britain. This highly influential book developed a historical overview of domestic violence in Britain and an explanation based on historical inequalities between men and women in marriage and in society. However, it also contained a kernel of research into reported domestic violence in police stations in Glasgow in the late 1970s and an empirical study of the circumstances which triggered violent episodes (see Cavanagh, in Pahl, 1985). This research contained the first published figures on the incidence of reported domestic violence in Britain. It found that 25% of reported crime in sample police stations was in fact incidents of domestic violence. This figure was shocking at the time but has since been replicated. Indeed, higher incident rates have been found elsewhere: for example, as high as 50% in a more recent study (Cretney and Davis, 1996). Of course, such findings are subject to change because of local variation and are possibly affected by the growth of reporting in more recent years, as a result of changing policing practice. However, this figure of 25% has acted as a baseline for incidence statistics and for campaigning for action on domestic violence. In fact, it is still widely cited, including government sources (Women's Unit, 1999). Another significant early study on agency responses to domestic violence – this time, largely in the context of divorce (see Borkowski et al, 1983) – showed high rates of divorce attributable to domestic violence in its wider sense.

Civil law remedies and social legislation through Private Member's Bills

Important legislation was passed in the mid-1970s via Private Member's Bills as a result of lobbying and alliance building by Women's Aid, rather than as a result of government initiatives.

Civil protection laws

In cases of domestic violence, the 1976 Domestic Violence and Matrimonial Causes Act and the 1978 Domestic Violence and Magistrates Courts Act introduced non-molestation orders and orders to oust or exclude the perpetrator from the family home for protection. However, judicial discretion limited their scope, while case law sometimes moved in contradictory directions. National Judges Directions, which are sent to all judges in the court system, limited the application of powers of arrest to cases where there had been severe physical abuse. Exclusion and ousting orders were limited to three months in the first instance and required regular applications for renewal rather than being permitted to operate for the time required for a property settlement in divorce or separation proceedings. The application of the law where the woman was not married to her attacker had to be confirmed on appeal because of concerns over the property rights of the men involved (an issue which was raised again when the law on civil protection was strengthened in 1996). Enforcement was often ineffective where there were no powers of arrest involved, and often when there were because of failure to ensure that police were informed of such injunctions (Barron, 1989; Law Commission, 1992; Hague and Malos, 1993).

The 1977 Housing (Homeless Persons) Act

In view of the problems arising with protection under the criminal law and through civil legislation, emergency and temporary accommodation was – and still remains – of vital importance for the safety of many of the women and children involved. From the start, the accommodation was provided almost exclusively by voluntary, community-based Women's Aid refuges that had little or no secure funding. Therefore, Women's Aid acted in conjunction with housing campaign groups in securing the inclusion of domestic violence as a reason to be considered homeless in the 1977 Housing (Homeless Persons) Act, also initially a Private Member's Bill (now replaced by the 1996 Housing Act and the 2002 Homelessness Act).

The homelessness legislation was heavily dependent for its implementation on local discretion, and was sometimes applied ungenerously (Binney et al, 1981; Malos and Hague, 1993). Nevertheless, as we shall see later in this chapter, the limited security it offered was attacked as a 'perverse incentive' and a queue jumper's charter in the final period of the Conservative government and weakened by the 1996 Housing Act (Malos and Hague, 1993, 1998; Morley, 2000).

Policy and practice oriented research from the early 1980s

The 1980s saw the beginning of more formal research, which was part of a developing critique of service provision and of the reaction of statutory agencies to women experiencing domestic violence and their children. Such studies investigated services, policies, and the application of legislation in a number of important social policy areas, most notably in the beginning: housing and refuge, and policing and the civil and criminal justice systems. An important aspect of this research was that it involved links between activists, academics and sometimes practitioners. This was often because the researchers themselves combined activism and an academic background or occupation, and because feminist analyses were being pioneered within the social sciences and humanities. While this strand of research continued, others were added over time:

- social services, child protection and child welfare;
- 'prevention' (perpetrator programmes, education);
- health;
- the impact of domestic violence on children, and how these are, or are not, taken up by children's services (Abrahams, 1994; Mullender and Morley, 1994).

Housing research and its impact

In the late 1970s the Department of the Environment funded a study of refuges and housing issues (Binney et al, 1981). This was a significant departure in that the researchers were Women's Aid activists rather than academic researchers, although they did have third-level qualifications. Although it was designed to study the impact of the new 1977 Housing (Homeless Persons) Act, it also looked at other issues for women experiencing domestic violence who had left violent relationships.

The next systematic study of the operation of the Homelessness Act in domestic violence situations was funded in 1990 by the Joseph Rowntree Foundation (Malos and Hague, 1993). There was also other relevant research on homelessness funded by the Department of the Environment in the late 1980s and early 1990s (for example, Evans and Duncan, 1988; Bull, 1993). However, the range of services carried out in refuges have not been widely researched except by or through the Women's Aid movement itself (Women's Aid Federations, 1992, 1997; see also Abrahams forthcoming).

In cooperation with activists and advocates, especially Women's Aid, such research was influential in changing the advice in government Codes of

Guidance and encouraging the development of Local Housing Authority and Housing Association policy and practice, and the beginnings of domestic violence awareness training for staff. However, the undoubted impact of this work has to be measured against the reduction of the public, rented sector, the introduction of the right to buy council housing at a generous discount after the 1980 Housing Act, and the more financially stringent approach to social rented housing introduced by the Conservative government after 1979.

Research on policing

Although physical and sexual violence against women was, in law, a crime (although, at that time, rape was a crime only if it occurred outside of marriage), the women's movement had highlighted the fact that it was rarely taken seriously and that women themselves were often treated with hostility by the police. Women's Aid, Rape Crisis and anti-rape groups gave women subjected to these experiences support. Their complaints were followed up by public campaigns backed by substantiating evidence from researchers, and followed through by media revelations and television documentaries (Hanmer and Maynard, 1987; Edwards, 1989; Hanmer et al, 1989; Smith, 1989; Hague and Malos 1993; Hague et al, 1996). This body of work documented the failure of the police to protect women who called them in an emergency. Police were shown often to be indifferent or hostile when women reported rape and sexual assault or other forms of violence, whether from partners and other known men, or from strangers.

Over time, such evidence brought about significant changes in policing policy in some areas. The impact was felt in a number of individual police authorities because of combined pressure from activists and researchers (often the same people) and media coverage[6]. By the second half of the 1980s, the Home Office had begun to issue national guidance to police on taking violence against women seriously (Home Office, 1986; Smith, 1989). The first Home Office circular – *Violence against women* (1986) – was followed by influential new guidance specifically on domestic violence (Home Office, 1990). The importance of this later circular was that it covered the need for improved practice in recording incidents and in actively seeking both to protect victims and to prosecute perpetrators. Police forces were encouraged to appoint domestic violence officers or set up domestic violence units, and to work in liaison with Women's Aid and other agencies. Such developments encouraged joint working and the growth of domestic violence forums, which had already been initiated in some areas (Hague et al, 1996).

Research on the criminal and civil justice systems

Research on the treatment of violence against women in the criminal justice system ran parallel to that on policing. It was often directed at critiques of the prosecution process and judicial decision making relating, for example, to sexual offences and rape (Lees, 1997; Gregory and Lees, 1999) which played an important part in changing the law on rape within marriage. Similarly, both research and campaigning were highly important in highlighting the injustices of the treatment of women who killed[7] violent husbands, often after years of abuse, as compared with that of husbands who killed their wives (see, for example, Russell and Radford, 1992; Nadel, 1993; Ahluwalia and Gupta, 1997). At a slightly later point, documentation and research on the failings of the civil protection legislation led to strengthened legislation in the mid-1990s (Barron, 1990; Law Commission, 1992).

Moving from the margins into the mainstream

The 1980s to the mid-1990s

Alliances between activists, advocates, researchers, and others that had led to the development of legislation and policy, continued and strengthened throughout the 1980s. In the decade from the mid-1980s onwards there was an important policy shift. A phase of partial inclusion of violence against women in mainstream government policy directives was initiated through the two Home Office circulars of 1986 and 1990. The latter (Home Office 60/1990) went much further in relation to domestic violence than its predecessor:

- it emphasised the duties of police officers to take reports of domestic violence seriously;
- it called for local police authorities to introduce pro-arrest and pro-prosecution policies – instead of 'no-criming' such cases;
- local police authorities were to introduce domestic violence liaison officers or units to develop inter-agency work, and to ensure that adequate records were kept of calls, attendance at incidents and of any injunctions in force.

This was a stage beyond Private Member's Bills, since a government ministry took up the policy initiatives developed in a number of police authorities in order to apply the existing criminal law, and the policing powers within it, to the situation of women experiencing violence. The 1990 Home Office circular was followed by a number of parliamentary initiatives, including the 1993 House of Commons Home Affairs Committee Inquiry, to which a large number of individuals and organisations gave evidence (House of Commons, 1993; Hague and Malos, 1993, 1998). This gave further impetus to cooperation between voluntary and statutory organisations, to investigations into issues relating to inter-agency and multi-agency cooperation (National Inter-Agency Working Party, 1992), and to the development of multi-agency work, protocols and guidelines by other agencies (Hague et al, 1996; Harwin et al, 1999).

The more active role of central government and statutory agencies was partly a consequence of the developments described earlier in this chapter, and also arose from the greater international profile of issues of gender inequality and violence against women. As signatory to international declarations and protocols (United Nations, 1993a, 1993b, 1995), the British government had an obligation and incentive to show progress in tackling issues arising from discrimination and violence against women.

The mid-1990s onwards: the inter-agency circular on coordination of support for women experiencing domestic violence

The development, strengths and weaknesses of multi-agency work

The Home Office circular of 1990 was followed in 1995 by a circular on inter-agency coordination of action on domestic violence at local level issued by the Home Office on behalf of a wide range of government ministries (Home Office and Welsh Office, 1995)[8]. The inter-agency circular emphasised the need to ensure the safety of women and children and to develop action across the full range of agencies and services and listed a range of actions that required the participation and cooperation of a very wide range of local statutory and voluntary agencies. The Home Office was given the overall responsibility to coordinate central government policy, chairing the Official and Ministerial Inter-departmental Groups on domestic violence. Membership of these groups included the full range of legal and social ministries and the Treasury (Home Office, 1995, p 9, Section 4.1).

It was clear that responsibility for the success of multi-agency approaches to domestic violence could not lie with local agencies alone but would need sufficient resources and, in some cases, encouragement from the relevant ministries to carry them out. Until relatively recently, however, there has been little specific advice from ministries, other than the Home Office, to local agencies on how to work within a coordinated multi-agency strategy on domestic violence issues (but see Ball, 1995; Department of Health, 2000). Research on multi-agency initiatives by both myself and my colleagues found that the work was often taken on by committed individuals making time in an already overcrowded schedule with no clear mandate for developing better practice within their organisation (Hague et al, 1996; Malos, 1999). Even in relatively well established multi-agency initiatives, there is still patchy participation by some statutory agencies, such as the Department of Health (Hague et al, 1996; Department of Health, 2000; Williamson, 2000).

The issue of earmarked resources for multi-agency work is still a difficult one and can affect the quality of the work. In addition, the lack of a national strategy on the part of government for funding both multi-agency work and refuge services can lead to implicit competition between multi-agency initiatives and the vital front line services provided by the Women's Aid Federation and refuges.

Legislation

Despite a significant commitment to the issue of domestic violence, particularly in relation to policing the criminal law, the character of some policy and legislation in the 1990s became increasingly ambivalent. This was due, in part, to the Conservative government's concern both to reduce public spending and to cut back on the role of the state in welfare. This indicates the need to scrutinise legislative and policy changes for their detailed impact in relevant policy areas and to remain vigilant to detect negative or contradictory implications of government action, rather than relying solely on declarations of good intent.

The 1996 Housing Act

The most glaring example of possible side effects was the 1996 Housing Act. (Ironically this was already drafted when the 1995 inter-agency circular was being issued.) In its original form it would have removed the right for homeless people, including women experiencing domestic violence and their children, to be allocated permanent public or social housing by the 1977 Homelessness Act, and would have limited the provision of temporary housing to six months.

The current New Labour government confirmed the discretion of local authorities to give due weight to homelessness and specifically homelessness in relation to domestic violence in determining the priority of applicants on housing waiting lists. It has now backed this up by legislation (after considerable delay) in the shape of the 2002 Homelessness Act. Nevertheless, there is still scope for discretion on the part of unsympathetic housing officers and housing authorities. Coupled with the reduction (and sometimes elimination) of public rented housing in a number of local authority areas, this means that this important safety net has been seriously weakened since the 1970s (Malos and Hague, 1998; Morley, 2000).

The 1996 law, however, has enabled women who are already in social-rented accommodation to obtain sole tenancy under the provisions against anti-social behaviour, which includes domestic violence. This can be helpful when it is successfully combined with effective protection to enable women and children to continue to occupy their homes, or with tenancy transfer (Malos and Hague, 1998; Morley, 2000).

The 1996 Family Homes and Domestic Violence Bill

The enactment of initial legislation for domestic violence and civil protection orders came from women's desire for protection without having to initiate divorce or take criminal proceedings. However, there were growing criticisms of the legislation in action, particularly by Women's Aid. Related research (Barron, 1990) had a significant influence on the Law Commission report (1992) on the legislation. This report ultimately led to strengthened and rationalised provisions in part IV of the 1996 Family Law Act. However, enacting the Law Commission's proposals illustrates the difficulties still facing attempts to strengthen protection and support for women experiencing domestic violence and their children.

Some of the commission's proposals proved to be enormously controversial, since various sections of the media and journalists, such as John Torode and William Oddie, as well as certain men's organisations such as the UK MEN's Movement (UK MEN'S Movement, 2002) claimed that they unfairly attacked the rights of men to their homes. The bill was unique historically, in that it was withdrawn by the then Conservative government part way through the legislative process because of fears that its paper-thin majority would be lost.

The 1996 Family Law Act (FLA)

The FLA carried both positive and negative implications for women experiencing domestic violence. Like the 1996 Housing Act, the FLA illustrates the need for a detailed scrutiny and critique of such legislation in the process of drafting and passage through the parliamentary process. Part II, concerning divorce, would have introduced delays in initiating and finalising divorce as well as pressure to mediate and to settle issues prior to divorce proceedings which could have increased the danger of post-separation violence (Hester et al, 2000). Therefore, there is considerable relief among those concerned with domestic violence that the implementation of these sections of the Act has been indefinitely postponed (Lord Chancellor's Department [www.lcd.gov.uk]; pers. comm.).

Part IV of the FLA, however, based on the previously withdrawn Family Homes and Domestic Violence Bill, greatly strengthens civil protection orders, although it is more complex than intended because of amendments introduced while the bill was going through parliament (Lord Chancellor's Department, 1997; Edwards, 2001b).

The new law widens the scope of protection orders by extending the range of possible applicants, which now includes both adults and children. The adults do not necessarily need to be married or currently living in the same household but they must have lived in the same household at some time. Both non-molestation and occupation orders may be 'ex parte' in the first instance; therefore it is no longer possible for a man to prevent the granting of protection orders by failing to come to court. Additionally, there is an obligation to attach a power of arrest to both non-molestation and occupation orders unless the court is satisfied that the applicant will be adequately protected without it. A power of arrest may also be attached to 'ex parte' orders, and, if breached, the order may be enforced by a new procedure of issuing a warrant for arrest instead of relying on contempt of court proceedings (Hester et al, 2000; Edwards, 2001b). A judge or magistrate may invoke action under the FLA in any family proceedings. In addition, the FLA allows third-party applications (by police or social workers, for example) but these have not yet been implemented (Humphries and Kaye, 1997; Humphreys et al, 1997).

The weakness of the FLA lies in the greater complexity introduced into the original bill in parliament, and the fact that it does not normally extend any protection to those who have never lived with their abusers. In addition, in its passage through parliament, the bill was amended to introduce distinctions between 'entitled' persons with a legal claim on the property, where orders were initially for a longer period and may be extended indefinitely, and 'non-entitled' persons, where occupation orders would be shorter in the first instance and much more temporary overall.

Research on the use of the FLA (Edwards, 2001) shows that there have been marginally more non-molestation orders than before. There have also been more occupation orders than previous ouster orders; however, it is not possible to make a direct comparison because of the wider scope for orders under the new law. The greatest improvement has been in the use of powers of arrest, which are attached to 75% of occupation orders and 80% of non-molestation orders. This is compared to one-third previously but the proportion was rising to a half in the year before the FLA, illustrating the possible tendency of impending legislation to affect court practice in some instances before it is passed or implemented. The research found that the courts are taking a more robust view of enforcement. In addition, undertakings (such as keeping the peace) which have been criticised for ease of evasion are also used more (Barron, 1990, pp 21-2, p 123; Law Commission, 1992). The research also reveals wide variations between courts in granting of orders and of attachment of powers of arrest with some areas sampled showing very low use.

The 1997 Protection from Harassment Act (PHA)

The PHA was intended for use against 'stalkers' and therefore not formulated for use in domestic violence. However, it does have a number of important potential impacts (Hester et al, 2000; Edwards, 2001; Lord Chancellor's Department [www.lcd.gov.uk]). In particular, it has the potential to fill a gap left in the protection offered by part IV of the FLA. Under the PHA, it is not necessary for the abuser to have lived with the complainant, so the PHA can therefore be used by women experiencing violence from known men, who could not use the FLA.

There are also a number of important innovations in the legislation. It recognises a whole range of types of coercive and intimidating behaviour, which do not necessarily fall under conventional definitions of violence and harassment. Use of the PHA can be triggered by an accumulation of incidents or behaviours rather than a single severe incident, as in previous law. The Act recognises the possible links between seemingly innocuous acts – the sending of unsolicited cards, letters, and flowers or unsolicited telephone calls – and their potential escalation into more obvious forms of harassment – such as lingering in the street, or near a woman's place of work, calling at the house or moving on to possible breaking and entering, physical or sexual abuse or even murder.

Additionally, action under the law can be either civil or criminal. In civil actions, damages can be awarded, or an injunction granted forbidding harassment. Where a judge has reasonable grounds for belief that an injunction has been breached, a power of arrest can be attached. Indeed, in civil proceedings there may be difficulty over legal aid as in proceedings under the FLA.

A case can rely, not only on the complainant's testimony, but also on an accumulation of evidence. This technique of evidence building may have application in criminal assault proceedings, and recent changes to Crown Prosecution Service guidelines suggest that in criminal proceedings for domestic violence, or possibly sexual offences, evidence should be sought from neighbours and others, rather than insisting on the women's testimony as the main evidence.

In general, the use of the PHA has been greater than originally anticipated, but as with the FLA there are great variations in use between regions with some using it sparingly. It is probable that much of the use comes from its applicability to domestic violence and violence and harassment by known men, but it is not possible to quantify this from the court statistics because the different categories of case are not distinguished in the returns (Edwards, 2001a).

The 1998 Crime and Disorder Act

Although this act is not explicitly concerned with domestic violence, it introduces 'crime audits', which can draw attention to safety measures for women experiencing domestic violence (among other things). It also calls for partnerships between the police and other agencies and consultation with the community, so providing an opportunity for developing imaginative community safety measures in a multi-agency setting. The current Home Office Crime Prevention Programme, which is funding a significant number of intervention projects on violence against women, including domestic violence, has proved to be a means of using such local crime audits. It allows both community safety partnerships and multi-agency forums to develop imaginative interventions designed to enhance the safety of women and children and reduce repeated violent offences.

Current research developments

A large number of researchers are evaluating the intervention projects programmes in a coordinated evaluation research programme funded by the Home Office. As this indicates there are some signs that the lack of recognition of domestic violence and violence against women as a field of research in its own right has begun to change. Recently the Economic and Social Research Council (ESRC) has funded a number of such studies[9]. Others have been included in integrated programmes of research, such as those carried out under the ESRC programme 'Listening to the voices of children' (Mullender et al,

2000, 2002: forthcoming) and the more recent Violence Initiative which included three studies of different aspects of domestic violence (Morley, 2000; Mezey and Bewley, 2001; Stanko, 2002; Hague et al, 2003: forthcoming). This also included research on homicide (Dobash et al, 2002a, 2002b, 2002c) and on sexual violence (Stanko et al, 2002). The forthcoming work of Walby and her colleagues is directed to remedying the lack of large-scale survey data mentioned above (Walby and Myhill, 2001; Hague et al, 2001). In addition, the government – through the Department of Health, the Lord Chancellor's Department and the government's Women's Equality Unit – is funding related research.

Since the mid-1990s, a growing body of policy and legislation has aimed at developing an overall intervention strategy (Home Office, 1995, 2000a, 2001; Women's Unit, 1999). This has been accompanied by research evaluating and scrutinising the implementation of such developments, some of which is encouraged by the government. However, much remains to be done to ensure effective intervention based on clear understandings of the needs of women experiencing domestic violence, and their children.

The impact of domestic violence on children

Child protection proceedings

To date research with regard to child protection is still less developed and is difficult to conduct because of the sensitivity of the subject. However, since the mid-1990s, a small body of published research has built up on this subject (Mullender and Morley, 1994; Hague et al, 1996; Mullender et al, 2000; Mullender et al, 2002: forthcoming; Harne, 2002: unpublished). In addition, a specific body of work examines the impact on women and their children of the granting of contact orders following divorce to fathers who are violent within the family (Hester et al, 1998).

Guidance has been offered to local authorities, guardians *ad litem* and reporting officers in relation to the seeking of occupation orders under part IV of the Family Law Act by the Department of Health Circular (1997). The circular showed understanding of the complex issues involved, the need for informed consent of the non-abusing parent in seeking to apply for orders, and of support for mothers in situations of domestic violence within statutory social services responsibility for child protection.

There is still a danger, however, that awareness of the impact of domestic violence on children will lead to removal of children should the mother be perceived to be failing to protect them, rather than exploring ways to support the mother in safeguarding the children and herself (Hester and Pearson, 1998; Mullender et al, 2002: forthcoming).

Orders under the 1989 Children Act

Another problematic area is that relating to court ordered contact with fathers following separation after domestic violence. The 1989 Children Act was drawn up to recognise both the child's 'best interests' and developing international protocols on children's rights. The law promoted the expectation that children had a right to contact with both parents in cases of divorce or separation, and this has created problems of decision making where there has been either child abuse or domestic violence.

In making decisions under the Children Act, a welfare checklist – including a consideration of the wishes and feelings of the child – must be considered. Currently, however, there is no specific item on the welfare checklist that invites consideration of issues of a child's legitimate fear for their mother's safety when considering contact with a father who has been violent to the child's mother, despite the growing concern about the impact on children of living with such violence. There is some evidence that judges regard the child's 'right' to contact as primary. This often takes the form of an imperative that contact should take place, and sometimes, in effect, equate the child's 'best interests' with the father's right to see the child. In the end, the child's expressed wishes and feelings against contact (or at least direct face-to-face contact) are often attributed to the influence of the mother's 'implacable hostility' to the father and therefore ignored[10].

Research on child contact in cases of domestic violence (Hester and Radford, 1997; Hester and Pearson, 1998; Edwards, 2001b; Saunders, 2001) suggests that, where contact is granted, there is a high risk of harm either to children, their mothers, or both. Additionally, recent court judgements and an influential expert witnesses report (Sturge and Glaser, 2000) have all found that there is a need for great caution in making such orders.

The Lord Chancellor's Department held a wide-ranging consultation in 1999 following widely expressed concerns on court judgements. At the time of writing the government has introduced an amendment to the 2002 Adoption and Children Bill which would introduce the need for judges to take into account any harm a child may suffer not only by direct abuse but also to witnessing the suffering caused by violence to others (Advisory Board on Family Law, 2001a, 2001b). This would also amend the 1989 Children Act and the Family Proceedings rules so as to apply to all child contact cases. This is a highly charged political issue, and one which tends to divide along gender lines, with well connected pressure groups for father's rights, mounting counter-campaigns to those of feminist and children's organisations. Resolution will not depend on research evidence alone.

Criminal law

Despite changes to policing practices and the law, there are major problems in relation to prosecution and law enforcement concerning domestic violence, as with sexual offences and other forms of violence against women. These include wide variations between areas and the fact that pro-arrest policies have not necessarily led to a high proportion of prosecutions or to a significant increase in successful prosecutions. Women still report 'no-criming' or the unjustified reduction of charges, for example from 'grievous bodily harm' (GBH) to the much less severe 'actual bodily harm' (ABH), leading to suspicions of plea bargaining in some cases. Police practice has received the most scrutiny and there are currently a number of detailed research programmes designed to help to improve practice (for example, Hanmer et al, 1999) but results are very uneven (Edwards, 2001a).

Crown Prosecution Service policies and problems with using the courts

Some of the inability to take cases through to prosecution results from the reluctance of women to appear as witnesses, but some is due to the reluctance of the CPS to take cases forward if they perceive them to be potentially unsuccessful − or else *not in the public interest*. Police in the more proactive police authorities often express frustration at such attitudes. The CPS, on the other hand, may be cautious because of their knowledge of the attitude of judges − or their perceptions of such attitudes − or may be critical of the quality of evidence produced by the police. There is also a lack of sensitivity to the possibility of intimidation where women and witnesses withdraw statements, or a lack of understanding of other more subtle but pervasive pressures, such as the attitude of other family members, or women's reluctance to be responsible for the imprisonment of their children's father (Cretney and Davis, 1996). The CPS have recently adopted new guidelines (Crown Prosecution Service, 2002a, 2002b) but it is as yet too early to gauge their impact. Support-to-court measures have been effective in other Western countries, such as Australia, New Zealand, and some states or municipalities of the US.

A number of other such problems with the policing prosecution and court process are all too familiar to those supporting women and their children who have experienced domestic violence. A comprehensive multi-agency approach at the level of government ministries would be of benefit here, both for the civil and criminal law. Domestic violence awareness programmes, and training for magistrates and the judiciary on the implications of new statue law and on changing agency practice (including of multi-agency approaches), would also be potentially beneficial, as it has been in other professional arenas. This would help to counteract the tendency in British law, which is based on precedent, to decant new law into old bottles[11].

Funding of refuges and related services

There are welcome signs that the present New Labour government recognises the importance of front-line services, such as those provided by the Women's Aid federations and refuges. However, there is still no clearly earmarked funding that recognises the special circumstances and the related costs of providing for the safe emergency and temporary housing, and particularly for the support and advocacy, offered by the grossly under-funded Women's Aid and refuge movement (Abrahams, work in progress), as well as for other community-based organisations concerned with violence against women in general, including those working on rape and sexual abuse. It is unlikely that the government's new 'Supporting people' initiative will remedy this, since its approach to the subject is all too formulaic, and despite the efforts being made to fine tune the provision (DETR, 2000; Women's Aid, 2000). In general, policy and legislation still underplays the specific importance of personal support and advocacy for women experiencing violence, especially in relation to the allocation of resources. Few recognise the limitations of the law's protection and the greater difficulty women, who need to leave violent relationships immediately, have in gaining access to safe and affordable long-term housing within the diminished public and social housing sector of the last 15 years or more.

Conclusions

Recent policy and legal developments in Britain, and the election of New Labour in 1997, has led to a more comprehensive policy approach and increased research, particularly on the evaluation of policy and services. In addition, there have been attempts to define and measure both violence against women in general and domestic violence in particular. There is a general understanding that domestic violence is not a simple category in itself and that it involves intimate relationships other than marriage and cohabitation. It is not necessarily confined to heterosexual relationships and may include same-sex violence and violence of women towards men. It is increasingly recognised that sexual violence and rape, as well as a great range of non-physical coercion, is encompassed by domestic violence and that there is an intermeshing between domestic violence and other forms of violence against women. Research shows a high prevalence and incidence of domestic violence, which is still significantly under-reported. Whether physical or sexual violence or serious coercion and psychological violence are considered, such violence and coercion is much more likely to be directed by men against women. It may affect, depending on the definition of violence adopted and the duration examined, between one quarter and one third of women's relationships with male partners over time.

Looking at the last 20 to 30 years, there have been enormous gains in the direction of making violence against women, and domestic violence, more visible and less publicly acceptable. A high priority is given to the more individualised path of action through the legal system, underestimating the need for material services and support for women and children trying to rebuild their lives following violent relationships. There is still a need for greater recognition of the vital importance of support based on collective and mutual social provision, and for earmarking resources for this. Such support needs to embrace community-based services, such as those pioneered by Women's Aid and by women's services and campaigns on violence against women generally.

Additionally, it would be valuable to use the national inter-departmental domestic violence committees to scrutinise forthcoming and existing legislation for its likely impact on women experiencing all forms of violence. This may help to avoid the problems that have arisen in the past from introducing major pieces of legislation without considering their unintended secondary impact.

Each of these is essential in tackling the remaining consequences of public indifference experienced by women and children living with domestic violence, which was so pervasive in the first three quarters of the 20th century. They are equally essential in allowing us to move forwards, both to provide effective services and to begin the process of developing an awareness that challenges the widespread acceptance of the unequal power relationships between men and women which underpins violence towards women.

Notes

[1] Britain's situation contrasts with other countries' statistical resources, such as Canada (see Johnson 1998a, 1998b; Hague et al, 2001).

[2] Some of the results of these and other studies are summarised in Hester et al, 2000.

[3] British Home Office figures report 292,000 incidents in 1981; 1,178,000 in 1993; 990,000 in 1995; 834,000 in 1997; 761,000 in 1999; and 499,000 in 2000 (Home Office, 2001, Table A2.1).

[4] The survey in 2000 gave a repeat victimisation rate of 57% of victims – the highest for any type of crime (Home Office, 2000b).

[5] For further discussion see Hague and Malos, 1993, 1998 (especially chapter 1, pp 11–16); Hester et al, 2000.

[6] For instance, in West Yorkshire: the series of horrific murders known as the 'Yorkshire Ripper' cases, and later in the Metropolitan Police Division, where it was also influenced by the documentation of racist incidents (Patel, in Harwin et al, 1999).

[7] Legally homicide can be classified as either murder or manslaughter but women have been more likely to be convicted of murder than men in domestic homicide cases.

[8] The circular has since been revised and reissued (Home Office, 2000).

[9] See, for example, the work on violence and gender by Hanmer (Hanmer et al, 1987, 1997, 1999) and Hearn (2002); see also Harne, forthcoming.

[10] Sometimes the mothers are imprisoned for refusing to comply with the order (O'Hara, 1994; Hester et al, 1997; Women's Aid, 1997).

[11] As appears to have happened to a large extent in the interpretation of children's 'right' to contact with both parents in situations of domestic violence, sometimes against the evidence of possible harm and the expressed wishes of the children (Hester and Pearson, 1998).

References

Abrahams, H. (work in progress) *A long hard road to go by: A study of the support work carried out in women's refuges*, unpublished, School for Policy Studies, University of Bristol.

Advisory Board on Family Law, Children Act Sub-Committee (2001a) *Guidelines on good practice on child contact in cases where there is domestic violence*, London: Family Policy Division, Lord Chancellor's Department.

Advisory Board on Family Law, Children Act Sub-Committee (2001b) *Making contact work*, London: Family Policy Division, Lord Chancellor's Department.

Ahluwalia, K. and Gupta, R. (1997) *Circle of light*, London: Harper and Collins.

Ball, M. (1995) *Domestic violence and social care: A report on two conferences held by the Social Services Inspectorate*, London: DoH.

Barron, J. (1990) *Not worth the paper...? The effectiveness of legal protection for women and children experiencing domestic violence*, Bristol: Women's Aid Federation of England.

Binney, V., Harkell, G. and Nixon, J. (1981) *Leaving violent men*, London: Women's Aid Federation of England.

Borkowski, M., Murch, M. and Walker, V. (1983) *Marital violence: The community response*, London: Tavistock.

Bull, J. (1993) *Housing consequences of relationship breakdown*, London: HMSO.

Cobbe, F.P. (1978) 'Wife torture in England', *Contemporary Review*, April, pp 55-87.

Coote, A. and Campbell, B. (1982) *Sweet freedom: The struggle for women's liberation*, London: Picador.

Cretney, A. and Davis, G. (1996) 'Prosecuting "domestic" assault', *Criminal Law Review*, vol 42, March, pp 162-74.

Crown Prosecution Service (2001a) *Guidance on prosecuting cases of domestic violence*, London: Crown Prosecution Service.

Crown Prosecution Service (2001b) *Policy for prosecuting cases of domestic violence*, London: Crown Prosecution Service.

DETR (Department of the Environment, Transport and the Regions) (2000) *Supporting People*, London: HMSO.

DoH (Department of Health) Circular (1997) LAC (97) (15), London: DoH.

DoH (2000) *A resource manual for healthcare professionals*, London: DoH.

Dobash, R.E. and Dobash, R.P. (1980) *Violence against wives*, Shepton Mallet: Open Books.

Dobash, R.E. and Dobash, R.P. (1992) *Women, violence and social change*, London: Routledge.

Dobash, R.E., Dobash, R.P., Cavanagh, K. and Lewis, R. (2002a) *Homicide in Britain: Focus on male offenders*, Research Bulletin no 1, Manchester: Department of Applied Social Studies, University of Manchester.

Dobash, R.E., Dobash, R.P., Cavanagh, K. and Lewis, R. (2002b) *Homicide in Britain: Interviews with men*, Research Bulletin no 2, Manchester: Department of Applied Social Studies, University of Manchester.

Dobash, R.E., Dobash, R.P., Cavanagh, K. and Lewis, R. (2002c) *Homicide in Britain: Interviews with women*, Research Bulletin no 3, Manchester: Department of Applied Social Studies, University of Manchester.

Dominy, N. and Radford, L. (1996) *Domestic violence in Surrey: Towards an effective inter-agency response*, London: Roehampton Institute/Surrey Social Services.

Edwards, S. (1989) *Policing domestic violence*, London: Sage Publications.

Edwards, S. (2001a) 'New directions in prosecution', in J. Taylor-Browne (ed) *What works in domestic violence*, London: Whiting and Birch, pp 211-38.

Edwards, S. (2001b) 'Domestic violence and harassment: an assessment of The Civil Remedies', in J. Taylor-Browne (ed) *What works in domestic violence*, London: Whiting and Birch, pp 187-210.

Evans, A. and Duncan, S. (1988) *Responding to homelessness local authority policy and practice*, London: HMSO.

Gordon, L. (1989) *Heroes of their own lives*, London: Virago.

Gregory, J. and Lees, S. (1999) *Policing sexual assault*, London: Routledge.

Hagemann-White, C. (2001) 'Measuring what? A review of violence against women prevalence studies in Europe', Special issue of *Violence against women: European perspectives*, vol 7.

Hague, G. and Malos, E. (1993) *Domestic violence: Action for change*, (2nd edn, 1998), Cheltenham: New Clarion Press.

Hague, G., Kelly, L. and Mullender, A. (2001) *Challenge violence against women: The Canadian experience*, Bristol: The Policy Press.

Hague, G., Malos, E. and Dear, W. (1996) *Multi-agency work and domestic violence*, Bristol: The Policy Press.

Hague, G., Mullender, A. and Anis, R. (2003: forthcoming) *Is anyone listening? Women survivors of domestic violence*, London: Routledge.

Hanmer, J. and Maynard, M. (eds) (1987) *Women, violence and social control*, Basingstoke: Macmillan.

Hanmer, J., Radford, J. and Stanko, E. (1989) *Women, policing and male violence*, London: Routledge.

Hanmer, J., Griffiths, S. and Jerwood, D. (1999) 'Arresting evidence: domestic violence and repeat victimisation', *Police Research Series*, Paper 104, London: Home Office.

Harne, L. (2002) 'Violence, power and the meaning of fatherhood in issues of child contact', Unpublished PhD thesis, Bristol: School for Policy Studies, University of Bristol.

Harwin, N., Hague, G. and Malos, E. (1999) *The multi-agency approach to domestic violence*, London: Whiting and Birch.

Hester, M. and Pearson, C. (1998) *From periphery to centre: Domestic violence in work with abused children*, Bristol: The Policy Press.

Hester, M. and Radford, L. (1997) *Domestic violence and child contact arrangements in England and Denmark*, Bristol: The Policy Press.

Hester, M., Pearson, C. and Harwin, N. (2000) *Making an impact*, London: Jessica Kingsley.

Home Office (Annual) *Criminal statistics for England and Wales*, London: HMSO.

Home Office (1986) *Violence against women*, (Circular), Home Office.

Home Office (1990) Home Office Circular 60/1990: *Domestic Violence*.

Home Office (1999) *Research study 191*, London: Home Office.

Home Office (2000a) *Multi-agency guidance for addressing domestic violence*, London: Home Office.

Home Office (2000b) *Statistical bulletin 18/00*, London: Home Office.

Home Office (2000c) *Reducing domestic violence: What works*, Briefing Notes, London: HMSO.

Home Office (2001) *Statistical bulletin 18/01*, London: Home Office.

Home Office and Welsh Office (1995) *Inter-agency circular: Inter-agency coordination to tackle domestic violence*, London: Home Office.

Humphreys, C. and Kaye, M. (1997) 'Third party applications for protection orders: opportunities, ambiguities and traps', *Journal of Social Welfare and Family Law*, vol 19, no 3, pp 403-21.

Humphreys, C., Kaye, M. and Harwin, N. (1997) *Third party orders*, Bristol: Women's Aid Federation of England.

Johnson, H. (1996) *Dangerous domains: Violence against women in Canada*, Toronto: Nelson Canada.

Johnson, H. (1998) 'Rethinking survey research on violence against women', in R.E. Dobash and R.P. Dobash (eds) *Rethinking violence against women*, London: Sage Publications.

Law Commission (1992) *Domestic violence and occupation of the family home*, Report 207, London: HMSO.

Lees, S. (1997) *Ruling passions: Sexual violence, reputation and the law*, Buckingham: Open University Press.

Lord Chancellor's Department (1997) *Marriage and the Family Law Act 1996: The new legislation explained*, London: Lord Chancellor's Department.

Lord Chancellor's Department (1997) *Domestic violence: The new law: A guide to part IV of the Family Law Act 1996*, London: Lord Chancellor's Department.

Lord Chancellor's Department (1999) *Consultation on child contact issues in domestic violence*, London: HMSO.

Lord Chancellor's Department (2002) *Amendment to the Adoption and Children Bill*, London, (www.lcd.gov.uk).

McGibbon, A., Cooper, L. and Kelly, L. (1989) *What support?*, London: Hammersmith and Fulham Council/Polytechnic of North London.

Malos, E. (2000) 'Supping with the devil? Multi-agency initiatives on domestic violence', in J. Radford, M. Friedberg and L. Harne (eds) *Women, violence and strategies for action*, Buckingham: Open University Press.

Malos, E. and Hague, G. (1993) *Domestic violence and housing: Local authority responses to women and children escaping violence in the home*, Bristol: Women's Aid Federation of England and School of Applied Social Studies, University of Bristol.

Malos, E. and Hague, G. (1997) 'Women, housing, homelessness and domestic violence', *Concepts of home*, Women's Studies International Forum Special Issue, vol 20, no 3, pp 317-410.

Malos, E. and Hague, G. (1998) 'Facing both ways at once? The effect of the Housing Act 1996 on legislation and policy for the safety of women and their children escaping domestic violence', in D. Cowan (ed) *Housing participation and exclusion*, Aldershot: Dartmouth Press, pp 234-48.

Malos, E., Hague, G., Hester, M., Thiara, R. and Crisp, D. (2002: unpublished) *Interim report to the Home Office on the multi-service domestic violence interventions*, Home Office Crime Reduction Programme.

Mama, A. (1996) *The hidden struggle, statutory and voluntary sector responses to violence against black women in the home*, London: Whiting and Birch.

Mezey, G.C. and Bewley, S. (2001) *An exploration of the effects of domestic violence in pregnancy*, End of Award Report, Swindon: Economic and Social Research Council.

Mirlees-Black, C. (1995) *Home Office Statistical Bulletin 18/01*, London: Home Office Research, Development and Statistics Directorate.

Mirlees-Black, C. (1999) *Domestic violence: Findings from a new British Crime Survey self-completion questionnaire*, (Research Study, 191), London: Home Office, Research, Development and Statistics Directorate.

Mooney, J. (1994) *The hidden figure: Domestic violence in North London*, London: Middlesex University and London Borough Of Islington, Police and Crime Prevention Unit.

Morley, R. (2000) 'Domestic violence and housing', in J. Hanmer, C. Itzen, S. Quaid and D. Wigglesworth (eds) *Home truths about domestic violence*, London: Whiting and Birch, pp 228-45.

Mullender, A. and Morley, R. (eds) (1994) *Children living with domestic violence*, London: Whiting and Birch.

Mullender, A., Hague, G., Imam, U., Kelly, L. and Malos, E. (2002) *Children's perspectives on domestic violence*, London: Sage Publications.

Mulvey Roberts, M. and Mizuta, T. (eds) (1994) *The wives: The rights of married women*, London: Routledge/Thoemmes Press.

Nadel, J. (1993) *Sara Thornton: The story of a woman who killed*, London: Gollancz.

National Inter-Agency Working Party (1992) *Domestic violence: Report of a National Inter-Agency Working Party*, London: Victim Support.

ENVEFF (National Survey on Violence Against Women in France) (2001) *Population and societies*, vol 364, January.

O'Hara, M. (1994) 'Child deaths in contexts of domestic violence', in A. Mullender and R. Morley (eds) *Children living with domestic violence*, London: Whiting and Birch, pp 57-66.

Pahl, J. (ed) (1985) *Private violence and public policy: The needs of battered women and the response of the public services*, London: Routledge and Kegan Paul.

Parton, N. (1985) *The politics of child abuse*, Basingstoke: Macmillan.

Pizzey, E. (1974) *Scream quietly or the neighbours will hear*, Harmondsworth: Penguin.

Prato Conference (2001) *Leggere le differenze*, Monash University Centre, Prato, November.

Rose, H. (1985) 'Women's refuges: creating a movement', in C. Ungerson (ed) *Women and social policy*, Basingstoke: Macmillan, pp 243-59.

Russell, D. and Radford, J. (1992) *Femicide: The politics of woman killing*, Buckingham: Open University Press.

Saunders, H. (2001) *Making contact worse? A report of a National Survey of Domestic Violence Refuge Services into the enforcement of contact orders*, Bristol: Women's Aid Federation of England.

Smith, L. (1989) *Domestic violence: An overview of the literature*, Home Office Research Studies 107, London: HMSO.

Stanko, E. (2000) *The day to count. Details of the occurrence of reports of domestic Violence reported in the UK in one day* (www.domesticviolencedataorg/5_research/count/count.htm).

Stanko, E., Crisp, D. and Lucraft, C. (1998) *Counting the costs: Estimating the impact of domestic violence in the London Borough of Hackney*, London: Crime Concern.

Stanko, E., O'Beirne, M. and Zaffito, G. (2002) *Taking stock: What do we know about interpersonal violence?*, ESRC Violence Research Programme, Egham: Royal Holloway University of London.

Statistics Canada (1993) *The violence against women survey*, Ottawa: Ministry of Supply and Services.

Sturge, C. and Glaser, D. (2000) 'Contact and domestic violence: the experts' court report', *Family Law*, vol 30, September, pp 615-29.

UK MEN'S Movement (2002) 'The 1996 Family Law Act', printed/accessed at 11/13/02, www.mm.org.uk.

United Nations (1993a) *Strategies for confronting domestic violence: A resource manual*, New York: United Nations Department of Information.

United Nations (1993b) *Convention on the elimination of discrimination against women: Directive on violence against women*, New York: United Nations Department of Information.

United Nations (1995) *Beijing declaration and platform for action: Adopted by the Fourth World Conference for Women*, New York: The United Nations Department of Information.

Walby, S. and Myhill, A. (2001) 'New survey methodologies in violence against women', *British Journal of Criminology*, no 41, pp 502-22.

Williamson, E. (2000) *Domestic violence and health*, Bristol: The Policy Press.

Women's Aid Federation (1992) *Written evidence to the House of Commons Public Affairs Committee Inquiry into domestic violence*, Bristol: Women's Aid Federation of England.

Women's Aid Federation (1997) *Women's Aid Federation briefing paper on child contact and domestic violence*, Bristol: Women's Aid Federation of England.

Women's Aid Federation (2000) *Briefing paper on supporting people*, Bristol: Women's Aid Federation of England.

Women's Unit (1999) *Living without fear: An integrated approach to tackling violence against women*, London: Central Office of Information, Cabinet Office (www.womens-unit.gov.uk).

SIX

Domestic violence in Japan: perceptions and legislation

Yoko Shoji

Introduction

Exposing the problem of domestic violence has been one of the most important and also difficult policy areas that many societies have faced at the end of the 20th century. This is especially so since the special nature of domestic violence is that it is often hidden behind the private relationships between individuals. Now, positioned clearly as an issue on the agenda of the UN, the seriousness of the problem has been recognised in many societies, requiring urgent policy responses. In this context, policies and legislation aimed at the eradication of domestic violence have been put into practice in various forms in several societies. In Japan, however, it has only been in recent years that domestic violence has come to be recognised as a social problem (see Otto [Koibito] kara no Boryoku Chosa Kenkyukai, 1998). As a result, special legislation to cope with the issue has yet to be enacted by the Japanese authorities.

There is a significant gap between Japan and Western societies (such as Britain, for example), where domestic violence was put firmly on the social agenda by the women's movement of the 1970s and became an important issue on the policy agenda in the 1980s. Consequently, legal systems to tackle the problem have been developed (for more discussion, see Chapter Five of this volume). This discrepancy cannot be attributed simply to the characteristics of family relations in Japanese society. Nor can it be explained by the Confucian traditions specific to East Asian culture, since other similarly situated countries, including Korea (Republic of Korea) and Taiwan, enacted special legislation concerning domestic violence earlier than Japan (Asia Taiheiyo Jinken Joho Center, 2001). In this context, this chapter investigates the reasons behind the delayed action by the Japanese government in tackling this problem, and then will move on to discuss how to develop methods to deal with the issues of domestic violence.

In order to set out the background to domestic violence in Japan, this chapter first presents the prevailing situation. A careful analysis of the occurrence and outcomes of domestic violence – which is in fact more common than is commonly understood – is important particularly for two reasons. First, many people in Japan – including policy makers and implementers – currently view domestic violence as rare or special incidents, and therefore negligible. Such misconceptions, however, must be challenged: further research will be the key to help correct such commonly held misconceptions. Second, confronting the issue and openly discussing it may aid in the recovery of victims, who are often led to believe that their predicaments are too special to be understood by professionals and other people, and that they themselves (and their partner) are to blame for the problem. As a result of this second problem, victims rarely report incidents of domestic violence to the police or relevant support agencies, and therefore delay public recognition of the universality of the problem and the need for a society-based solution.

The nature and level of domestic violence in Japan

Following the 'Declaration on the Elimination of Violence against Women' at the UN General Assembly in 1993, tackling 'violence against women' was also discussed as one of the most prominent issues that needed an urgent response at the forth World Conference on Women held in Beijing, China in 1995. At the same time, in Japan, eliminating violence against women was mentioned as one of the eleven priorities of the 'Joint Participation Plan of Men and Women for 2000'. However, it was also pointed out that the lack of existing data obscured the actual situation of violence against women (Konishi, 2001). For instance, according to police reports, 120 to 130 women are murdered by their husbands annually in Japan, which indeed indicates the reality of domestic violence. However, in a society where the nature and concept of domestic violence, or violence against women in the private sphere, has rarely been understood or recognised, the media tends to portray the violence as 'part of the process in the breakdown of a relationship leading to homicide'. Such reports obscure the real causes and process of the offence. Moreover, since existing research conducted by private institutes tends to focus on surveying victims of domestic violence, such available data quantify in limited terms only the extent of the problem and also do not comprehensively ascertain the actual situation of the victims. Therefore, such constraints clearly highlight the importance of the government as a central body, who has the power to influence the mass media as well as the general public, to conduct further and detailed research.

In response, the first research on domestic violence by Japanese policy makers was conducted by the Tokyo Metropolitan Government in 1997. The official statistics on domestic violence available so far had been police records on the number of wives being murdered by their husbands; and statistics relating to the causes of divorce, particularly the number of cases in which wives mentioned 'violence' as a reason for divorce. The research by the Tokyo Metropolitan Government was designed with the help of experts in this field of study, and in order to be able to facilitate cross-national comparison, questionnaires were adapted from research conducted in other developed societies. The results of the research project were reported widely in the media, and indeed this in turn provided an opportunity for the raising of consciousness in society in general. In the interim, the first-ever national survey on domestic violence was also conducted by the Prime Minister's Office (currently, the Cabinet Office) in 1999, and was followed by numerous local government surveys. Apart from looking at the impact of the survey results published in the media, it is also worthwhile considering the significant increase in the number of published articles regarding domestic violence appearing in newspapers since the 1997 survey by the Tokyo Metropolitan Government. Since this watershed in 1997, the number of newspaper articles reporting 'violence by husband' has more than doubled, from 82 articles in 1997 to 147 in 1998, and 172 in 1999. A keyword search using 'domestic violence' in all newspapers brought up only six articles in 1997; however, the increase has been even more dramatic since, rising from 74 in 1998 to 198 in 1999, and to 468 articles in 2000. This indicates that the issue of domestic violence was reported seven times more frequently in 2000 than in 1997. It is reasonable to conclude, therefore, that the issue of domestic violence is increasingly being recognised by the general public as one of several social problems which need urgent responses.

Perceptions towards and experiences of domestic violence

Using the results of the first comprehensive survey on domestic violence by Tokyo Metropolitan Government (Tokyo Metropolitan Government, 1998), this chapter presents some of the key findings:

• the experiences of women suffering violence by their husband or male partner;
• the perceptions of men and women towards domestic violence.

The first stage of this research was conducted between July and August 1997 using a questionnaire, and 4,500 men and women living in Tokyo were approached to participate. Face-to-face interviews with 52 female victims of domestic violence were conducted in November 1997. The questions asked were about the types and degree of violence the women received from their husband or male partner, and what kinds of assistance the women required when they faced violence from their husband or partner. The final stage of the research in early 1998 involved key informant interviews with officers and staff in 16 public institutions and private organisations including the police, a magistrate court, hospitals and welfare offices.

Figure 6.1 indicates gender differences in perceptions towards domestic violence. This figure shows the percentages of the respondents who answered they 'would not forgive their husband or male partner for his act' by gender. It is interesting to note that there was a large discrepancy in perceptions towards violence between men and women. In all the acts specified in this questionnaire, a higher percentage of female respondents considered that acts done to them were 'unforgivable' than male respondents. On the other hand, the majority of

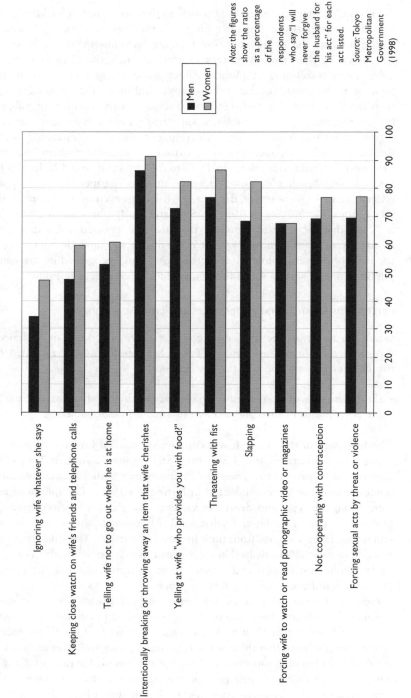

Figure 6.1: Attitude toward the acts committed by a husband against his wife in Tokyo (%)

Note: the figures show the ratio as a percentage of the respondents who say "I will never forgive the husband for his act" for each act listed.

Source: Tokyo Metropolitan Government (1998)

the male respondents did not think that acts such as 'ignoring wife, whatever she says' and 'keeping close watch on wife's friends and telephone calls' constituted 'unforgivable' acts. A high percentage of both male (86.3%) and female (91.2%) respondents agreed that the act of 'intentionally breaking or throwing away an item that the wife cherishes' (for example, burning a wife's music LPs) was 'unforgivable'. This clearly suggests that the respondents considered mental violence could cause an equal or greater level of damage to the victims than physical violence. Indeed, this confirms the varying definitions of domestic violence not only including physical violence, but also extending to various dimensions of violence including mental violence, financial abuse, sexual violence, and neglect (Otto [Koibito] kara no Boryoku Chosa Kenkyukai, 1998; Cabinet Office, 1999; Danjo Kyodo Sankaku Shingikai, 1999; Hester et al, 2000). Other areas of mental violence, such as 'yelling at wife, "Who provides you with food?"' and 'threatening with fist' were also considered 'unforgivable' by both the male and female respondents. Compared with the female respondents (82.4%), lower percentages of the male respondents (68.2%) thought 'slapping' unforgivable. Moreover, over 60-70% considered sexual violence, such as 'not cooperating with contraception' and 'forcing wife to carry out sexual acts by threat or violence', unforgivable. The reason why the act of 'not cooperating with contraception' scored such high percentages can be partly attributed to the Japanese health care system, which has only recently issued a license for the pill. In Japan, the limited contraceptive choices available meant that the condom is the most common form of contraception, and it certainly requires the cooperation of the male partner. Consequently, the percentage of abortions among all pregnancies in Japan in 1997 was 22.1%, which is high compared to other developed countries (Prime Minister's Office, 1999). (See Chapter Twelve of this volume for a discussion of Japanese women's sexuality.)

What was the frequency and extent of violence that women have actually experienced in domestic situations? Seventeen types of violence listed in Figure 6.2 are classified into three categories: physical violence, mental violence, and sexual violence. Approximately 10-15% of the female respondents experienced mental violence such as 'yelling at wife, "Who provides you with food?"', physical violence such as slapping and kicking, and sexual violence – 'not cooperating with contraception' – at least once or twice. Figure 6.2 also reveals that 17.2% of the respondents had experienced at least one of these violence categories. Three to five per cent of the respondents were victims of frequent violence by their husband or partner. A high percentage of the respondents had experienced mental violence such as 'ignoring wife, whatever she says' in both frequency categories. Among physical violence, 'threatening with a fist', 'slapping' or 'pushing, grabbing and poking with a finger' were mentioned frequently. One per cent of the respondents was however threatened by their husband or male partner wielding a kitchen knife, and 3% of the respondents reported serious acts of violence to the extent that they could not rise to their feet. Women who had experienced beating, kicking or other forms of physical violence were observed widely regardless of their age, educational background,

Figure 6.2: Wives who have experienced an act of violence carried out by husband or partner in Tokyo (%)

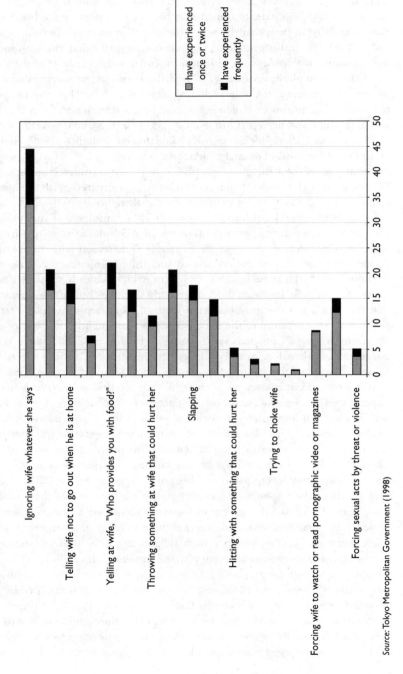

Source: Tokyo Metropolitan Government (1998)

or annual income of their own and their husband or partner. The data challenges the myth that domestic violence is largely a problem among the low-income and uneducated sections of Japanese society (see also Yoshihama, 1999). The 1999 survey conducted by the Prime Minister's Office also revealed that one in 20 women have experienced life-threatening violence (Prime Minister's Office, 2000; also see *Asahi Shimbun*, 26 February 2000, p 1). Despite being recognised as a social problem in Japan in recent years, the extent of violence which Japanese women experience may not be far from that of their Western counterparts.

Of the respondents who have experienced an act of violence, approximately 40% did not try to talk to someone about it. Regardless of age, the reasons given for their inactivity included "did not think it was serious enough to consult someone" or they thought it was *their* own fault. Only approximately 15% of the respondents had actually consulted someone about the incidents, and approximately 6% wanted to consult with someone but did not do so. The results clearly indicate the misconception among the women themselves about domestic violence, which they believed to be rare or special incidents and therefore easy to overlook. Of those women who have talked to someone, 70% talked to their friends, and 60% to their family and relatives. Only 2-3% of the victims have actually reported their suffering to the police or other public offices, symbolising the current underdeveloped support system or the existing barriers preventing access to justice as well as the lack of available services.

Almost all of the female victims interviewed in the second stage have suffered physical violence such as beating and kicking, as well as mental and sexual violence. Approximately 80% of the women have been physically injured as a result of violence by their husband or partner. The majority of the women mentioned 'trifling matters' as the main trigger of violence: "He was not pleased with what I said or did" or "It was an everyday quarrel at first but later led to the use of violence". In the case of households with children, the husband's violence was often extended to the children. Of the 45 female respondents who had children, 29 women reported that the violence used by their husband extended to their children as well. The number and type of violence against children reported included 31 cases of physical violence and 25 cases of mental violence. While the former included beating, kicking, and pulling the child's arm, the latter included extremely violent language, belittling, and shouting. The impact of the use of violence on children mentioned most by the female respondents included hatred for and fear of their father (18 respondents), followed by distortion of character and emotions (11 respondents), and refusal to attend school (nine respondents). Furthermore, the research revealed that the majority of the female victims wished to leave their husband or partner and earn their own living. However, those women who wanted to divorce their husband as soon as possible were also concerned about the consequences of the divorce. Possible economic effects is the most common and significant concern for those who wish to leave their partner but cannot. Adverse influences on their children can be the reason for both leading to divorce and remaining in marriage.

This is partly because divorce is still not widely accepted as a social norm in Japan.

Finally, in terms of public assistance provided for the victims of domestic violence, many of the female respondents wanted public institutions to take steps to emphasise and diffuse the idea that violence is a crime, even if it is used by a husband against his wife in the private sphere of the household. They also wanted to change public attitudes towards violence. Moreover, many of the women requested the provision of safe public shelters for the victims of violence, since there is currently no such provision should women want to flee domestic violence. Expansion of the advice and counselling services for the victims was also frequently recommended. The key informant interviews also confirmed the present limitations on roles and systems of public organisations such as the police, welfare offices and hospitals in taking necessary action. Since those organisations usually prioritise their (main) functions other than dealing with cases of domestic violence, their involvement in the issue is currently limited.

Considering the voluntary agencies that play more active roles in this field in Britain, there would be many areas, in which Japanese institutions could learn from the experiences of the British counterparts. The hallmark of action on domestic violence in Britain has been its growth from a grassroots movement emerging from the women's movement and the important part that dedicated independent voluntary sector organisations continue to play, even though they are increasingly drawing on government funding and working in a multi-agency framework alongside statutory organisations with broader or different remits (Hague et al, 1996).

Delayed policy responses to domestic violence and its causes

Policy responses to domestic violence in Japan remain relatively limited at present. When victims of domestic violence seek help and assistance from the police, welfare offices, or women's centres run by local governments, the women are usually provided only temporary shelter within facilities run by the women's centres or at support facilities for single-mother households. Apart from the public shelters, only 30 private shelters are currently operating in Japan. Although they supplement the shortage of public shelters to a minor extent, such privately operated shelters are often run by female voluntary activists and are likely to suffer a great deal of financial constraint and lack of human resources. Furthermore, in the current climate, both types of facilities inevitably play only a passive role by helping female victims and their children temporarily to flee from violent husbands and fathers.

Why is there such a delay in responding to this emerging issue in contemporary Japan? In Western societies such as Britain and the US, the women's movements of the 1970s directly influenced the development of policy and responses to the issues of domestic violence (Coote and Campbell, 1982; Rose, 1985; Hague and Malos, 1998; Kaino, 2002). In order to examine the reasons behind the delayed action by the Japanese government, the necessary analysis must come from the perspectives of both 'family policy' and 'policy for women' in Japan. This delay cannot be simply attributed to the characteristics of the Confucian traditions specific to East Asian societies; that is, by relating the problem of domestic violence to the nature of family relations as well as in relation to women's traditional position in the family and society. The fact that such delayed action is not attributable to the characteristics of East Asia is evident when examining the progress made in neighbouring Asian societies such as South Korea and Taiwan, that enacted special legislation against domestic violence in 1998. Other societies, including Singapore and Malaysia, are also following suit and are in the process of establishing legislation. Therefore, the problem is likely to be embedded in Japanese society itself and in the way in which social systems have been developed in Japan. In this context, two particular perspectives are chosen to explore the reasons behind the delayed response:

- the principles of (social) security and family policy;
- the strategies adopted by women themselves in their social movements.

When we examine the issue from the perspectives of Japanese socioeconomic systems, it is necessary to point out the underlying principles of the male breadwinner family model and family dependency in the systems. For instance, the 'family-as-a-unit' – rather than the individual – is often the foundation of society and always used for a basis to measure people's needs under Japanese social welfare and social security systems. In a society with the male breadwinner model, where gender roles are clearly defined with husband as breadwinner and wife as domestic labourer and carer, it is very difficult for women to become financially and mentally independent. Tax and pension systems operate under the principle of a 'family-as-a-unit' and favour the continuation of marriage (Shinozaki, 2002). Through marriage, women acquire the position and status of a housewife. These housewives are usually granted access to social security, health services and social position through their spouse's employed status and welfare contributions. For women, the position of a housewife provides not only financial stability from her husband in marriage but also an entitlement to a widow's pension after his death. Losing the position as wife may therefore also mean the loss of social security in the future. Under the current pension system, if their spouse is employed and has an occupational pension scheme, his contributions automatically cover those of his wife for the basic national pension scheme without any extra contributions. Such a system reinforces women's dependency on men.

Moreover, even for 1994 – the UN's 'international year of family' – the approaches taken by both national and local governments in Japan were totally lacking the notion of *campaign for human rights* (which was the main focus of the UN). Instead, the government focused firmly on the importance of the mutuality and harmony in the family rather than rights of individuals. Not surprisingly, a model of a 'happy extended family' was used for the campaign posters by the government. Second, in relation to women's rights advocates in Japan, policy responses addressing the concerns of women have always been made as a result of external pressure such as the pressure put by the UN, rather than any that emerged internally (for more discussion see Chapter Eleven). Although the number of women's rights advocates have also expanded since the 1970s in Japan, their movements have been firmly focused on breaking down existing gender roles within the family and society while overlooking the violence within the family. Therefore, such movements have not yet reached the point of influencing the development of effective policy responses.

Current situation and legislation

Until recently, the Japanese government did not acknowledge the importance of special legislation to counter domestic violence. Until the autumn of 2000, in order to protect the victims of domestic violence under a protection order [*hogo meirei*], the views expressed by the Ministry of Justice and the Supreme Court have been making use of existing laws, and criminal law in particular. There was also a debate concerning protection orders since laws applicable only to women may be a breach of the rights of gender equality defined in the Japanese Constitution. Since Korea began developing legislation before Japan, it is worthwhile examining their strategies (Nikkan Josei ni taisuru Boryoku Project Kenkyukai, 2001; Shinozaki, 2002).

While placing an emphasis on the 'peace and stability' of the family, legislation to counter domestic violence in Korea was not developed without consideration being given to the views of both men and women. In addition, the Korean government locates protection orders somewhere between civil law and criminal law. This approach allows, for example, wives to make a statement, even though they may not wish to take a legal charge against their husbands. Indeed, it is a real challenge to expose the problem of domestic violence, which is hidden in the private relations between individuals in the 21st century. Korea is currently going through a period of legislative reform – a new direction is being taken with an emphasis more on human rights than on 'peace and stability' of the family and it is notable that this agenda was put forward by the women's rights advocates themselves.

In Japan, nonetheless, since the UN Women's Forum held in New York in 2000 called for legislative action to prevent domestic violence, the climate has begun to change. In the process, lawyers' groups and women's organisations have consistently criticised the substantive and procedural deficiencies of the proposed law. The largest problem stems from the fact that detailed information regarding the proposal has not been made available to the public. Lawmakers need to recognise that, while detailed consideration of the legal aspects of tackling the problem of domestic violence is important, education of the public concerning the issue and the accompanying legislation in the process of development is another important factor. Indeed, informing and involving the public in the process will bring a positive impact. Therefore, while the content of the bill is no doubt important, a campaign against domestic violence that attracts public attention and fosters the participation of many people from all walks of life is also essential.

The first legislation to counter domestic violence in Japan finally passed the national legislature in April 2001, and went into effect nationally in October 2001. The Law on Prevention of Spouse Violence and Protection of Victims DV Boshi Ho (Haigu-sha Kara no boryoku boshi • higai-sha hogo ho) allows district courts to issue six month restraining orders against abusers and to be able to evict abusers from the home for as long as two weeks. Abusers who violate the court orders can receive as much as one year in jail and a fine up to one million yen (£5,000). Anyone who makes a false report of domestic violence can also be fined up to ¥100,000 (£500). The law makes no distinction between couples who are legally married and those who cohabit (www.womensnews.org, 25 February 2002). The new law also requires local governments to provide financial assistance to organisations that assist victims of domestic violence, and it provides for the national government to establish new facilities to support victims. It established for the first time that spousal battery is a criminal offence.

The significance of this law is the introduction of protection of victims and at the first time legal ground is provided to cases of domestic violence. In the past, due to the ambiguity of domestic violence between the civil and criminal boundaries, it was difficult to gain police corporation as criminal offence and was not common to receive an interim order under the civil law. Since the law's enactment, there has been an increasing number of reports to the police as well as arrests under bodily injury and assault within couples which suggest the law successfully and effectively started uncovering existing violence in society. According to the information by the National Police Agency (21 February 2002), police issued 185 protection orders within three months of the law's enactment, a very significant increase indeed.

However, several problems concerning the new law have also been pointed out and will continue to be debated until the planned review in three years time. Problems include:

- people can file an injunction order against violence from current partners (spouses and unmarried cohabitants) but not from former partners;
- types of violence applicable are limited to 'serious physical violence' and do not include mental or sexual abuse, and proof is needed;
- protection covers spouses only, and not the children or the wife's parents.

Conclusion

When examining domestic violence, the impact of domestic violence on children – and not only on women – needs to be considered (Kaino, 2001; Hasegawa,

2002). Domestic violence is indeed violence against women and children who are in a sense caught in the trap of an 'intimate family domain'. Even if children did not receive direct violence, witnessing violence against their mother at home equally damages their mental wellbeing. The danger is that violence can perpetuate throughout the life-course of children; consequently, they may develop distrust of other human beings. Those children who have experienced violence at home may repeat this violence when they grow up although there is no deterministic law that suggests this will automatically be the case (Emery, 1982; Fantuzzo and Lindquist, 1989; Fonargy et al, 1994; Edelson, 1999). In order to prevent the experiences of domestic violence from becoming a catalyst to increased levels of violence in society, early intervention in the case of children would be an important approach (Nihon DV Boshi Joho Center, 1999).

'Survivor', the term used by the victims and practitioners to describe those women who have experienced domestic violence, may symbolise the fact that domestic violence is a violation of human rights. Those women are at risk of being damaged mentally and even being murdered, and living a life without life (or a living death). Even when at risk of being murdered, why do they not run away from their violent husbands or partner? Why do they not bring charges before the law courts? These are indeed points of debate for the policy makers. The reality is that female victims often have nowhere to go and no one to rely on. Japanese women often do not have sufficient financial means to live independently. Moreover, there is not always a safe or easy means of escaping from their violent husband. These issues tend to be analysed using the theory of *co-dependency* in the psycho-medical model. There is, however, a certain danger in relying heavily on a medical model for explanation (see for example, Hague and Males, 1998). Nevertheless, using such a model may be valuable in treating the victims of post-traumatic stress disorder (PTSD).

The elimination of domestic violence requires the establishment of socioeconomic systems for women including revisions to the social security and legal systems, as well as the creation of a powerful women's rights advocacy to help the victims to understand better their situations and support them in taking more positive action to tackle this personal, yet increasingly prevalent social problem.

References

Asia Taiheiyo Jinken Joho Center (ed) (2001) *Domestic violence ni taisuru torikumi to kadai* [*Measures for and issues of domestic violence*], Asia Taiheiyo Jinken Review 2001, Gendai Jinbun sha, Tokyo.

Cabinet Office (1999) *Living without fear*, London: Cabinet Office.

Coote, A. and Campbell, B. (1982) *Sweet freedom: The struggle for women's liberation*, London: Picador.

Danjo Kyodo Sankaku Shingikai (1999) *Josei ni taisuru Boryoku no nai Shakai wo Mezashite* [*Towards society without violence against women*].

Edelson, J. (1999) 'Children's witnessing of adult domestic violence', *Journal of Interpersonal Violence*, vol 14, pp 839-70.

Emery, R. (1982) 'Interparental conflict and children of discord and divorce', *Psychological Bulletin*, vol 92, pp 310-30.

Fantuzzo, J.W. and Lindquist, C.U. (1989) 'The effects of observing conjugal violence on children: a review and analysis of research methodology', *Journal of Family Violence*, vol 4, no 1, pp 77-94.

Fonargy, P., Steele, M., Steele, H., Higgitt, A. and Mayer, L. (1994) 'The theory and practice of resilience (Emmanuel Miller Memorial Lecture 1992)', *Journal of Child Psychology and Psychiatry*, vol 35, no 2, pp 231-58.

Hague, G. and Malos, E. (1998) *Domestic violence: Action for change* (2nd edn), Cheltenham: New Clarion Press.

Hague, G., Malos, E. and Dear, W. (1996) *Multi-agency work and domestic violence*, Bristol: The Policy Press.

Hasegawa, K. (ed) (2002) *DV Boshi Ho Katsuyo Handbook*, Osaka: Tokishobo.

Hester, M., Pearson, C. and Harwin, N. (2000) *Making an impact: Children and domestic violence*, London: Taylor and Francis.

Kaino, T. (ed) (2001) *Domestic violence boshi ho* [*Domestic Violence Prevention Act*], Kogaku sha.

Kaino, T. (2002) *Domestic violence*, Fuma shobo, Tokyo.

Konishi, T. (2001) *Domestic violence*, Hakusui sha, Tokyo.

Nihon DV Boshi Joho Center (1999) *Domestic violence heno Shiten: Otto Koibito kara no Boryoku Konzetsu no tameni* [*Views towards domestic violence*], Osaka: Tokishobo.

Nikkan Josei ni taisuru Boryoku Project Kenkyukai (2001) *Katei-nai no 'josei ni taisuru bouryoku' boushi ni kansuru shakai system kaihatsu no tame no Nihon Kankoku Kyoudou Kenkyu* [*Japan–Korea joint project for developing social system to prevent 'violence against women' at home*], Toyota Foundation.

Otto (Koibito) kara no Boryoku Chosa Kenkyukai (1998) *Domestic violence shinban: jittai, DV-ho kaisetu, vision* [*Domestic violence (new edn): facts, explaining Domestic Violence Act, and vision*], Tokyo: Yuhikaku.

Prime Minister's Office (1999) *The present status of gender equality and measures: Third report on the plan for gender equality 2000*, Tokyo: Prime Minister's Office.

Prime Minister's Office (2000) *Danjo kan ni okeru Boryoku ni kansuru Chosa* [*Survey on violence between men and women*], (www.sorifu.go.jp/danjyo/yoron/bouryoku/bouryoku.html).

Rose, H. (1985) 'Women's refuges: creating a movement', in C. Ungerson (ed) *Women and social policy*, Basingstoke: Macmillan.

Asia Josei Koryu Kenkyu Forum (ed) (2002) *Asia no domestic violence* [*Domestic violence in Asia*], Akashi shoten, Tokyo.

Tokyo Metropolitan Government (1998) *Josei ni taisuru Boryoku Chosa Hokoku Sho* [*Survey report on violence against women*], Tokyo: Daitou Insatsu Kougyou.

Yoshihama, M. (1999) 'Domestic violence: Japan's "hidden crime"', *Japan Quarterly*, vol 46, no 3, July-September (www.asiamedia.ucla.edu/Deadline/ViolenceAgainstWomen/articles/Yoshihama.htm).

SEVEN

Housing and social inequality in Britain

Mark Kleinman

Introduction

This chapter looks at trends in social inequality in Britain and how the operation of the housing system and housing policy has contributed to this. It is divided into three parts. In the first, it looks at the development of housing policy in Britain from the mid-1970s on. It argues that the late 1970s and early 1980s were a turning point which committed British policy to a path of 'bifurcation', leading to an increase in inequality, and an entrenched process of tenure polarisation. To some extent, the trends observed in Britain – the expansion of homeownership, the residualisation of the social rented sector and the switch from supply-side ('bricks and mortar') subsidies to demand-side (means-tested) support – are in common with trends observed in other European countries. However, there are important aspects that are very specific to Britain, such as a rejection of social corporatism, a stress on economic individualism and a weak role for private renting. This chapter argues that there is no single reason for the particular path taken by housing policy in Britain. Rather, there is a variety of contributing factors: social and economic changes interrelate with policy innovations and development.

The second part of this chapter looks more generally at the growth of social and economic inequality over the same period. In Britain, income inequality grew rapidly between 1977 and 1990, when it reached its highest postwar level. During this period, inequality increased faster in Britain than anywhere else in the world (with the exception of New Zealand). This increase was driven by three factors: growing inequality of earnings; an increase in the number of people dependent on benefits; and a widening gap between those with earnings and those on benefits. One important change has been an increase in the numbers both of 'no-earner' and 'multiple-earner' households. Nearly one in five British households with children has no working adult, significantly higher than all other European countries. As a result of the increase in inequality, poverty and social exclusion have also increased in Britain over the last 25 years.

The third part of this chapter looks at the current policies tackling inequality and social exclusion, including the contribution of housing and regeneration policies. In its first three and a half years in office, New Labour has followed policies of 'redistribution by stealth'. While explicitly rejecting some of the rhetoric of previous Labour governments, in order to reassure middle-class voters, successive budgets and other policies have redistributed income towards poorer households, towards families, and in particular towards working households. Housing policy has not radically changed however: the promotion of owner-occupation and the ending of local authorities' direct role in providing housing remain key goals. New Labour has emphasised regeneration and other area-based policies as ways of tackling social exclusion. The strengths and limitations of this approach are discussed. And finally, the chapter examines some of the likely future issues for housing policy.

Housing policy in Britain, 1979-97

Housing occupies a unique place in public policy: neither fully part of the welfare state, nor fully part of the free market. To use Esping-Andersen's (1990) term, housing in Western Europe was never 'decommodified'. In contrast to health, education, social insurance and pensions, housing has always been "the wobbly pillar under the welfare state" (Harloe, 1995).

In Britain, the 1980s and 1990s – dominated by Conservative governments – saw a major shift in housing policy. There were some elements of continuity with housing policies under the previous Labour governments (1964-70, 1974-79). Labour had already in the 1960s accepted the growth of owner-occupation and the duty of governments to promote it. In its 1965 White Paper, the Labour government declared that "the expansion of building for owner-occupation ... is normal; it reflects a long-term social advance which should generally pervade every region"(Malpass and Murie, 1994, p 70). This was contrasted with the role of public house building, which was to meet 'exceptional' needs (Malpass and Murie, 1994). Labour's Housing Policy Review in 1977 famously declared that "For most people owning one's home is a basic and natural desire which for more and more people is becoming attainable" (DoE, 1977, para 7.03).

The mid-1970s also saw a major change in attitudes to public spending and economic policy. At the Labour Party Conference in September 1976, Prime Minister Jim Callaghan explicitly repudiated the received Keynesian wisdom of the postwar period:

> We used to think that you could just spend your way out of a recession, and increase employment, by cutting taxes and boosting government spending. I tell you in all candour that the option no longer exists, and in so far as it ever did exist, it worked by injecting inflation into the economy. (Smith, 1987 p 65)

A more decisive break with the postwar consensus came in 1979, when Labour's 'reluctant monetarists' were succeeded by a radical Conservative administration which embraced monetary control and reductions in public expenditure not as unfortunate necessities, but as articles of faith. This shift was reinforced by further election victories in 1983, 1987 and 1992. The consequences went beyond the purely electoral. In the 1980s, there was growing acceptance of the idea that inequality is a necessary prerequisite for growth. Hence the 1980s and 1990s have left the post-1997 New Labour government with a double legacy: in terms of outcomes, a huge growth in social and economic inequality; and at the ideological level, a greater acceptance of an unequal society.

In the General Elections of 1979 and 1983, housing was an important factor in the gains made by the Conservatives (but was less so in later elections), particularly among skilled manual voters. The Conservatives projected a powerful image of Britain as a property-owning democracy, and the release of council tenants from 'municipal serfdom' through the creation of a 'right to buy'. Labour's response, by contrast, often appeared defensive and contradictory, without a coherent and positive alternative. By the mid-1990s, New Labour had learned the political lessons. In 1997, New Labour projected itself as the champion of aspiring working and middle-class homeowners ('Mondeo Man') and not just defenders of a shrinking municipal proletariat. In Britain, as in Japan (see Chapter Eight of this volume), homeownership had become a symbol of belonging to mainstream society.

In the 1980s and 1990s, despite the Conservative rhetoric, there was no 'rolling back of the state' with regard to welfare in most cases, but housing was a major exception (Kleinman, 1996). Public expenditure on housing was significantly reduced, and was shifted away from general subsidies towards means-tested, personal support. Similarly, expenditure was moved away from new construction towards repair and renewal of the existing stock. The ideology of the New Right emphasised individual choice and consumer freedom. This was expressed in housing policy in two ways. First, homeownership was encouraged and supported, and secondly, spending on council housing was reduced. The growth of council housing was halted and then reversed, and its role became primarily that of welfare tenure providing a housing safety net for the poor.

Public housing was residualised. Continuing sales under the 'right to buy' and transfers of rented stock to non-profit but independent housing associations meant that the general climate moved remarkably rapidly towards a consensus that the era of council housing was coming to an end. Partly, this came about through the success of some councils in voluntarily privatising their rented stock through large-scale voluntary transfer (a policy generated by the local authorities themselves as an essentially defensive measure in the face of ever more financial and legal restrictions imposed by central government). However, there were also wider political and cultural changes involved. By the mid-1990s, council housing was seen as a discrete service, to be provided to 'customers', rather than part of the local state, still less as a component of the social wage, or as an example of 'decommodification'. In part, this resulted from specific legislation, such as the 1989 Local Government and Housing Act, which 'ring-fenced' local authority housing accounts, making them more similar to private sector trading accounts, and through the extension of compulsory competitive tendering to housing management in the early 1990s. These legal changes took place in a climate which was already hostile to the idea that council housing should be provided as anything other than a customer-driven service.

Furthermore, while the introduction in 1979 of a 'right to buy' for council tenants had seemed a bold and radical move against a background of continuity in the welfare state, by the early 1990s, the marketisation of the welfare state had become commonplace. The limited devolution of public housing to some similar-looking housing associations and a few trusts and cooperatives looked rather tame when compared to the internal market of the National Health Service, where hospital trusts and fund-holding general practitioners acted as cost centres; opted-out schools; huge resources channelled through new quangos, such as Training and Enterprise Councils (TECs), and the large profits and salaries generated by the newly privatised utilities. Suddenly, it was the continued *existence* of large-scale council housing, rather than its disappearance, that began to look unlikely:

> It seems increasingly certain that the combination of financial pressures, stock transfers and diversification of management will bring to an end the era of municipal landlordism in Britain. (Cole and Furbey, 1994, p 206)

The prospect of complete demunicipalisation – that is, the end of public housing – became increasingly realistic. The process of transferring housing stock away from local councils to housing associations and other bodies, which had begun under the Conservatives, continued and indeed accelerated under Labour. More than 250,000 homes have been transferred since 1997. If transfers continue at this rate, traditional council housing will disappear in little more than a decade (*Financial Times*, 26 February 2001).

The financing arrangements for housing associations – non-profit independent providers of social housing – changed in the late 1980s, so that they were required both to raise a proportion of their finance from the private sector ('mixed finance') and to bid competitively for funds. The more competitive regime and the need for asset-backing to secure private finance led to concentration in the sector, with merger activity and faster growth by the larger associations. Greater risk-bearing increased the importance of financial control and management and called into question the governance structure of associations, based around unpaid voluntary committee members.

Although there was no dramatic policy change in the owner-occupier sector, a series of measures had cumulative effects which brought about major system change. Through the 1980s HM Treasury pursued a covert policy of reducing the real value of mortgage tax relief, which it saw (correctly) as an open-ended and expensive subsidy. Over the decade, there were a number of indirect and marginal changes, such as lack of indexation and more restricted availability, the cumulative effect of which was considerable. By the early 1990s, tax relief had become in effect, a flat-rate subsidy to owner-occupiers, capped in nominal terms. In the 1990s, the policy became more overt, as part of a more general strategy to bring the ballooning British budget deficit under control. The rate of mortgage interest tax relief was limited from 25% to 20% in 1994 and to 15% in 1995. This paved the way for further reduction and eventually complete abolition by New Labour after 1997.

Hence, in the 1980s, fiscal support for owner-occupation was reduced, and yet the period saw an owner-occupied housing boom. How can we explain this? Three factors are important: rises in real income; the deregulation of the mortgage market; and the lack of rental alternatives. In Britain, real earnings rose by 21% between 1980 and 1989, compared with, for example, a rise of only 8% in real earnings in France. Demographic factors were also relevant: household growth peaked at 180,000 per annum in England in the 1986-91 period. Deregulation brought competition into Britain's mortgage market, which led to much easier availability of housing credit and a sharp rise in loan-to-value and loan-to-income ratios. At the same time, social housing output fell rapidly and the private rented sector continued to decline.

The result was an unsustainable boom in the second half of the 1980s. Average British house prices rose by 126% in the six years between 1983 and 1989, and by 178% in London. Thereafter, there was a dramatic turnaround: prices fell nationally by 16% between the first quarter of 1989 and the first quarter of 1993. In London prices fell by 30% over this period. The slump continued till the mid-1990s, and left a legacy of over-indebtedness, negative equity, mortgage arrears and repossessions. In 1989, two thirds of all first-time buyers borrowed more than 90% of the purchase price of the dwelling, and astonishingly, one third borrowed more than 100%. This high level of gearing was disastrous when coupled with subsequent falls in house prices, rises in unemployment and high real interest rates during the period of Exchange Rate Mechanism (ERM) membership between 1990 and 1992. More than one million homeowners were left with negative equity (outstanding debt exceeds current market value), and the total value of negative equity in the first half of 1992 was estimated at £6 billion. Possessions peaked at 75,000 per annum in 1991 before falling to an annual rate of about 50,000 in the first half of 1994.

From a policy aspect, the most interesting thing was not what the government did, but rather what it did *not* do. The actions it took were extremely limited. The government did not respond to the distress of lenders, builders, the housing lobby and elsewhere by increasing its support to owner-occupation, either through extending mortgage interest relief or by introducing mortgage benefit. Rather surprisingly, the government stuck, by and large, to the implications of its own rhetoric: a market system means that individuals make and live by their own decisions.

In the 1990s, homeowners were confronted by a very different set of economic conditions to those of the 1970s and 1980s. Inflation was lower, earnings growth was lower and real interest rates (even outside the ERM) remain high. There was growing awareness that finally the British government (Conservative or New Labour) was serious about counter-inflationary policy, and was no longer prepared to tolerate – or even encourage – house-price inflation as somehow different from, and morally superior to, other sorts of inflation. Nevertheless, in the second half of the 1990s, house prices recovered, and there were 'mini-booms' at the end of the decade in parts of London and elsewhere, so that house-price inflation reached perhaps 17-18% in 2000. By early 2001, the New Labour government could prepare for an election in far more favourable economic circumstances than that experienced by any previous Labour government – low inflation, low unemployment, an expanding economy, and house prices on an upward, but apparently sustainable, course. They duly got their electoral reward in June 2001, winning a second term with another huge majority of 167 seats.

Housing polarisation and social inequality

The public housing sector in Britain has been, and still is, much larger than in Japan. While public housing in Japan was less than 5% of the total stock in 1998 (see Chapter Eight of this volume), in Britain, even after 20 years of 'right-to-buy' sales and stock transfer, 16% of households were council tenants with a further 6% in the housing association sector.

However, over the course of the 1980s and 1990s the housing system in Britain became far more polarised between relatively affluent homeowners and poor council tenants. By the beginning of the 21st century, council tenure was closely identified in both popular imagination and by policy makers with poverty and 'social exclusion'. Between 1981 and 1991 the proportion of all household heads in Britain in full-time work fell from 58% to 54%. Among council tenants, however, it fell from 43% to 25%, and among housing association tenants from 42% to 29%. Lone parents, as a proportion of all household types, rose from 7% in 1981 to 9% in 1991, but from 12% to 18% in the council sector, and from 9% to 13% in the housing association sector.

In the council sector, the proportion of economically inactive households increased from 42% in 1980 to 62% in 1992, and in the housing association sector from 52% to 59%. In 1972, the average income of mortgagors was 77% higher than that of council tenants; by 1992 it was 191% higher.

This polarisation came about for a variety of reasons. First, there are changes over time in the characteristics and attributes of social sector tenants compared with owners – for example, the ageing of households in the sector, and the increased likelihood of council tenants compared with owners to become unemployed. Second, there has been the process by which a section of the council tenant population – the more affluent – has been able to transfer tenure without moving, through the 'right to buy'. Third, there have been the effects of transfers of moving households between tenures and differential entry and exit into the two main tenures. On this latter point, in 1981 about two thirds of new entrants to the social sector were married, with 9% divorced or separated. In 1991, the proportion of new social tenants who were married fell to 25%, with 18% being divorced or separated.

What can we conclude about housing policy and social exclusion in Britain? If we define social exclusion exactly, then it remains the case that British housing policy is a force for social *inclusion*. The social sector, despite the pressure on it, remains geared to housing need: in particular, there is a legally defined right to housing, enforceable through the courts, for a defined category of households. Social housing provides a route to affordable permanent housing for a range of households that would be unable to secure accommodation in a purely private system. Similarly, homeownership, despite its casualties, meets the choices as well as the needs of millions of British households. Access to owner–occupation has widened considerably over the last two decades to include households for whom home ownership would not have been possible in earlier periods.

Nevertheless, housing policy in the last 20 years can scarcely be described as helping to create a more equal society. Poverty has been increasingly concentrated in the social sector. Policy has not only reinforced and supported this process, but has also undermined the very notion of social provision as an alternative to the market, rather than as a safety net, grudgingly supplied by the state from limited resources.

Greater social inequality by housing tenure is one component of a more general growth of social and economic inequality in Britain over the last 20 years. Income inequality grew rapidly between 1977 and 1990, reaching its highest postwar level. This increase in inequality was driven by three main factors (Atkinson, 1993). First, earnings for those in work became more unequal. Second, there was an increase in the numbers of households dependent on benefits. Third, the income gap between households with earnings and those dependent on benefits grew. Unlike the rest of the postwar period, over these 20 years, the poorest 20–30% did not benefit from economic growth.

The proportion of the population living in households below 50% of average (mean) incomes rose from 10% in 1979/80 to 25% in 1996/97 (DSS, 1999) (see Figure 7.1). In particular, there has been a large increase in the numbers of working-age households where no one is working, with the proportion doubling between the end of the 1970s and the end of the 1990s. This has been driven both by a fall in male unemployment rates and by a rise in single adult including lone parent families. Income inequality rose faster in Britain between 1977 and 1990 than in any other country (except New Zealand) (Joseph Rowntree Foundation, 1995).

The rise in income inequality experienced in Britain over the past 20 years was virtually unparalleled among OECD countries, and Britain has fared relatively badly in terms of other aspects of poverty and social exclusion as well. Nearly one in five households with children has no working adult, significantly higher than all other European countries. In Britain almost 20% of children are growing up in households with no working adults, compared

Figure 7.1: UK households in poverty (various definitions)

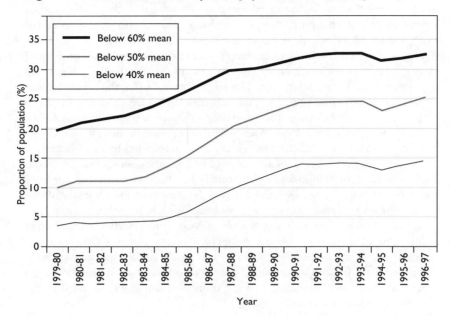

with 10% or less in Spain, the Netherlands, France, Germany, Italy, Greece and Portugal. Teenage birth rates are higher and education participation rates lower by comparison with other EU countries (Department of Social Security, 1999, p 30). Measured in all sorts of ways, poverty and social exclusion have undoubtedly increased in Britain over the last 25 years.

New Labour, inequality and housing

Poverty and redistribution

Since the election of New Labour in 1997, there has been a complex pattern of continuities with and differences from the previous administration. Public spending in the first three years was tightly controlled, with Chancellor of the Exchequer Gordon Brown proving himself to be, if anything, more fiscally orthodox than his conservative predecessors. Public spending fell from 41.2% of GDP in 1996-97 to 38.9% in 1998-99 and is planned to fall further to 36.9% in 2001. Spending over the term of New Labour's first parliament will average 39.4% of GDP, compared with 43.0% over the last Conservative administration of 1992-97 and 44.0% over the period 1979-97 (Institute for Fiscal Studies, 1999). However, this does not provide concrete evidence that the current government is a low spender. The role of government has changed, with some expenditure transferred from the public to the private sector; the impact of the economic cycle distorts the figures; and the distinction between government spending and tax relief is not always clear.

Moreover, in its second Comprehensive Spending Review, the government indicated a more expansionary approach to public expenditure, with particular emphasis on raising real spending on health and education. On these projections, total public spending will rise to 40.5% of GDP by the end of the review period in 2003/4.

A very strong theme of the New Labour government is the imposition of target setting, performance measures and evaluation of both outputs and outcomes on the public sector. Hence increases in expenditure on welfare services are linked to the achievement of specified targets, and to demonstrate efficiency and economy in meeting need. Schools, hospitals, social housing providers and other organisations are expected to 'compete' in terms of having their performance measured against their peers, and, increasingly, having funding streams dependent on successful performance.

David Piachaud of the London School of Economics has estimated what the effect of current government policies will be on the numbers in poverty in the period up to 2002 (Piachaud, 1999). He separately estimated the effects of government policies, such as the introduction of the Working Families' Tax Credit and the minimum wage, changes in Income Support and Child Benefit levels, and the combined effects of the three Labour budgets to date (September 1999), together with expected changes in the level of unemployment and demographic change. His results are reproduced in Table 7.1.

Piachaud's analysis shows that, on current policies, the numbers of people in poverty would fall by almost two million by 2002. However, he goes on to say:

> To put it in perspective, poverty would remain more than twice what it was in 1979. Child poverty will have been reduced over five years by some 800,000 or one sixth. This represents a most significant step on the Prime Minister's 20-year mission to end child poverty. Yet to achieve the goal would require an acceleration in the future. If the current rate of progress were maintained – a very big 'if' – only two thirds of child poverty would be abolished in 20

Table 7.1: Main changes in poverty (1997-2002)

Reduction in unemployment	−500,000
Effect of national minimum wage	−300,000
Budget measures to reduce child poverty	
Children	−800,000
Parents	−550,000
Relative decline in social security benefits to non-retired households without children	+300,000
Retired households	
	Little change
Overall change	−1.85 million

Source: Piachaud (1999)

years, and its extent would be no lower than it was 20 years ago in 1979. (Piachaud, 1999)

In its first term, New Labour explicitly repudiated both the policies and rhetoric of previous Labour governments in terms of redistributive taxation in order to attract the support of the floating voters of 'Middle England'. Nevertheless, in practice, successive budgets and other policies have aimed at redistributing income towards poorer households and towards families – a policy some have called 'redistribution by stealth'. How effective this has been is not yet clear. The Institute for Fiscal Studies has argued, that "Overall ... New Labour has been a redistributing government" (2000), pointing out that the lowest two deciles of the income distribution have gained most from Labour's first four budgets in office (1997-2000). However, other evidence shows rising income inequalities and rising health inequalities after 1997 (Lakin, 2001; Shaw et al, 2001).

Neighbourhood renewal and social exclusion

New Labour policies towards both social inequality and housing come together in its approach to what it calls 'neighbourhood renewal'. This was signalled very early as a key concern for the New Labour government. In a speech on a local authority estate in Southwark, London on 2 June 1997, just one month after the General Election, Prime Minister Tony Blair said there was a case in terms of both morality and enlightened self-interest to "tackle what we all know exists – an underclass of people cut off from society's mainstream, without any sense of shared purpose" (Kleinman, 2000). In December, Tony Blair set up a Social Exclusion Unit (SEU), based in the Cabinet Office. At the launch he argued:

> Social exclusion is about income but it is about more. It is about prospects and networks and life-chances. It's a very modern problem, and more harmful to the individual, more damaging to self-esteem for society as a whole, more likely to be passed down from generation to generation, than material poverty. (Kleinman, 2000)

Speaking to the Fabian Society in August 1997, Peter Mandelson, then Minister without Portfolio, and a key figure in New Labour's electoral landslide earlier that year, went further:

> There are 3 million people living in the worst 1,300 housing estates expressing multiple deprivation, rising poverty, unemployment, educational failure and crime. Behind these statistics ... are people who have lost hope trapped in fatalism. They are today's and tomorrow's underclass, shut out from society. (Kleinman, 2000)

In 1997, the Prime Minister gave the SEU the remit to examine "how to develop integrated and sustainable approaches to the problems of the worst housing estates, including crime, drugs, unemployment, community breakdown and bad housing". While not all the most deprived neighbourhoods consisted of social housing, council housing in particular dominated in many cases. The SEU published a report in September 1998 on the problems facing deprived neighbourhoods, recommending the development of a national strategy and setting up 18 Policy Action Teams (PATs). These PATs brought together civil servants, local officials, academics and local residents, investigated and reported on a variety of issues including jobs, skills, neighbourhood management, housing management and unpopular housing, anti-social behaviour, young people, and so on. In all, almost 600 recommendations were made.

Finally, in January 2001 a National Strategy Action Plan was launched. The action plan set a general target that, within 10-20 years, "no-one should be seriously disadvantaged by where they live". More specific targets were set for a whole range of social outcomes in deprived areas – for example, that no district should have a burglary rate more than three times the national average, and that no school should have fewer than 25% of pupils getting five good GCSE passes (national examinations usually taken at age 16). The plan also argued strongly for Local Strategic Partnerships – single bodies that bring together different parts of the public sector with private, voluntary and community sectors – and a greater role for micro-local neighbourhood management.

More generally, area-based policies are an important strand of the government's attack on poverty and social exclusion. The Single Regeneration Budget funds some 600 schemes in England, and the programme has recently been re-targeted to focus activity on the most deprived areas. There are about 100 Education Action Zones – which typically cover 2–3 secondary schools and their feeder primaries – as well as 15 Employment Zones and 26 Health Action Zones. The New Deal for Communities aims to regenerate the most deprived areas through improving job prospects, reducing crime, improving educational attainment and reducing poor health. Seventeen pilot areas have already been selected for the initiative, and more will follow. Other government initiatives include Sure Start, which aims to coordinate support for pre-school children, and initiatives set up under the overall umbrella of the National Strategy for Neighbourhood Renewal, including the Neighbourhood Renewal Fund, and support to community empowerment and neighbourhood management.

The plethora of area-based programmes is such that already by the late 1990s, some local authority areas could have up to eight separate initiatives within their boundaries. Furthermore, the government had to introduce mechanisms to coordinate between the programmes and prevent duplication. The Department of the Environment, Transport and the Regions (DETR) instigated a research study of six areas where a variety of area-based initiatives are running concurrently. The DETR has also set up a unit to exchange information on and coordinate the activities of the various zones. Indeed, the DETR has commissioned the Ordnance Survey to map the main area-based initiatives to establish the degree of overlap (Smith, 1999).

New Labour's approach therefore stresses area-based intervention and uses the rhetoric of social exclusion. However, in 1997, two thirds of all unemployed people in England lived *outside* the 44 'most deprived' districts identified in the SEU report. Even taking the broader category of the 65 local authorities targeted in Round Five of the Single Regeneration Budget – which together contain one third of the entire population – half the unemployed live outside the defined areas of deprivation (Smith, 1999). It is crucial to bear in mind that there is no statistical contradiction in having a level of concentration (that is, over-representation) of deprivation within areas while at the same time the bulk of the deprivation is not spatially concentrated.

Moreover, although the approach borrowed the European discourse of 'social exclusion', in practice the analysis drew much from the US debate on the 'urban underclass'. The underlying metaphor is clear: an urban underclass is a social group, separate and different from the mainstream, and living in particular neighbourhoods and housing estates. While it is true that many residents in areas of concentrated poverty can be excluded in different ways from the wider society, there is no evidence of a complete rupture either with social norms or with the workings of the national economy. In the US, Wilson concluded, on the basis of his research into Chicago's 'ghetto poor' that "despite the overwhelming joblessness and poverty, black residents in inner-city ghetto neighborhoods actually verbally endorse, rather than undermine, the basic American values concerning individual initiative" (1996). Similarly, Morris's study of unemployed and employed households in Britain found "no direct evidence ... of a *distinctive* culture of the 'underclass'" (1993).

The same generally holds true for the economy. The *variance* in unemployment rates by region, by class or by ethnic group is strongly related to the *level* of unemployment. Hence the likelihood of finding work among the most disadvantaged households and in the most deprived communities is directly connected with the strength or weakness of the national and regional economies. Such persons and areas continue to have above-average unemployment rates through periods both of growth and of recession. However, these rates move in phase with the national economic cycle. For example, Freeman and Rodgers (1999) investigated the impact of the current US boom on the labour market outcomes of less-educated men. They concluded that:

> the 1990s boom has substantially improved the labor market outcomes of young non-college-educated men; and helped the young African American men who are the most disadvantaged and socially troubled group in the US. Young men in tight labor markets in the 1990s experienced a noticeable boost in employment and earnings. (Freeman and Rodgers, 1999)

In fact, a similar point is made at area level by the authors of the Neighbourhood Renewal National Strategy Action Plan, who state that unemployment has fallen faster than the national average in 19 out of the 20 highest unemployment areas.

While area-based policies have a role to play, it seems clear that they can only be effective if they accompany national policies to address the root causes of poverty, inequality and social exclusion, which lie in labour market disadvantage, in lack of educational opportunities and in family breakdown.

Housing policy and politics

Questions of housing, social inequality and neighbourhood renewal are not the only housing issues on the agenda. There is a continuing population loss from most British cities to suburbs and to rural areas. About 90,000 people per year leave London and the six major cities in England. There are particular problems of decline in many northern cities.

London is different. After decades of decline, the population of Greater London first stabilised, and then began increasing in the 1980s. Between 1961 and 1983, the resident population of London fell from 7.977 million to 6.765 million. From then it increased to 6.890 million in 1991 and to 7.187 million in 1998. London's population is projected to continue to increase in the future. This population growth has come from increased international migration as well as from natural increase (excess of births over deaths). The increase in international migration encompasses a range of groups including EU nationals, highly skilled professionals and also rapidly growing numbers of refugees and asylum seekers. It is estimated that the number of refugees and asylum seekers now living in London is between 240,000 and 280,000, including almost 40,000 children in London schools (Aldous et al, 1999). Increasing population and continuing economic growth has put considerable pressure on the London housing system, with particular concerns about essential but moderately-paid workers, such as teachers and nurses, being driven out by high house prices and housing rents.

Nationally, there is a requirement to house an extra 4.3 million households in the 25 years to 2021. The greatest housing pressures are in the south-east. Here there have been continuing struggles between central government and local authorities (particularly the counties) over the scale and extent of new housing and hence population growth. In effect the earlier 'inner versus outer' London struggles concerning housing provision have been displaced even further. The arena for these struggles is the Secretary of State's Regional Planning Guidance (RPG 9) for the south-east which provides the regional framework for the preparation of local authority development plans outside London and the Mayor's Spatial Development Strategy in London. The regional planning body, SERPLAN (South East Region Planning Council), comprising the local authorities, proposed a figure of 33,000 new dwellings per year. This was rejected by the government who commissioned an independent panel to conduct a public examination into the draft RPG 9. The figure proposed by the panel was considerably higher, at 55,000 new dwellings per annum, provoking a furious political response. Ultimately, the government compromised at 43,000 additional houses per year outside London, and 23,000 within London.

The western part of the south-east region continues to be characterised by very high levels of development pressures and full or even over-full employment. By the end of 2000, local politicians were actively campaigning for policies of job *diversion* from the area, arguing that continuing influxes of higher paid employees were squeezing teachers, nurses and other public service workers out of local housing markets, creating problems for service delivery.

The Government's Urban White Paper in 2000 set the goal of "encouraging people to remain in, and move back into, our major towns and cities, both for the benefit of our urban areas and to relieve the pressure for development in the countryside" (ODPM, 2000). There has been some success in revitalising city centres as places to live in, as well as places of work, shopping and leisure, in London, Leeds, Manchester and Bristol. However, it is the suburban, fringe and rural areas which, in general, continue to see the greatest housing demand. The contrast between relatively affluent, owner-occupied outer areas, and deprived inner-ring suburbs characterised mainly by rented housing continues to be a dimension of social inequality expressed through the housing market.

Conclusion

According to a MORI poll before the 2001 General Election, housing issues have never been less important to voters. Only one in six people thought housing was an issue that would influence the way they would vote in that election. This contrasts with 1996, when 30% of voters said housing was very important in deciding their vote. Council and housing association tenants in 2001 were twice as likely as homeowners to see housing as an important issue. Housing was, however, a more significant issue for those living in London, where one in three rated it as important.

In its second term, Labour is under pressure to deliver on core issues such as the health service, education, and poverty. Housing policy per se will be less important. However, it will be relevant because of the increased concentration of poverty and the spatial polarisation associated with increased social inequality. The wider issues of the future of towns and cities and the need for an 'urban renaissance' will also involve difficult issues about the location, price, and type of new housing.

References

Aldous, J., Bardsley, M., Daniell, R., Gair, R., Jacobson, B., Lowdell, C., Morgan, D., Storkey, M. and Taylor, G. (1999) *Refugee health in London: Key issues for public health*, The Health of Londoners Project, June, London: Health of Londoners Project.

Atkinson, A.B. (1993) 'What is happening to the distribution of income in Britain?', London School of Economics ST/ICERD Welfare State Programme Discussion Paper WSP/87.

Cole, I. and Furbey, R. (1994) *The eclipse of council housing*, London: Routledge.

Department of Social Security (1999) *Opportunity for all: Tackling poverty and social exclusion: First Annual Report 1999*, London: The Stationery Office.

Esping-Andersen, G. (1990) *The three worlds of welfare capitalism*, Cambridge: Polity Press.

Freeman, R.B. and Rodgers, W.M. (1999) 'Area economic conditions and the labor market outcomes of young men in the 1990s expansion', NBER Working Paper 7073, April.

Harloe, M. (1995) *The people's home?*, Oxford: Basil Blackwell.

Institute for Fiscal Studies (1999) *Green Budget 1999*, London: Institute for Fiscal Studies.

Institute for Fiscal Studies (2000) *Budget briefing 22nd March: The distributional impact*, (www.ifs.org.uk/gbfiles/distribution/sld001.htm).

Kleinman, M.P. (1996) *Housing, welfare and the state in Europe*, Cheltenham: Edward Elgar.

Kleinman, M.P. (2000) 'Include me out? The new politics of place and poverty', *Policy Studies*, vol 21, no 1, pp 49-61.

Lakin, C. (2001) 'The effects of taxes and benefits on household income 1999-2000', *Economic Trends*, vol 569, pp 35-74.

Malpass, P. and Murie, A. (1994) *Housing policy and practice*, (4th edn), Basingstoke: Macmillan.

Morris, L. (1993) 'Is there a British underclass?', *International Journal of Urban and Regional Research*, (Special Issue: 'The new urban poverty and the underclass'), vol 17, no 3.

ODPM (2000) 'Our towns and cities: the future. Delivering on urban renaissance', London: ODPM.

Piachaud, D. (1999) 'Progress on poverty', *New Economy*, September, vol 6, no 3.

Joseph Rowntree Foundation (1995) *Inquiry into income and wealth*, York: Joseph Rowntree Foundation.

Shaw, M., Dorling, D. and Davey-Smith, G. (2001) 'Did things get better for Labour voters? Premature death rates and voting in the 1997 election', University of Bristol, Townsend Centre for International Poverty Research.

Smith, D. (1987) *The rise and fall of monetarism*, Harmondsworth: Penguin.

Smith, G. (1999) 'Area-based initiatives: the rationale and options for area targeting', LSE STICERD Centre for the Analysis of Social Exclusion (CASE) Paper 25, London: London School of Economics and Political Science.

Wilson, W.J. (1996) *When work disappears*, New York, NY: Knopf.

EIGHT

Housing policy and social inequality in Japan

Yosuke Hirayama

Introduction

Housing policy does not serve to improve the housing condition for all people. Under a specific set of social, economic and political conditions, it allots resources to certain groups, which in turn contribute to the formation of social inequality. In relation to housing, boundaries that place certain groups at an advantage and others at a disadvantage are socially drawn. These boundaries are not fixed but are redrawn depending on changes to various conditions.

This chapter examines the role of housing policy in creating social inequality in Japan. Housing policy in Japan has placed importance on the formation of a social mainstream. The Conservative party (Liberal Democratic Party) has been in power for most of the postwar period, and their housing policy has directed resources to family households with middle to upper incomes, and encouraged them to own their own home. In principal, people are expected to secure their housing through the market by themselves. For middle-class households, acquiring their own housing and accumulating assets is considered to have a stabilising effect on the social mainstream. The government has been implementing housing policies as a means of accelerating the mass construction of owner-occupied houses and as a driving force of economic development backed by its strong relationship with the construction and housing industries, and real estate developers. There has been little direct provision of public housing for low-income households in the past. Such housing policies have produced social inequalities, with boundaries between those on low incomes and those with higher incomes; between single and family households; and also between renters and homeowners.

The mainstream-oriented housing policy has been rationalised under the conditions of economic development, by an increase in the middle-class and also by the large proportion of family households that make up the whole population. Modern Japan, however, has entered a period of rapid and profound change in which various currents can be detected: from state intervention to deregulation; from Keynesian to neoliberalism; from economic growth to a destabilised economy; and also from a cohesive society to a fragmented society.

The framework of housing policy established in earlier periods of strong economic growth has lost its effectiveness due to fundamental changes in socioeconomic conditions. Japan has been in the grip of a prolonged recession since the burst of the 'bubble economy' at the beginning of the 1990s. Prices of land and housing have dropped and owner-occupied housing has lost its security as an asset. Furthermore, Japan's demographic is becoming skewed by an increase in the elderly population and a decrease in the birth rate. The proportion of conventional family households is in decline, and single households, elderly-only households, and couples without children are increasing. The construction, real estate and housing industries continue to press the government to deregulate the housing market. Circumstances surrounding housing policies have changed and policy direction is becoming less and less transparent.

As a consequence, the Japanese definition of 'social mainstream' is ambiguous. This is not meant to mitigate social inequalities, but rather to reconstruct them. What is emerging is a more complex structure of social inequalities set by traditional boundaries as well as by new ones based on more varied and complicated criteria. The first part of this chapter highlights how Japanese housing policy reflects and reinforces the social mainstream, expanding homeownership and contributing to economic growth. The second part provides a clearer picture of the actual state of social inequalities formed by such housing policies. The final part of this chapter then considers how best to reconstruct the relationship between housing policies and social inequalities in present-day Japan.

Framework of housing policy

Social mainstream-oriented housing policy

Housing policy in Japan was systematised in the period immediately after the Second World War (Hayakawa and Ohmoto, 1985). The framework was designed mainly to speed up the formation of the social mainstream. Immediately after the war, Japan began to address fundamental reforms centring on demilitarisation and democratisation under orders of the US General HQ. Industry and the economy had completely collapsed and people were living in extreme poverty. Cities devastated by the war had lost large amounts of housing stock. It was estimated that approximately 4.2 million housing units across the nation, equal to one fifth of all housing at that time, were needed. Support for the people thought to form the core of society was given priority under housing policies in order not only to address the housing shortage but also to construct a new state and to encourage the rebuilding of industry and the economy. People strongly voiced their demands for housing. Housing policy, however, did not reflect any social activity by those who needed housing, but was organised by a national 'top-down' system driven by the necessity to build a new society within as short a space of time as possible.

The Ministry of Construction, which has jurisdiction over housing policy, was established in 1948. They systematised housing policy on 'three pillars':

- the 1950 Housing Loan Corporation Act;
- the 1951 Public Housing Act;
- the 1955 Housing Corporation Act.

The Housing Loan Corporation (HLC), a government agency, mainly provides individuals with a long-term and low-interest loan for the building and acquisition of their own home. Public housing, which is subsidised by the central government, and constructed, owned and managed by local government, is provided for low-income people at a subsidised rent. The Housing Corporation (HC) was also founded as an agency of the state to construct rental housing and condominiums for middle-income households in large cities.

Housing policy began to evolve helping family households with middle income to secure housing. These households were considered to have played a key role in stabilising society, by rebuilding industry and developing the economy. Single people were excluded from the HLC and public housing measures, since they were not considered to have a problem in terms of overcrowded living conditions, and did not count as members of the mainstream of society. Once they were married and had children, housing policy came into play. Moreover, public housing measures did not include the lowest income households (although it was supposed to provide for those on low incomes). There was a controversy between the Ministry of Construction and the Ministry of Welfare over the jurisdiction of public housing. The Ministry of Construction, which eventually took control of public housing, thought that low-income people were the concern of public assistance by the Ministry of Welfare. The calculation of rent was based on construction expenditure and did not alter according to the dwellers' income. In this context, public housing was provided to households with the ability to pay rent rather than to those below the poverty line. The HC took the role of supporting the increasing number of white-collar working households in large cities. The HC also constructed some rental housing for single people in the 1950s. It was not, however, because the HC acknowledged the shortage of housing for single people as a priority, but rather because the number of units constructed was increased by reducing the size of unit and then decisions were taken to provide those units for single people.

Housing policy produced modern houses and a new landscape for the social mainstream. Before the Second World War, most houses were built in a Japanese style: *tatami*-matted rooms; a dining room; an arrangement of rooms where privacy was not of paramount importance; and a drawing room which was considered much more than a space for family members to gather. In urban inner cities, low-rise wooden terraced houses were built closely together.

Modern houses built in the postwar period, in stark contrast, were provided for nuclear families of parents and children. They introduced the dining kitchen where people sat at the table on a chair; an individual's room was securely private; and the living room was there more for the family to be together than for entertaining guests. The HC developed multi-family housing estates – *Danchi* – where concrete structures and open spaces were combined on a large scale. Also, the HLC developed a standard housing design and distributed it to those who intended to build their own houses to further popularise modern housing design. The HLC's low-interest loans further accelerated the formation of suburban areas with single-family homes. With its modern housing for modern families, *Danchi* for salaried workers, and suburban residential districts for modern nuclear families, policy played a role in defining how housing in postwar Japan should be.

Homeownership-oriented housing policy

Japan's recovery and development in the postwar years was remarkable. During the period from 1955 to the oil crisis of 1973, the average annual GDP growth was as high as 10%. Immediately after the oil crisis, the economy began to grow again and continued to grow at a high level until the burst of the 'bubble economy'. This 'bubble' was the result of speculative investment in real estate and the stock market from the latter half of the 1980s.

One of the factors that supported economic growth was the mass construction of housing. Housing was in serious shortage from the end of the Second World War until the beginning of the 1970s. The number of households had increased enormously by the mid-1970s and rapid urbanisation took place. The average annual increase of households swelled from 185,000 in 1950-55, to 466,000 in 1955-60, to 682,000 in 1960-65, and to 758,000 in 1965-70 (Izu, 1999). The proportion of urban population in the total population jumped from 37.7% in 1950 to 63.9% in 1960 and to 72.1% in 1970. Therefore, there was a tremendous demand for housing behind the mass construction. The housing industry developed rapidly to increase the construction of urban condominiums and suburban single-family homes. Over 90% of housing investment came from the private sector, and this came to have an important position in the macro-economy.

By 1968, the amount of housing stock exceeded the total number of households nationwide for the first time, and by 1973 a crude surplus became a common feature of every prefecture. Housing demand was met in quantity for the first time in the 30-year postwar period. The quality of housing, however, was mostly inferior and good quality housing was still scarce; nevertheless, mass construction continued. Large-scale housing construction has been a prominent feature in Japan right up to the present time. The number of new constructions per 1,000 people was 3.27 in Britain in 1993, 4.42 in France in 1992, and 4.98 in the US in 1993. In Japan, on the other hand, it was as much as 12.02 in 1993 (Sumita, 2000).

Of the 'three pillars' of housing policy, the government has constantly encouraged the building of owner-occupied housing using low-interest loans provided by the HLC (van Vliet and Hirayama, 1994; Hirayama and Hayakawa, 1995). The ratio of homeownership shifted to about 60% between 1963 and 1998. Despite rapid urbanisation and the increasing number of households, the ratio of homeownership was kept at a certain level due to the measures used to accelerate housing acquisition. The ratio of private rental housing has been the second highest at around 25%, although private rental housing has not been a priority tenure of housing policy. Among the whole housing tenure, the ratio of public housing and HC housing have been very low, at around 5% and 2%, respectively (Table 8.1).

Housing policy was aimed at the expansion of homeownership with a specific combination of social, economic and political conditions. By obtaining their own house, family households with middle to high incomes were expected to form the social mainstream. Houses were market commodities and the principle was clear that people should obtain their own housing by self-reliance. To maintain economic growth, an increase in the construction of owner-occupied housing was regarded as a necessity. Private financial institutions made inroads into the housing loan market allowing the provision of finance to expand. In order to acquire a house, households usually combined loans made available by the HLC and banks. The HLC's low-interest loan withdrew capital from family finances, expanded the bank's financial market, and stimulated private housing investment. By raising the demand for housing, the government was able to stay in power supported by the construction and housing industries, and real estate developers.

Table 8:1: Housing tenure in Japan

Year	Owned houses (%)	Public rented houses (owned by local government) (%)	Public rented houses (owned by public corporation) (%)	Private rented houses (%)	Company houses (%)	Total (including tenure not reported) n
1963	64.3	4.6		24.1	7.0	20,374,000
1968	60.3	5.8		27.0	6.9	24,198,000
1973	59.2	4.9	2.1	27.5	6.4	28,731,000
1978	60.4	5.3	2.2	26.1	5.7	32,189,000
1983	62.4	5.4	2.2	24.5	5.2	34,705,000
1988	61.3	5.3	2.2	25.8	4.1	37,413,000
1993	59.8	5.0	2.1	26.4	5.0	40,773,000
1998	60.3	4.8	2.0	27.3	3.9	43,892,000

Source: Statisitics Bureau; 1963 Housing Survey of Japan, 1993 Housing Survey of Japan, and 1998 Housing and Land Survey of Japan

In terms of single households, the HLC began to lend to single people aged 40+ in 1981 and 35+ in 1988, and finally rescinded the age limitation in 1993. The HC, which had not built housing for single people between the 1960s and the mid-1970s, started providing housing for single people in 1976. The reason why housing policy changed to implement a measure for single people was not only to address their housing needs but also to stimulate housing demand and increase the amount of construction.

With the oil crisis in the early 1970s as a turning point, housing policy became more of a measure to stimulate the economy, putting more stress on encouraging people to buy their own houses with a loan provided by the HLC. The ratio of houses with the HLC's loans increased from 41% in the 1951-55 fiscal year to 54% in the 1971-75 fiscal year, to 69% in the 1976-80 fiscal year and to as much as 76% in the 1981-85 fiscal year (Table 8.2).

With the exception of the oil crisis period, the prices of land and housing in Japan increased rapidly until the burst of the 'bubble economy'. This acceleration rate well exceeded the rate at which incomes and commodity prices rose. The economic stimulation programme generated a large amount of investment into the housing market to rapidly push up housing prices. By the mid-1970s, it had become difficult for ordinary workers to purchase their own homes. Therefore, the HLC repeatedly eased restrictions on loans to improve take-up rates. The repayment term for wooden houses was extended from 18 to 25 years and that for non-wooden houses from 25 to 30 years in 1978. The Step Repayment System, in which the amount of repayments is set at a low level for the first five years, was introduced in 1979. A virtuous cycle was formed in which the improvement of lending conditions encouraged house acquisition,

Table 8.2: Housing new starts (thousand unit) in Japan (1961-2000)

Fiscal year	Housing by housing loan corp-oration A	Public housing by local govern-ment and public corp-oration B	Publicly founded housing of other types C	Publicly founded housing D=A+B+C	Private housing	Total n	D/N *100 (%)	A/E *100 (%)
1961-65	392	189	213	794	2,684	3,478	22.8	49.5
1966-70	697	352	465	1,514	4,522	6,036	25.1	46.1
1971-75	1,154	447	455	2,056	5,784	7,840	26.2	56.1
1976-80	1,967	339	297	2,603	4,658	7,261	35.9	75.6
1981-85	1,994	258	280	2,532	3,360	5,892	43.0	78.8
1986-90	2,085	210	272	2,567	5,562	8,129	31.6	81.2
1991-95	2,653	211	292	3,156	4,161	7,317	43.1	84.1
1996-00	2,171	179	312	2,662	3,929	6,591	40.4	81.5

Source: Ministry of Construction

which then increased demand for owner-occupied housing and boosted housing prices, and when it became difficult to obtain a house, lending conditions were again adjusted.

Inside or outside

A ladder to homeownership

Since housing policy defined homeownership as social mainstream housing, it put pressure on resources to be allocated to where they would be best utilised. Consequently, there has been little construction of public housing and no institutional support for private rental housing. This has resulted in generating a large disparity between those who own their homes and those who do not. According to the Housing and Land Survey in 1998, a significant difference in the floor area was observed between 121 square meters of an owner-occupied housing unit and 44 square meters of a rental housing unit. Regarding the housing standard stipulated by the government, the proportion of housing under the minimum housing space standard was 1.3% in owner-occupied housing and 11.3% in rental housing, and the proportion under the targeted housing space standard was 41% in owner-occupied housing and 69.3% in rental housing. Owning property in the housing market was a particularly good way of accumulating wealth since values of land and housing had always increased (that is, until the burst of the 'bubble economy'). Therefore, to obtain housing meant to many people an eventual capital gain. In addition, the income of households generally determines the type of tenure. Among households who own their housing the proportion of those with higher incomes compared with other tenures is high (Table 8.3). Under Japanese employment practices,

Table 8.3: Annual income by housing tenure in Japan (1998)

Annual income (million yen)	Owned houses (%)	Public rented houses (owned by local government) (%)	Public rented houses (owned by public corp-oration) (%)	Private rented wooden houses (%)	Private rented non-wooden houses (%)	Company houses (%)	Total (%)
1-3	21.2	54.6	26.6	47.0	38.3	13.2	28.0
3-5	23.1	30.1	32.8	29.1	29.5	28.0	25.1
5-7	19.0	10.2	21.0	12.6	15.0	23.9	17.1
7-10	20.0	3.3	12.9	6.3	8.7	21.9	15.4
10+	15.7	0.6	4.3	2.6	3.9	11.3	10.9
Not reported	1.1	1.2	2.5	2.5	4.6	1.7	3.5
Total	100.0	100.0	100.0	100.0	100.0	100.0	100.0

Source: Statistics Bureau; 1998 Housing and Land Survey of Japan

Table 8.4: Home ownership rate (in Japan) by main earner's age and sex (1998)

Age	Total	Male	Female
Total	60.0	63.7	43.7
up to 24	3.3	3.3	1.6
25-29	12.7	14.6	5.0
30-34	29.0	31.7	11.7
35-39	48.6	51.5	25.1
40-44	62.4	65.7	37.0
45-49	69.7	73.0	46.7
50-54	73.2	76.3	53.3
55-59	76.7	79.8	58.5
60-64	79.1	82.4	62.3
65+	80.6	84.9	69.8

Source: Statistics Bureau; 1998 Housing and Land Survey of Japan

income usually increases with maturity. Therefore, the rate of homeownership tends to increase with the age of household heads. The rate of homeownership among female-headed households, however, is significantly lower in any age groups compared with their male counterparts (Table 8.4).

When considered as social policy, housing policy is generally expected to allot more public capital to people with low incomes. However, the emphasis on homeownership resulted in concentrating public support for middle- and upper-income groups. Therefore, a 'filtering' system was conceived to rationalise the situation. For example, a young family may rent a house of relatively poor quality since their income tends to be low. As the family advances in age, their income is likely to increase so that they are likely to be able to improve their housing situation. Eventually, the family should be able to purchase a house. Once they own a house, it often means they make a capital gain, which enables them to move from a small property to a larger one, such as from a condominium to a single-family home. Support for the middle- and upper-income groups was considered to improve the housing circumstances of the lower-class by the chain reaction of such moves. This system defined how a life-course should develop in the social mainstream and required people to climb up a 'housing ladder' by self-reliance. Not all people, however, can reach the stage of acquiring their own home. Indeed, those with low incomes have been excluded from the system.

Those who could claim that they were a part of mainstream society owned a house. Homeownership was not only defined in a material sense, but also represented the new social status and attitude of its owner. It symbolised middle or high-level income, a stable job and credibility, and ownership of a real estate asset. Homeowners were supposed to respect the order of society, to take care of their family, to work hard, and to accept the concept of self-help. The suburban single-family home meant that the owner had reached the top of the housing ladder. A homeowner represented a symbol of 'the inside' – that is, belonging to mainstream society.

It was often a sense of uneasiness that spurred people into obtaining a house. Purchasing a house and a patch of land at an early age – the younger the better – could lead to asset creation. To ease their anxieties about their old age, people believed it was necessary to have assets in the form of housing since older people were often rejected as tenants of private rental housing. Owner-occupied housing was regarded as security of tenure. Middle-class families also liked to express their social 'attitude'. It was necessary to show a desire to belong to the order to receive a certain position within society. The steady rise in land and housing prices forced people toward housing acquisition, and joining the housing ladder helped them to deal with such uneasiness.

Family and company

Japan's modernisation took place in the postwar years. The housing market was formed, private investment was invited to the market, and housing began to be seen as a commodity. The government established a housing policy system. It was, however, not only the relationship between individuals, government and the market, which decided an individual's housing conditions. Various 'communities' – represented by the family and the company – influenced the individual's housing options. In Japan, an individual does not only exist as an individual with a direct relationship with the market and government, but also lives with a strong connection with their family and company (see Chapter Two of this volume). Therefore, the market, public policy as well as family and company together brought about social inequality in terms of housing provision.

The type of company that individuals belong to has a strong influence on whether or not the individuals can obtain a house (Ohmoto, 1996). Postwar Japanese society is sometimes called a 'company society' – many companies have adopted lifelong employment and seniority systems to form the models of 'company as a community' and 'company as a family'. Many employees and their families lived their lives belonging to and dependent upon their company. Large corporations often had systems of internal saving and low-interest loans for housing acquisition for their employees. These systems reinforced the 'company society'. Employees of large corporations benefited greatly with regard to housing acquisition. Small to medium-size companies, however, usually did not have such saving and loan systems. Even if they did, the conditions were not as good as those offered by large corporations. According to research conducted by the Japan Federation of Employers' Associations in 1984, the proportion of companies, employing 30-99 people, with saving and loan schemes for housing were 35% and 72%, respectively; this increased to 90% and 100% in companies with over 5,000 employees.

In pre-war Japanese society, the extended-family household predominated. As a result of the postwar modernisation, the number of nuclear families increased, although the relationship between several generations within a family was still strong (see also Chapter Four of this volume). According to the Housing Demand Survey in 1983, 27% of older people lived with their children and 33% lived in the same municipalities as their children without sharing an accommodation. Even in cases where parents and their adult children form separate nuclear family households, a mutual-help relationship often exists between the two generations. For example, children help their older parents with domestic chores, and in return, parents take care of their grandchildren.

Social inequality in housing tends to be passed to the next generation by the family system. A younger household may receive financial support from their parents when obtaining a house. Gift tax, where parents financially support their children for housing acquisition, is free for a gift of up to five million yen (£25,000) − ¥200 = £1 − and very low for amounts up to 15 million yen (£75,000). Therefore, children of wealthy parents are at an advantage. Owner-occupied housing is not only an asset for the owner household but also can be inherited by the next generation. With the decreased fertility rates of recent years, the possibility that the young generation will inherit their parents' housing is becoming higher (Hirayama and Hayakawa, 1995). For instance, the 1993 Housing Demand Survey on housing inheritance for households living in rental housing indicated that 30% of the respondents would inherit a house from their parents. Although they do not currently own housing, there is a potential disparity concerning the possibility of housing inheritance.

Segregated socio-space

Segregated socio-space has been created in urban areas. The mainstream-oriented housing policy has placed people either 'inside' or 'outside' of society, frequently allotting resources only to those inside. People who are placed 'outside' may not easily find a way in, resulting in some specific socio-spaces existing separately from those within the mainstream society.

There are dilapidated districts where *mokuchin* and *nagaya* are built closely together. *Mokuchin* is privately rented, multi-family housing in a wooden structure, constructed en masse between 1960 and 1970. *Nagaya* is wooden terraced housing, constructed prior to the Second World War, and which remain concentrated in areas that escaped from war damage. Both *mokuchin* and *nagaya* are in a severely run-down condition. The unit space is very small, and there is no proper road infrastructure around them. They are built very close together, and dwellers hardly receive adequate sunshine or ventilation. Since no investment for material maintenance or improvement has usually been made, these houses have rapidly become dilapidated. The dwellers of *mokuchin* used to be young workers who flocked into cities by the 1970s but are now mainly occupied by low-income households and older people. The ratio of older residents is also very high in *nagaya*.

Although the numbers of *mokuchin* and *nagaya* are declining, they still remain concentrated in certain districts of inner cities forming distinctive socio-spaces outside the housing ladder system. It is difficult to redevelop these areas partly because most owners of *mokuchin* are older people and those on low incomes, and have neither the financial ability nor the intention to invest in rebuilding their houses. The property-rights situation in *nagaya* is also extremely complex, which makes their redevelopment difficult: land-ownership rights, and leaseholds for land and units are mixed and locked together in a single building. In many cases of both *mokuchin* and *nagaya*, it is not easy to redevelop the sites according to newer building regulations since the sites are often extremely small and not adjacent to existing roads.

There are also areas in a city where minority groups are concentrated. Mainstream society has constructed a clear boundary between themselves and others and has therefore promoted segregation. The main examples of districts outside the mainstream are *burakumin* districts, Korean districts, and *yoseba* districts. In some areas of a large city, these districts are placed close together or overlap each other. *Burakumin* and Korean districts exist in both urban and rural areas.

Burakumin are said to be descendants of an outcast group under the caste system of the feudal era, and have continued to be discriminated against in marriage and employment even in modern times. Generally, they lived in crowded, shack-like housing that was in a state of severe disrepair. The Slum Clearance and Redevelopment Act was enacted in 1927 and revised as the Housing Improvement Act in 1960. Under these laws, local governments, through subsidies from the central government, have cleared slums and constructed improved rented housing for the former slum residents. These Acts were not particularly intended for *burakumin* districts; however, since most of the slums were in *burakumin* districts, the Act was implemented to redevelop them. The actual conditions of their neighbourhoods were gradually improved by the construction of improved housing. Such improved housing, however, served to reinforce the area's segregation. The improved housing is already showing signs of deterioration and the maintenance and prevention of delapidation remains a major issue.

In the Korean districts live those who were brought to Japan as labourers by force during the Second World War, and their second and third generations mainly live as permanent residents. Having been discriminated against in Japanese society, they have built a community based on strong cooperation. Ikuno in Osaka is the largest Korean district with approximately 40,000 Korean residents, a quarter of the total population in the area. The Japanese government had excluded non-Japanese residents from housing policy for a long time. It was not until the 1980s that the government decided to grant those formally registered, long-term residents the same status as Japanese citizens in relation to housing policy. Some local governments, however, still restrict non-Japanese residents from moving into public housing, and quite often, private landlords and letting agencies refuse to rent their properties to them.

Yoseba districts are where casual labourers gather together in a large city, and where brokers provide the labourers with manual work on a daily wage basis (these districts are discussed in detail in Chapter Ten of this volume). The day labourers do not have permanent accommodation but lodge in a 'flop-house' at a daily rate. The rooms of such houses are extremely small, usually no more than five square meters. *Yoseba* labourers have often cut-off relations with their family, and their employment conditions are unstable, low-paid and severe. They are also often subject to various other discriminations. Kamagasaki is the largest *yoseba* in Osaka with approximately 200 flophouses, and an estimated 25,000 to 30,000 labourers make the area their living base. Approximately 6,000 people lodge in flophouses in the Sanya *yoseba* in Tokyo.

Residualised public housing

Public housing, which was available to a wide range of households including the middle-income group when it was launched, began its process of residualisation shortly after the establishment of the 1951 Public Housing Act. The Act limits its target recipients to the lowest income group. The government brought out housing policy that was geared towards accelerating the provision of owner-occupied housing, while making public housing residual. People were required to secure their own housing through the market by themselves and to climb up the housing ladder.

Public housing is located outside of the social mainstream and forms an isolated socio-space (Hirayama, 1990). Its construction is therefore at a low level. The ratio of public housing to total housing was as little as 4.8% (see Table 8.1). Fifty-five per cent of households living in public housing were on an annual income of less than three million yen (£15,000) (see Table 8.3). Developments were constructed on a large scale on the fringes of cities; their function was to gather together people on low incomes. Public housing has been residualised as follows:

1. Income criterion for moving into public housing has been lowered. At the time of the 1951 Public Housing Act's launch, the majority of the households (the lowest 80% of all the income groups) qualified for public housing. However, this percentage dropped to 33% in the 1970s, and to 25% after the Act's amendment in 1996. As the number of residents with low income increased, local governments were put under pressure to lower the rent, but due to a lack of state subsidy, their financial burden became greater.
2. The 1959 amendment established a system whereby a household whose income exceeded a certain amount had to make an effort to move out of public housing. Furthermore, a 1969 amendment made it possible for local governments to formally request those with higher incomes to move out. Although the original rent for public housing was set, based on a calculation of the construction cost of the building, the 1996 amendment introduced the system of calculating rent based on the tenants' income. As a result, households with an income above a fixed amount have to pay a market rent. Nowadays, therefore, losing the economic advantage of living there, they became more likely to move out of public housing.

3. Finally, the government has increasingly put importance on the criteria for the welfare categories that qualify people for public housing. There has been an increase in the provision of special public housing catering for older people, people with disabilities, and single-parent households. Although public housing originally excluded single people, it began to accept single older residents in 1980, as older people were qualified under the revised welfare categories. Young and middle-aged single people are still excluded from public housing. After the 1996 amendment of the Public Housing Act, the income criterion was relaxed for older households up to the lowest 40% of the total income group, where local governments thought it right to do so.

The revised welfare categories have been rapidly introduced to public housing. Indeed, public housing has been for the 'worthy poor' and justified as long as it is residualised. In a society where self-reliance is the predominant principle, heavily subsidised housing is socially and politically unstable. An increase in public housing was regarded as a danger threatening this principle. It is difficult to be recognised as the 'worthy poor' simply by being a low-income household. The main purpose of public housing until the 1960s was therefore for young people to secure their first house. Young households were regarded as the 'worthy poor' since they were expected to move out of public housing to obtain their own housing after a short period as their incomes increased. In this context, public housing was used as a stepping stone to the social mainstream. Public housing since the 1970s, however, lost its role of providing a route into the mainstream: separated socio-spaces began to form and the average period of living in these areas became longer. Today, public housing is provided for classes with very low income, older people, and people with disabilities. Limiting the income criteria and using welfare categories for residents imply a means of procuring agreement for the justification of public housing.

Restructuring of social inequality

Changes in the conditions of housing policy

Japan is in a period of transformation brought on by a number of reasons: economic globalisation; financial deregulation; the formation of more competitive business environments; the change in population structure by increased longevity and decline in the birth rate; the fragmentation of the social structure; as well as expansion of neoliberal ideology. In this context, the predetermined framework of housing policy is losing its effectiveness due to the rapidly changing circumstances.

The 'bubble economy' of the late 1980s brought about an abnormal rise in land and housing prices. The prices of land and housing constantly went up in the postwar period and prices were decided in anticipation of further increases, which led to a speculative 'bubble' forming. The governments of the 1980s adopted neoliberal policies and deregulated finances, urban planning and land policy (Hayakawa and Hirayama, 1991). The speculative bubble, which had been swelling in the past, suddenly expanded, due to a series of deregulations. All kinds of industries – not only the real estate industry – rushed into land speculation. The 'bubble economy' burst at the beginning of the 1990s, however, and land and housing prices have been on the decline ever since. A major drop in the value of real estate is now being observed for the first time in the postwar period (Hasegawa, 2001; Yamada, 2001).

The Japanese economy is no longer stable. The business climate has been sluggish for a long time and the economy showed little growth in the 1990s. Unrecoverable debts generated by the burst of the economy are obstacles for economic recovery. It is now unclear whether the 'company community' can be maintained. Many companies are restructuring by downsizing and abandoning the lifelong employment and seniority wage systems as the economy is globalised and a more competitive business environment is formed. Employment is now becoming more mobilised, the unemployment rate is increasing and income is being destabilised.

Housing policy to expand numbers in owner-occupied housing was effective only under conditions of economic growth, rising housing prices, and stable employment with steady income increases. Even if it was a financial burden to purchase a house, repayments of the loan were expected to ease as income increased, and the property value of the house was – without question – anticipated to rise. However, the property value of privately owned houses is currently at risk, while incomes are not increasing and stability of employment remains weak.

Mass construction of housing used to be considered an engine of economic growth. In the past, there was massive demand for housing due to an expansion in population and its concentration in urban areas and an increased number of households. Urbanisation, however, peaked in the late 1970s and housing demand began to shrink. It has been estimated that Japan's population will start to decrease after reaching its peak in 2006. The rate at which households increase will continue to decline every year henceforth. Therefore, there is no doubt that maintaining past levels of mass housing construction will be difficult.

The filtering system in housing policy has assumed a life-course of a stereotypical household within the social mainstream. Life-courses, however, have become diversified due to the postponement of marriage and a rise in the number of people who choose not to marry and people who do not have children even if they do get married. The central target of housing policy was the family household, which was expected to form the mainstream. However, the proportion of nuclear-family households, made up of parents and their children, is dropping and the number of single-person households, couple-only households, and elderly-only households is rising. According to the Housing and Land Survey in 1998, the percentage of nuclear-family households was 33% nationally and 29% in Tokyo, while those of single households were 24% and 37%, respectively. The number of single-person households has already exceeded that of nuclear-family households in Tokyo. The filtering system is proving dysfunctional where social structure is becoming more fragmented.

An increase of 'parasite singles' is one factor in the decline in housing demand and in the weakening of the filtering system (Yamada, 1999, 2001). 'Parasite singles' are persons aged 29-34 and living with their parents, and they accounted for ten million of the population in 1995. Two fifths of men and one third of women aged 25-29, and one fifth of men and one eighth of women aged 30-34 were 'parasite singles' in 1995. They enjoy many advantages, such as not having to pay housing costs or food expenses and their housework is done for them, often by their mothers. Fearing a decline in their quality of life should they become independent or get married, 'parasite singles' prefer to live for long periods in their parents' house.

The expansion of owner-occupied housing has been stretched to its limit. Since urbanisation rates peaked in the late 1970s and the policy which encouraged homeownership continued, the rate of owner-occupied housing was anticipated to rise. In reality, however, the homeownership rate has hardly changed, shifting from 61.1% in 1988 to 59.6% in 1993, and to 60% in 1998. Looking at owner-occupied housing in terms of the age of the main income earner of the household, the drop in the homeownership rate among young households is noticeable (Table 8.5). Increases in the number of single households and 'parasite singles', and the postponement of marriage have helped to reduce the rate. The number of people who can inherit their parents' houses has increased, which may have caused a fall in the rate. It is becoming economically easier to purchase a house as housing prices fall. However, people are increasingly wary of purchasing houses as income and employment have been less stable and so is the property's future value.

Table 8.5: Home ownership rate (in Japan) by main earner's age

Age	1983	1988	1993	1998
Total	62.0	61.1	59.6	60.0
up to 24	7.6	4.5	3.1	3.3
25-29	24.8	17.8	13.0	12.7
30-34	45.5	38.3	31.6	29.0
35-39	59.8	56.6	51.9	48.6
40-44	68.2	66.0	64.2	62.4
45-49	73.1	71.7	70.1	69.7
50-54	77.0	75.1	73.8	73.2
55-59	80.1	79.3	77.1	76.7
60-64	78.3	80.3	79.9	79.1
65+	76.1	76.8	79.1	80.6

Source: Statistics Bureau; 1983 Housing Survey of Japan; 1993 Housing Survey of Japan; 1998 Housing and Land Survey of Japan

The emerging new structure of social inequalities

The definition of Japan's social mainstream has become increasingly vague. This does not mean, however, the mitigation of social inequalities concerned with housing; rather, it means the restructuring of them. New boundaries have been drawn on top of the traditional ones, which makes the structure of social inequalities even more complex. Given that the previous boundaries simply divided the social mainstream into 'inside' and 'outside', newly drawn ones are more complex and continuously shifting.

The circumstances of homeowners are no longer equal. Property values differ greatly according to when their house was purchased. The market price of housing sold in the 'bubble economy' period is dropping sharply – the price of a condominium is declining more than that of a single-family home. Households who bought a condominium in the 'bubble economy' period are suffering from capital loss and negative equity (Hirayama, 2001). Those who want to obtain their own house usually purchase a single-family home in the suburbs. Throughout the 'bubble economy' period, however, as housing prices jumped to unprecedented levels, condominiums were constructed even in the suburbs. The market value of such 'suburban bubble condominiums' has now dropped significantly. In the current prolonged recession, more and more households are becoming unable to repay their housing loan. For example, the number of HLC loans unable to be repaid rose from 4,820 in 1990 to 17,958 in 2001. People pursued homeownership in the past to be free from various anxieties but many now realised housing itself may be a cause for unease.

According to the data concerned with housing using loans by the HLC, the market value of condominiums constructed in the bubble period has been reduced by half. The average price of a newly built condominium was ¥50.9 million (£254,500) in Tokyo in 1991, which dropped to ¥24.4 million (£122,000) in 1999, and the capital loss calculated as a disparity between the figures was as much as ¥26.5 million (£132,500) as of 1998. New condominiums in Osaka in 1992 cost ¥44.9 million (£224,500) on average and their value dropped to ¥21.1 million (£105,500) by 1999, which generated a capital loss of ¥23.8 million (£119,000) (Figure 8.1).

The Nippon Credit Bank Research Institute estimated the negative equity of condominiums in the Tokyo metropolitan area (NCB, 1999). In 1990, the average price of a new condominium was ¥60.7 million (£303,500) and the average loan of households who purchased one was ¥42.5 million (£212,500). Its value decreased to ¥25.6 million (£128,000) and the outstanding balance in 1997 was ¥34.6 million (£173,000). The outstanding balance exceeded the commodity value and the negative equity, and the disparity between these was as much as ¥12 million (£60,000). In all metropolitan areas, the number of households who acquired a newly built condominium between 1988 and 1994 was about 280,000. The negative equity generated was ¥1.4 trillion (seven billion pounds) in total and the capital loss created was ¥6.6 trillion (£33 billion) in total.

Figure 8.1: Capital loss in condominiums in Tokyo and Osaka

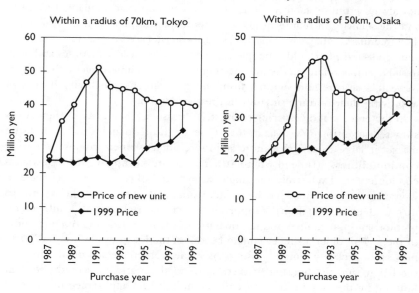

Source: Housing Loan Corporation

The construction, real estate and housing industries have been putting pressure on the government to bring about changes in housing policy, emphasising the necessity of leaving housing to market forces in an extension of the neoliberalism ideology. The HC was reorganised into the Housing and Urban Development Corporation in 1981 and again into the Urban Development Corporation in 1999. This was because private developers and the housing industry strongly criticised the HC's housing supply, since they believed it was taking business from them. The new Urban Development Corporation had to dramatically reduce the number of housing schemes. In addition, the Renters and Leaseholders Act was amended in 2000. Tenants were previously allowed to live in their rental accommodation indefinitely, and landlords could not easily evict their tenants. As a result of the amendment, however, it has become possible for landlords to rent the house only for a limited period. The private sector had been criticising the protection of tenants since it prevented redevelopment and housing investment due to the difficulty of implementing rent increases or eviction of long-time tenants (Morimoto, 1998).

A free market, according to neoliberalist theory, promotes rational housing provision (Iwata and Hatta, 1997). The direction toward centralisation of housing provision under the market principle, however, generates a paradox that can lead to the dualisation of 'inside' (where the market works) and 'outside' (which the market excludes). Inside, the deregulated market is a situation that does not always promise stability. Today, homeownership is accompanied by risks, and the security of tenure in privately rented accommodation is weakening. The free market draws boundaries by various criteria – such as income, credit and age – and places older people as well as those on low incomes and with unstable employment on the outside. Those, whose ability to access the market is weak, lose care and support from the government and their chances of improving their housing situation is greatly reduced.

In the process of diversifying social structure, social inequality by gender has attracted attention (Yazawa, 1996). One of the tendencies in the housing market in large cities is that more and more single women are now acquiring condominiums. (Indeed, there is a real estate company that constructs condominiums exclusively for single women in Tokyo.) The percentage of women in employment has been increasing, and some may choose not to marry. Despite the Equal Opportunity Act, the stability of employment, promotion opportunities and remuneration of women still do not equal those of men. The older a single woman becomes, the less possible it is for her to move into privately rented housing. As single women are at a disadvantage in the labour and the housing markets, some of them attempt to stabilise their housing by the acquisition of a condominium. The appearance of the new condominium market reflects this gender inequity.

Large cities attract foreign residents, both long-term/permanent residents and newcomers who have flown in from overseas, accelerating the fragmentation of the social structure. Among them, a great diversity in terms of nationality, occupation, legal status, ethnicity and the duration of their stay in Japan can be observed. For example, the US elite work in global enterprise offices in the metropolitan centre; Filipino women work in entertainment districts; illegal labourers are exploited on construction sites and in factories; and Chinese students may work part-time in restaurants. With the exception of South American-Japanese, the government has not accepted unskilled labourers from overseas. However, it is currently considering offering permits since it anticipates that, due to the future decrease in the working population and an increase in those with higher education, there will be a shortage of unskilled labourers. Unskilled labourers from overseas will further fragment the social structure in large cities.

There is a great disparity in the housing situation of such foreign residents according to their ability to access the market, their ethnic community and the resources of their workplace. For example, elite workers live in luxury high-rise apartments while *mokuchin* are occupied by low-income workers, and illegal workers are packed into cramped quarters. Districts are easily recognisable where newcomers are highly concentrated. A pattern of low-rent housing and work opportunities attracts migrant workers, and the formation of ethnic communities also draws more migrant workers.

At the very bottom of society in large cities, the number of homeless people has been increasing since the late 1990s (Iwata, 2000; see also Chapter Ten of this volume). Research conducted by local governments indicated that 5,800 people were homeless in Tokyo in 1999, and a further 8,660 in Osaka in 1998. A complex combination of unemployment, debt, bankruptcy, illness and breakdown of relationships caused by social and economic changes are explanations offered for the phenomenon. Although *yoseba* districts have been providing single manual labourers with jobs and a basis for living, its traditional function is weakening due to the fact that labourers are ageing and the availability of day labour is decreasing. Labourers with weakened physical strength find it much harder to find a day job. The homeless population includes many former *yoseba* workers.

In Shinjuku, Tokyo, there is a number of high-rise office buildings, and homeless people live in the parks between them. In Osaka Castle Park, 500 homeless families built a 'tent city' next to a large business park. Today's social inequalities are symbolised by such a juxtaposed landscape where business spaces for the global economy and spaces for homeless people are located next to each other with a clear boundary between.

Conclusions

Housing policy in postwar Japan has pursued the formation of a social mainstream. The core of society was defined and symbolised by the unification of modern housing and the modern family, the creation of assets by homeownership and people's diligent attitude to climb up the housing ladder. A society, which emphasises a specific direction, however, strongly suppresses people outside its boundary. Housing policy has generated social inequalities by concentrating resources on specific groups and excluding others.

Social and economic changes in recent years have blurred the definition of the social mainstream, which has become increasingly vague. The framework of housing policy has started to fragment, the sanctity of homeownership as an asset has been eroded, and one's life-course can no longer follow predetermined paths since the pathways themselves have become less clear. Public policy to establish a social mainstream has lost ground. Nobody today believes in the myth that Japan is a homogeneous society – that is, most of the people living in Japan are Japanese, belong to the middle-class, and share the same cultural values.

Social inequality in housing, then, cannot be mitigated but should be restructured to cater for a more representative population structure. Multiple boundaries are constructed by the continually shifting combination of many variables such as stability in employment and income, the time of housing acquisition, the balance of asset and debt, gender, ethnicity and so on. We are witnessing the appearance of a fragmented, destabilised and risk-filled society. New boundaries are complex and constantly shifting, and not only exclude those on the 'outside' but also fail to guarantee the stability of those once 'inside'. As the market is deregulated further, the safety net continues to collapse.

Under such new conditions, reorganisation of social inequalities will be repeated leading to an even more complicated situation.

References

Hasegawa, T. (2001) 'Bubble keizai no hassei to hokai, tochi hudosan shijo no kozo tenkan' ['The rise and collapse of the bubble economy and the restructuring of the urban land market'], in S. Harada (ed) *Nihon no toshi huo* [*Japanese urban laws*], vol II, Tokyo: Tokyo University Press, pp 61-77.

Hayakawa, K. and Hirayama, Y. (1991) 'The impact of the *Minkatsu* policy on Japanese housing and land use', *Society and Space, Environment and Planning D*, vol 9, no 2, pp 151-64.

Hayakawa, K. and Ohmoto, K. (1985) 'Toshi jutaku mondai shi gaisetsu' ['The history of the urban housing question'], in Tokyo shisei chosa kai [The Tokyo Institute for Municipal Research] (ed) *Toshi mondai no kiseki to tenbo* [*Urban questions: history and perspectives*], Tokyo: Gyosei, pp 233-76.

Hirayama, Y. (1990) 'Public housing segregation in Japan', Paper prepared for Housing Research Conference 12, Research Committee on Housing and Built Environment, International Sociological Association, Paris, 3-6 July.

Hirayama, Y. (2001) 'Housing in an unstable world: the case of Japan', Paper prepared for International Conference 'Managing housing and social change', Hong Kong, 16-18 April.

Hirayama, Y. and Hayakawa, K. (1995) 'Homeownership and family wealth in Japan', in R. Forrest and A. Murie (eds) *Housing and family wealth: Comparative international perspectives*, London: Routledge, pp 215-30.

Izu, H. (1999) 'Chiiki kozo no henka to jutaku shijo' ['Changes in regional structure and the housing market'], in H. Izu (ed) *Henbo suru jutaku shijo to jutaku seisaku* [*Transformation of the housing market and housing policy*], Tokyo: Toyo Keizai Shinpo Sha, pp 3-54.

Iwata, K. and Hatta, T. (1997) *Jutaku no keizaigaku* [*Housing economics*], Tokyo: Nihon Keizai Shinbun Sha.

Iwata, M. (2000) *Homeless, gendai shakai, fukushi kokka* [*Homeless people, modern society and the welfare state*], Tokyo: Akashi Shoten.

Morimoto, N. (1998) *Chintai jutaku seisaku to shakuchi shakuya hou* [*Rental housing policy and renters law*], Tokyo: Domesu Shuppan.

NCB Research Institute (1999) *News release*, Tokyo: NCB Research Institute, vol 14 September.

Ohmoto, K. (1996) 'Kyoju seisaku no gendai shi' ['Modern history of housing policy'], in K. Ohmoto and M. Kaino (eds) *Gendai kyoju: rekishi to shiso* [*Housing policy: history and ideology*], Tokyo: Tokyo University Press, pp 89-120.

Sumita, S. (2000) 'Jutaku seisaku: mass-housing kara multi-housing e' ['Housing policy: from mass housing to multi-housing'], *Kenchiku Zasshi* [*Journal of Architecture*], vol 115, no 1462, pp 30-33.

Van Vliet, W. and Hirayama, Y. (1994) 'Housing conditions and affordability in Japan', *Housing Studies*, vol 9, no 3, pp 351-67.

Yamada, M. (1999) *Parasite single no jidai* [*The time of parasite singles*], Tokyo: Chikuma Shobo.

Yamada, M. (2001) *Kazoku toiu risk* [*Risk family*], Tokyo: Kesio Shobo.

Yamada, R. (2001) 'Toshi tochi mondai no keizai kozo' ['Economic structure of urban land questions'] in S. Harada (ed) *Nihon no toshi hou* [*Japanese urban laws*], vol I, Tokyo: Tokyo University Press, pp 181-206.

Yazawa, S. (1996) 'Gender to toshi kyoju' ['Gender and urban housing'], in K. Kishimoto and A. Suzuki (eds) *Gendai kyoju: Kazoku to jukyo* [*Housing policy: family and housing*], Tokyo: Tokyo University Press, pp 83-107.

NINE

The production of homelessness in Britain: policies and processes

Patricia Kennett

Introduction

Homelessness represents one of the most acute forms – if not *the* most acute form – of social and housing exclusion in Europe today. In both a national and European context, there has been increasing recognition that a growing number of people are finding themselves in an increasingly hostile environment, particularly in relation to work, welfare and housing.

This chapter begins by addressing some of the debates surrounding definitions of homelessness. While the chapter is not intended to be a comprehensive review of the literature nor to expand debates, it does intend to emphasise the importance of this issue. It has particular implications for quantification and analysis of the causes of homelessness, as well as the solutions and provision considered necessary to tackle the problem.

Drawing on government statistics and recent research from the homelessness charity Shelter, the chapter looks at some of the pathways into and causes of homelessness. It concludes by focusing the discussion of homelessness within the context of broader structural factors: for example, changes in the economy, the labour market and a reorientation of the welfare state, which has given way to an increasingly polarised society in which poverty, unemployment and homelessness appear to have become accepted 'facts of life', reflecting a 'new common sense' in social policy.

Defining and enumerating homelessness

There is no universally accepted definition of homelessness. What constitutes homelessness and how many people are homeless is a debate which has been running for decades (see Bramley, 1988; Burrows et al, 1997; Jacobs et al, 1999). The term itself is fundamentally unstable:

> [A]ll statistical measures are socially negotiated, but in the case of homelessness
> – along with other key political issues like crime and unemployment – the

fragility of official definitions and measures is particularly stark. Societies with different socio-political traditions are likely to come to very different understandings of the term. (Marsh and Kennett, 1999, p 3)

However, Britain is unusual in having a statutory definition of homelessness. The operational definition applied by the government and local authorities in dealing with homelessness derives from the 1977 Housing (Homeless Persons) Act, incorporated into the 1986 Housing Act in England and Wales and 1987 in Scotland. The Act represented a fundamental shift in policy and practice away from the 1948 National Assistance Act which, according to Greve, had "inherited and perpetuated much of the philosophy of some of the practices of the hated Poor Law" (1997, p 1). The new legislation acknowledged homelessness as a housing – rather than a welfare – problem and gave housing departments responsibility for rehousing those considered to have met the statutory criteria.

However, the statutory definition is relatively narrow, and while it defines a concept of homelessness, it then delimits it to exclude certain categories. The Housing (Homeless Persons) Act imposes a duty on local authorities to secure accommodation for persons who are assessed as actually or imminently homeless, who are not *intentionally* homeless, who are in *priority need* and who have a local connection. Those in 'priority need' are: families with dependent children; pregnant women; people who are vulnerable because of old age and disability; young people at risk; victims of domestic violence; people made homeless by emergency (such as a fire); and, more recently, those leaving care. The following section of this chapter draws on government statistics for those categorised as statutorily homeless. The circumstances and characteristics of those homeless people not included in government statistics are then considered, drawing on the findings of a recent Shelter report.

Over the last 20 years, statutory homelessness reached its peak in 1992 when 179,410 households were accepted as homeless (in other words, they met the government's criteria for homelessness). As Figure 9.1 shows, the numbers proceeded to fall until 1997, but then began to increase thereafter. In 1999, the number of local authority homeless acceptances was approximately 134,000 households[1]. Furthermore, there is significant evidence to suggest that homelessness is highly significant for ethnic minority groups (Harrison, 1999). In 1998, 59% of households accepted by local authorities in inner London belonged to ethnic minorities.

The official definition then consists of those households, most often families with children, who have been accepted as homeless by a local authority. Approximately 70% of acceptances of those in priority need are households with dependent children or with a pregnant member. The most common immediate causes are illustrated in Figure 9.2. A consistent cause of homelessness has been that parents, relatives or friends have no longer been willing or able to provide accommodation. While remaining the major reason precipitating homelessness since the mid-1990s, other factors, such as breakdown of a

Figure 9.1: Local authority homeless acceptances in Great Britain (1980-99) (in thousands)

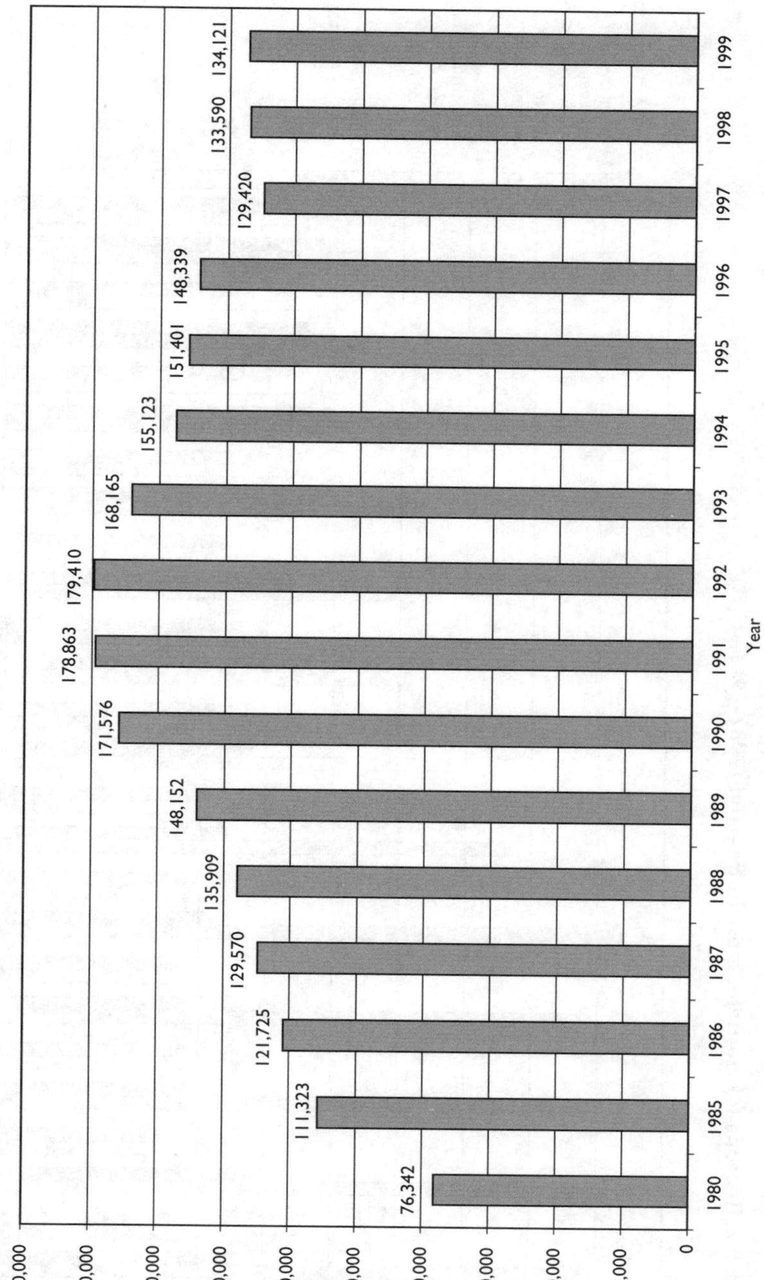

Source: Wilcox (2001)

Figure 9.2: Reasons for homelessness in England (1987-99) (%)

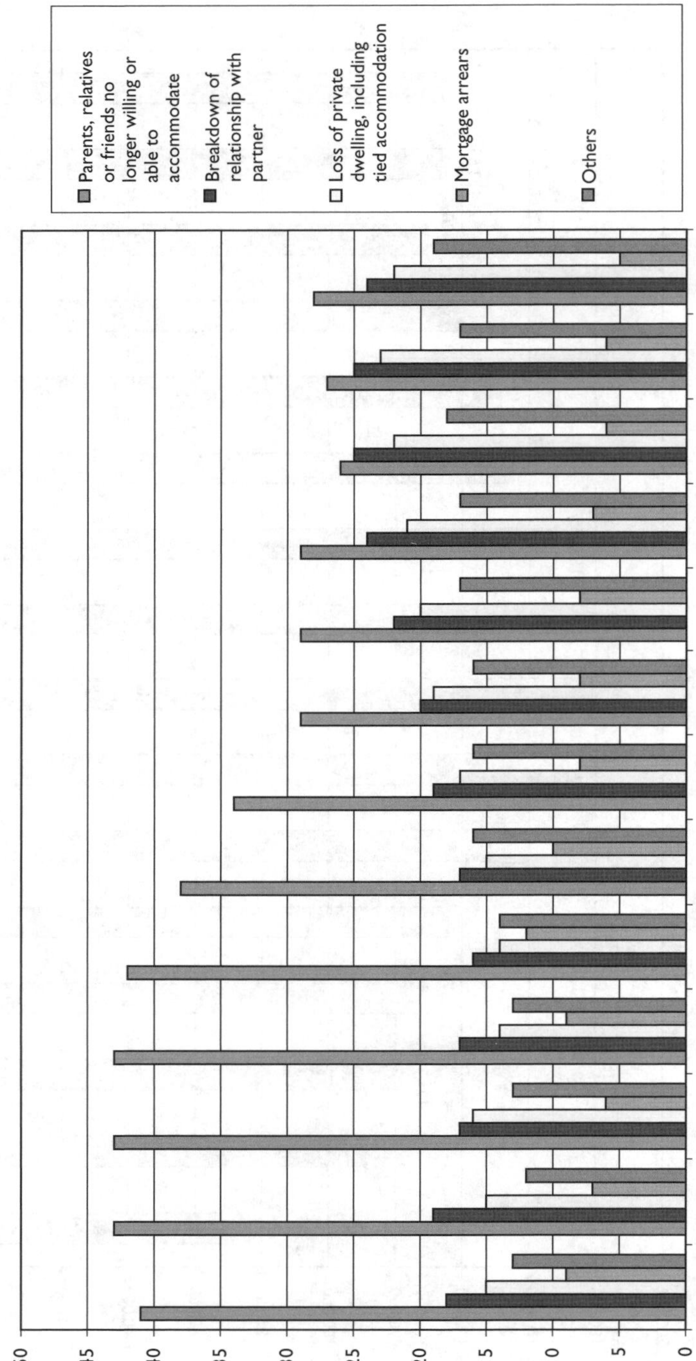
Parents, relatives or friends no longer willing or able to accommodate
Breakdown of relationship with partner
Loss of private dwelling, including tied accommodation
Mortgage arrears
Others
%
0
5
10
15
20
25
30
35
40
45
50
1987
1988
1989
1990
1991
1992
1993
1994
1995
1996
1997
1998
1999
Year

Source: Wilcox (2001)

relationship with partner and loss of private dwelling, have become almost as influential in affecting an individuals' or households' ability to maintain a home. The numbers experiencing homelessness due to mortgage arrears peaked in 1991. This coincided with a period of economic instability, recession and high interest rates in England, a situation that has been in reverse since the late 1990s. The numbers of statutory homeless people citing mortgage arrears as the immediate cause of their homelessness has reduced significantly since the early 1990s. However, in 2000 there were 22,610 repossessions, while 91,630 households were three to six months in arrears, 45,680 households were six to 12 months in arrears, and 18,830 households were 12 months or more in arrears (Wilcox, 2001).

While these figures provide a useful snapshot of the immediate causes of statutory homelessness, it could also be argued that in many ways the data simply represent administrative categories. Rather than revealing the complex processes that have precipitated these events, they often disguise them. For most people events such as losing a job, increased debt, or the breakdown of a relationship, will not result in such extreme consequences as homelessness. However, in the risk society of contemporary capitalism (Giddens, 1991; Beck, 1992; Culpitt, 1999), it is increasingly the case that for those with limited personal and financial resources and little by way of social networks or social capital on which to draw, the descent down the 'spiral of precariousness' (Paugam, 1995; Forrest, 1999) is given added momentum. Official figures do not reveal the complexity and diversity of these processes and individual pathways into homelessness.

It is also the case that there is considerable local discretion in the way the legislation is interpreted. Indeed, as Marsh and Kennett point out:

> [B]eyond a core of households whose circumstances would mean that they would be treated as homeless by the vast majority of local administrations, there is a range of households whose status as officially 'homeless' depends entirely upon which locality they find themselves in. Whether a household is considered by a local authority to be statutorily homeless and eligible for assistance is likely to depend on a number of contingent factors such as the political complexion of an authority or the demand for social housing locally. (Marsh and Kennett, 1999, p 3)

A negative effect of the legislation is that people who are assessed not to be in the priority need category generally do not get material help in finding accommodation. This mostly affects single homeless people and couples without dependent children. The total numbers falling into these categories are substantial. Shelter, for example, estimates that there are some 41,000 people who are living in hostels and squats who are not included in the official figures (Shelter, 2000). Homeless legislation clearly treats single-person homeless households with less priority than homeless households with children. To some extent, this reflects trends in most other areas of welfare legislation, which underpins the centrality and the primacy of the nuclear family within British society. Single-person households and households without children, although they account for a relatively large section of society, disappear when juxtaposed to the ideological acceptance of the family as the norm. When they do re-emerge, the tone is often one of individual blame and deviancy on behalf of the homeless person as demonstrated in more recent government policies directed at 'rough sleepers'.

It is generally single households and households without children, therefore, that make up the vast majority of those considered to be the *non-statutory* homeless. And it is from among this group that the majority of those sleeping on the street or in hostels are to be found. A recent study by Shelter sheds some light on the circumstances of 1,535 homeless people that used Crisis WinterWatch facilities between December 2000 and March 2001 (Shelter, 2001)[2]. Of the 1,535 people that stayed with the project, 1,285 were men and 232 were women. The vast majority (87.8%) described themselves as White British, and were aged between 25 and 34 (Table 9.1).

A great deal of research has highlighted that the health profile of homeless people is extremely poor, particularly in relation to substance misuse, mental health problems, sexual health problems and infectious diseases (Pleace and Quilgares, 1996; Power et al, 1999). These problems are particularly apparent among those who have spent some time sleeping on the streets:

> The effects of living on the street or in unfit accommodation impact on a
> person's health at the most basic levels .... The reasons for a higher incidence
> of these problems are very much connected to homeless people's physical,
> psychological and social situations. (Power et al, 1999, pp 7-8).

Table 9.2 indicates that the vast majority of respondents (94.2%) that stayed in the WinterWatch project had some form of 'problem'. The Shelter Report (2001) points out that many of the respondents had multiple needs and therefore

Table 9.1: Age range of those staying in WinterWatch projects

Age	Number	%
Under 18	13	0.8
18-24	330	21.5
25-34	534	34.8
35-44	344	22.4
45-59	259	16.9
60-69	27	1.8
70+	4	0.3
Not known	24	1.6
Total	1,535	100

Source: Shelter (2001, p 22)

Table 9.2: Problems experienced by those staying in the WinterWatch projects

Problem	Number	% of total
Alcohol	537	35.0
Drugs	537	35.0
Mental health	414	27.0
Issues with self-harm	121	7.9
Physical health	261	17.0
Physical disability	52	3.4
Benefits	306	19.9
Life skills	170	11.1
Involvement with the criminal justice system	444	28.9

Source: Shelter (2001, p 25)

cited more than one problem (therefore, the percentage tallies of Table 9.2 do not add up to 100). It is difficult to disentangle the relationship between the causes and effects of homelessness and health status. However, there can be little doubt that the isolation, stigma and hardships of life on the street have an extremely negative effect on social and physical wellbeing, resulting in more entrenched alienation and compounding the multiple aspects of social exclusion experienced by homeless people.

Table 9.3 indicates the types of accommodation used by the respondents who chose to answer the question in the month prior to coming into the WinterWatch project. It shows that a total of 14.6% of respondents had held some form of tenancy in the private rented sector (8.2%) or with the local authority (6.4%). Table 9.4 shows that 4.6% cited eviction from the public sector as the reason for their homelessness, and 7.9% the loss of their private rented sector tenancies. Table 9.3 shows that the two most likely forms of previous accommodation were sleeping on the streets (30.1%) or staying with

Table 9.3: Types of accommodation experienced during the previous month by those staying in WinterWatch projects

Type of accommodation	Number	%
Sleeping on the streets	462	30.1
Friends or family	361	23.5
Private rented sector	126	8.2
Hostel (rent charged)	122	7.9
Council flat	99	6.4
Prison/remand	99	6.4
Nightshelter	96	6.3

Source: Shelter (2001, p 23)

Table 9.4: Reasons for homelessness

Reason for homelessness	Number	%
Relationship breakdown	418	27.2
Released from prison	168	10.9
Eviction from the private rented sector	122	7.9
Tenancy breakdown	114	7.4
Financial circumstances	77	5.0
Eviction from public sector	71	4.6
Escaping violence/harassment	67	4.4

Source: Shelter (2001, p 23)

friends or family (23.5%). However, looking back over the last year it was reported that 1,172 respondents (76.4%) had spent some time sleeping on the street during that time. Relationship breakdown was cited as the major reason for becoming homeless (27.2%). However, leaving institutions such as prison, care, the armed forces or psychiatric hospitals were the reasons that precipitated the homelessness of 212 respondents (Table 9.4).

Homelessness in Britain concerns poverty and insecurity which, in turn, meshes with individual characteristics, resources, and social capital. Fundamentally, however, it is also about structural factors involving the housing market, employment opportunities, wage levels, demographic change, and policies relating to social security and housing benefit which shape the context within which homelessness emerges. This chapter now explores some of the policies and processes which contribute to the production of homelessness.

Understanding homelessness in Britain

Homelessness is not a new or transient phenomenon in Britain. The vagrants, indigents and 'wards of the community' of the 19th century, the transient workers and mobile poor of the early 20th century, and the 'victims' of the depression during the 1930s are all indications of the various ways in which the phenomenon has been constructed at different times. Following the Second World War, poverty and homelessness were seen as a thing of the past, and the prevailing ideology was that income and housing needs had been met. In 1960, only a few thousand households were accepted by local authorities as homeless, the great majority in London. The situation has been transformed since then and homelessness has emerged as a problem affecting different kinds of areas, from the inner city to rural villages, and has involved a widening spectrum of the population. The extent of homelessness, according to Marcuse (1993), can no longer be linked to changes in economic conditions, especially in the US. For Marcuse, homelessness today is:

large scale, permanent and independent of the short-term business cycle, a combination never before existing in an advanced industrial society. It represents the inability of the state to care for the most basic needs of significant segments of the population ... and their subsequent complete exclusion from or suppression in the spatial fabric of a technologically and economically advanced city. It may fairly be called 'advanced homelessness'. (Marcuse, 1993, p 353)

The end of full employment, the erosion of the welfare safety net, and the marketisation and residualisation of the welfare state, have all contributed to an environment in which a growing section of the population are finding it difficult to access and maintain adequate, secure, affordable accommodation.

The discourse of the postwar era was that the state would ensure that all citizens enjoyed a minimum standard of living, economic welfare and security as a matter of right. The welfare consensus emphasised an explicit commitment to state intervention through universal access to direct public provision. A Keynesian-led economy, with a commitment to full employment, an extensive role for the welfare state, and housing – although never fully socialised compared to other areas of welfare – as a social right through direct state provision, was characteristic of the postwar era. The trends were towards decreasing social inequality and the gradual inclusion of previously excluded or marginal populations. Personal disposable incomes rose, the rate of inflation was modest, the scale of unemployment was low, and the majority of the population was well housed. On the new housing estates, the move was towards a more fragmented, home-centred culture as rising working-class living standards started to establish themselves. This was a period in which growing middle-class affluence enabled the further development of home-owning suburbia, while the 'estate' provided mass housing for the 'respectable' working class. The boundaries of social rights were, however, constructed within specific narratives which reflected the privileged status of the white male worker and the partial citizenship of women and men from ethnic minorities. For the poor to be incorporated into the home ideal, they had to meet certain criteria relating to personal decency and the acceptance of established behavioural norms. Issues relating to class, race, gender, sexuality and household type have always been major considerations in how the home has been defined and who has been able to gain access to it. Women and ethnic minorities were unlikely to have equal access to the capital through which the suburban ideal could be achieved and were likely to be denied access to local authority housing waiting lists. Poverty and homelessness did exist, but by common consent were seen to involve a few people on the margins of society. For the majority of individuals the ideological commitment to equality and welfarism was compatible with the 'lived' experience at the micro-level. As Byrne explains:

[I]n the Fordist era, good council housing was the locale ... of an employed working class and movement into it from poor council housing and out of it to the cheaper end of the owner-occupied sector was simply an incremental matter. (Byrne, 1997, p 33)

As economic conditions deteriorated during the mid-1970s, the postwar consensus began to crumble. The institutional arrangements of the postwar period, which had supported a specific mode of integration, were increasingly perceived as barriers and impediments to the deployment of new methods of production and consumption. The term 'post-Fordism' has emerged as a shorthand for a multiplicity of explanations relating to 'new times'. These 'new times' have emerged in the context of changes in the labour market and labour process, the decline in manufacturing and the rise in service employment, the globalisation of capital, culture and ideology and the reorientation of the welfare state. By the late 1970s, previously relatively full employment economies were experiencing changes in the labour structure, and with it increasing unemployment. This trend was evident in many countries of the EU, and along with it poverty and social exclusion have been re-established as a public issue as the numbers of people living in poverty and experiencing homelessness has risen. A conservative estimate of 1.8 million people were considered to be homeless in the member states of the EU, in that they had used public or voluntary services for temporary shelter or had squatted or slept rough (Avramov, 1995).

During the 1980s and 1990s, attention turned from the 'invisible' poverty of the Fordist era to the more visible 'new homelessness'. A consistent feature, however, is the relationship between poverty and homelessness. It became commonplace in most British cities to see people begging in the street or huddled in shop doorways. In London, the makeshift constructions of cardboard city grabbed newspaper headlines, and indeed, it is this most visible aspect of homelessness that has become the focus of government policy.

Policies, processes, and the restructuring of welfare

The most profound shift in the restructuring of relations between state and civil society and the establishment of new forms of intervention were most evident during the Conservative era in Britain. However, following its election in May 1997, the New Labour government has pursued similar strategies indicating, according to Marquand, that New labour "has turned its back on Keynes and Beveridge" (Marquand, 1998, also quoted in Dean, 1999, p 221). According to Dean, "new Labour has combined the economic liberalism of the Thatcher/Reagan orthodoxy, with something approaching socially conservative Christian Democracy" (1999, p 221). For Prime Minister Tony Blair, the 'third way' is "the best label for the new politics which the progressive centre-left is forging in Britain and beyond" (Blair, 1997, p 1). This new orthodoxy reflects the 'communitarian turn' (Etzioni, 1995; Driver and Martell, 1997) of the 1980s, emphasising the institutions of civil society: the family, community and the notion of active membership. It is concerned with the promotion of a just society and the values of equal worth, opportunity for all, responsibility and community. Fundamental to these goals is a re-balancing of the social contract between the state and the individual, between rights and responsibilities. For Blair:

> [T]he demand for rights from the State was separated from the duties of citizenship and the imperative for mutual responsibility on the part of individuals and institutions. Unemployment benefits were often paid without strong reciprocal obligations; children went unsupported by absent parents .... The rights we enjoy reflect the duties we owe: rights and opportunities without responsibility are engines of selfishness and greed. (Blair, 1997, p 4)

Key policies of New Labour have been welfare-to-work and the New Deal programmes, through which the government seeks:

> a change of culture among benefit claimants, employees and public servants – with rights and responsibilities on all sides .... Our comprehensive welfare-to-work programme aims to break the mould of the old passive benefit system. (Blair, 1997, p 23)

Initially introduced to overcome the problem of unemployment among young people, the scope of the New Deal has been extended to include, for example, lone parents and those over 25 years-of-age. According to King and Wickham-Jones:

> The policy recast in fundamental fashion Labour's strategy to tackle poverty: previously, Labour administrations and social democratic thinkers had placed much weight on amelioration of general destitution through State-directed public spending programmes. New Labour, by contrast, emphasised paid work, seemingly to the exclusion of other approaches. (King and Wickham-Jones, 1999, p 271)

King and Wickham-Jones go on to point out that, in contrast to the commitment to universal and unconditional social rights which was central to the Labour Party's welfare agenda between 1945 and 1992, conditionality, compulsion and coercion appear to be the hallmarks of the policies of the Blair administration. Sanctions and penalties, such as loss of benefit, will fall on those who either refuse to participate or who are unable to finish the New Deal programmes. The implications of this move towards conditional citizenship are as yet unclear. Dean argues that one outcome might be that:

> more citizens will defect from their contract with the State, in the sense that they will 'disappear' into the shadowy world of the informal economy. If welfare reform does not work with the grain of everyday survival strategies the result may be more not less social exclusion. (Dean, 1999, p 232)

Contemporary homelessness then needs to address the questions of a transformed economic and labour market structure and a reorientation within the welfare state which in turn need to be analysed in the context of affordability and availability in a changing housing market. Focusing on these interrelated processes gives some idea of the complex array of processes that have given rise to groups of people, particularly those in major urban areas, young people and ethnic minorities, who are particularly vulnerable to homelessness.

Homelessness in Britain is a manifestation of housing need in its most extreme form. The social housing sector in Britain has changed substantially over the last 20 years. Although wide variations exist across the country the increase in the numbers of statutory homeless people has coincided with a decrease in local authority housing provision and an increasing emphasis on personal subsidy in the form of Housing Benefit rather than any 'bricks and mortar' subsidy. There are currently one million *fewer* dwellings owned by local authorities and registered social landlords than in 1997, and social housing now represents 21% (compared to 31% in 1997) of all housing (DETR, 2000). The local authorities' share of new construction plummeted in the 1980s as financial constraints were imposed on council building of new houses. And following the introduction of the 'Right to buy' in 1980, some 1.3 million council tenants in England have bought their own homes.

In relation to the switch in finance away from the direct provision of housing to income transfer schemes in 1978/79, £2.3 billion (1998/99 prices) was spent on Housing Benefit. By 1998/99, this figure had increased to £11.1 billion. There has been a virtual complete reversal of the balance of subsidies. In 1979 the distribution involved 84% bricks-and-mortar subsidy and 16% personal subsidy. In 1998/99 the distribution is 27% and 73%, respectively. The delivery of housing benefits is complex and confusing: only half of all local authorities in England and Wales are considered efficient in their administering of benefits (DETR, 2000).

The complexity, inefficiency, and inadequacy of housing benefit have important implications for an individual's ability to access and maintain housing, particularly in the private rented sector. An increase in average weekly rents by nearly 85% between 1990 and 1999 (from £45 to £83), combined with the increasing emphasis on personal subsidy, ensures that for many households the role played by the benefits agency is central to maintaining a home. Along with the inefficiency in the delivery of benefits, some 90% of private tenants assessed for housing benefit reported shortfalls between the benefit entitlement and their rent level, with 70% reporting shortfalls of £10 or more per week. Recent government recommendations have suggested linking housing benefit to anti-social behaviour, standard of accommodation, and housing management in this sector (DETR, 2000, p 52). The suggestion is that benefit rules will be adapted and reduced for 'unruly tenants', while the method of direct payment could be denied for landlords who failed to do what they could to control the behaviour of their tenants. The direct payment of Housing Benefit to the landlord occurs in some 70% of cases. Denying direct payments to landlords who do not let housing of an adequate standard, who do not take their management responsibilities seriously, or who are not a member of an accreditation scheme, would only serve to exacerbate the continuing decline in the supply of private rented dwellings to claimant households, and therefore further limit their housing opportunities (Wilcox, 2000).

The developments outlined earlier in this chapter are emblematic of the restructuring of welfare through deregulation and privatisation as well as an indication of the changing nature of the 'social contract'. There has been an explicit emphasis on market-based approaches for the delivery of services, the role of local authorities has become more focused on that of enabler rather than provider, and the 'desirability' and increased role for voluntary and private agencies in social policy has been enhanced. As Dean has argued, the burden of welfare provision has:

> shifted from the state to the informal, voluntary and commercial sectors and the character of welfare transactions has become, if not literally private, more akin to contractual relations in the marketplace. (Dean, 1999, p 218).

Nowhere is this more apparent than in the competitive city where both social and urban policies interact and where the emphasis has been on reducing public services and stressing the role of agencies alternative to local government, and the need for a mix of private, not-for-profit and voluntary inputs.

As cities compete between urban regions for increasingly mobile resources – jobs and capital – the fact that as many as 2,000 people are sleeping rough in many British cities contradicts and undermines the strategies of competitiveness, partnership and cohesion currently being pursued. One major government initiative to combat homelessness has been the Rough Sleepers Initiative (RSI), first instituted in London in 1990. This was accompanied by the Department of Health's Homeless Mentally Ill Initiative (HMII). The government committed £96 million for the first phase of the RSI (1990-93) to organise direct access accommodation, advice, outreach work, and some permanent housing association letting. However, the 1995 Consultation Paper reported that:

> [P]eople continue to sleep out at several main sites, for example, the Strand and the Bullring at Waterloo. Their evident plight is distressing not only for them but also for those who live, work and visit the centre of the capital, and it is frustrating for those who seek to promote London as a world-class centre for business and tourism. (DoE, 1995, p 4)

The initiative was extended for a further period and a greater emphasis was placed on "those sleeping rough or *with a clear history of sleeping rough*" (DoE, 1995, p 7, emphasis in original). In 1996, the RSI model was extended, first to Bristol (where 84 people were identified as sleeping rough), and then to Brighton, Birmingham, Bath, Chester, Cambridge, Exeter, Leicester and Southampton.

Around £200 million was committed to the initiative between 1990 and 1996 and a further £73 million until 1999.

Local authorities have developed a strategic role to facilitate services and provision for the homeless through housing associations and non-profit organisations by distributing funds for which organisations have to compete. It could be argued that the distribution of funds has been based more on the applicants' expertise in formulating a bid rather than real need, as each local authority has been required to document and 'prove' to the satisfaction of the Department of Environment that rough sleeping was a significant problem. Service providers "are the intermediaries through which flow the resources of relief to the homeless, and the people who outline how we should respond to this social phenomena" (Robertson, 1991, p 142). However, the professional providers, in turn, and through the bureaucratic process of bidding for funds, are required to supply information that appeals to the funding source, thereby encouraging the development of specialised programmes which catalogue the homeless according to a range of circumstances or individual vulnerabilities. The 'homeless problem' therefore becomes defined not in terms of structural causes but instead focuses on the pathological and individual characteristics of the homeless and their labelling as rough sleepers. As Cloke et al argue:

> Quantifying rough sleeping as a measure of the homelessness problem helps to sustain negative images and perceptions in which homelessness is reduced to a set of key issues centred around begging, street drunkenness and other perceived 'anti-social' behaviour. With such criminalisation and distortion of homelessness, it is hardly surprising that homelessness and homeless people are discussed in pejorative terms. (Cloke et al, 2001, p 270)

This major focus of the RSI has contributed to the perception of homelessness as 'rooflessness', and funding has not been directed towards those people living in insecure and inappropriate conditions. The emphasis on 'rough sleepers' has been perpetuated by the Social Exclusion Unit (SEU), which has set itself the target of reducing rough sleepers by two thirds by 2002 (Social Exclusion Unit, 1998). However, according to the Homeless Network:

> [I]t is our contention that without either a continuing supply of new accommodation, or a significant reduction in the flow of newly homeless people into London, we are likely to see the numbers of street homeless people increase sharply over the next 18 months. (Homeless Network, 1998, quoted in Social Exclusion Unit, 1998, p 12)

The strategies of the SEU, therefore, have done little to tackle the multifarious and structural processes through which people find themselves homeless. Instead, it is those sleeping rough who have become the objects of a narrowly defined set of policy solutions aimed mainly at restoring legitimacy in the competitive city. Carlen argues that "at the end of the twentieth century in England the management of homelessness is not merely about housing scarcity but has also become a site of struggle over social change" (1996, p 10).

Agencies seeking to work with the homeless have themselves become embedded in the entrepreneurial spirit of the city. With the emphasis on 'civic boosterism' (Ruddick, 1996) and through their involvement with local growth coalitions in the spirit of public-private partnerships, service providers have become, to some extent, the intermediary in the production of a new social urban space, in that they manage the tensions between the visible impoverishment and global cities. In this context, then, it seems likely that government strategies will do little to stem the flow of homeless people onto our streets. Nor will it support and maintain those attempting to reconstruct a life off the street.

Conclusion

Homelessness represents a continuous flow of people. While an emergency injection of cash or housing will assist those who are at present homeless it will do little or nothing to prevent more people from becoming homeless in the future. Current measures have tended to focus on only one extreme and visible aspect of homelessness – rough sleeping – and have done little to address issues of income maintenance or the availability of affordable housing. The result is that people are unable to find or retain housing at rents or prices they can afford, with security of tenure and with appropriate support.

Notes

[1] This figure represents the 111,750 households accepted as homeless in England and 4,171 in Wales in 1999. The 1990 figure of 18,200 households is used for Scotland, as 1999 figures were not available.

[2] The Shelter report from which these data are drawn forms part of the evaluation of the second year activities of the Millennium Plus Initiative. The Millennium Plus Initiative was established in 1999 to run for 3 years and represents a collaboration between Crisis and Shelter (Shelter Street Solutions funded by Nescafé). Millennium Plus is primarily concerned with developing comprehensive needs assessment strategies and to facilitate the rehousing of homeless people in appropriate, long-term accommodation. The data presented here are drawn from findings gathered in year two of the project (December 2000 to March 2001) and covers 18 WinterWatch projects.

References

Avramov, D. (1995) *Homelessness in the European Union – Social and legal context of housing exclusion in the 1990s*, Brussels: FEANTSA.

Beck, U. (1992) *Risk society: Towards a new modernity*, London: Sage Publications.

Blair, A. (1997) *The third way: New politics for the new century*, London: Fabian Society.

Bramley, G. (1988) 'The definition and measurement of homelessness', in G. Bramley, K. Doogan, P. Leather, A. Murie and E. Watson (eds) *Homelessness and the London housing market*, Occasional Paper 32, Bristol: SAUS Publications, pp 24-43.

Burrows, R., Pleace, N. and Quilgars, D. (eds) (1997) *Homelessness and social policy*, London: Routledge.

Byrne, D. (1997) 'Social exclusion and capitalism', *Critical Social Policy*, vol 17, no 1, pp 17-51.

Carlen, P. (1996) *Jigsaw: A political criminology of youth homelessness*, Buckingham: Open University Press.

Cloke, P., Milbourne, P. and Widdowfield, R. (2001) 'Making the homeless count? Enumerating rough sleepers and the distortion of homelessness', *Policy and Politics*, vol 29, no 3, pp 259-79.

Culpitt, I. (1999) *Social policy and risk*, London: Sage Publications.

Dean, H. (1999) 'Citizenship', in M. Powell (ed) *New Labour, new welfare state? The 'third way' in British Social Policy*, Bristol: Policy Press, pp 213-34.

DETR (Department of the Environment, Transport and the Regions) (2000) *Quality and choice: A decent home for all. The Housing Green Paper*, DETR: HMSO.

DoE (Department of the Environment) (1995) *Rough Sleepers Initiative: Future plans*, Consultation Paper linked to the Housing White Paper *Our future homes*, London: DoE.

DoE (1996) *Rough Sleepers Initiative: The next challenge*, Strategy Paper linked to the Consultation Paper *Rough Sleepers Initiative: Future plans*, London: DoE.

Driver, A. and Martell, L. (1997) 'New Labour's communitarianisms', *Critical Social Policy*, vol 17, no 3, pp 27-44.

Etzioni, A. (1995) *The spirit of community*, London: Fontana.

Forrest, R. (1999) 'The new landscape of precariousness', in P. Kennett and A. Marsh (eds) *Homelessness: Exploring the new terrain*, Bristol: The Policy Press, pp 17-36.

Giddens, A. (1991) *Modernity and self-identity: Self and society in the late modern age*, Cambridge: Polity Press.

Greve, J. (1997) 'Preface. Homelessness then and now', in R. Burrows, N. Pleace and D. Quilgars (eds) *Homelessness and social policy*, London: Routledge.

Harrison, M. (1999) 'Theorising homelessness and "race"', in P. Kennett and A. Marsh (eds) *Homelessness: Exploring the new terrain*, Bristol: The Policy Press, pp 101-121.

Jacobs, K., Kemeny, J. and Manzi, T. (1999) 'The struggle to define homelessness: a constructivist approach', in S. Hutson and D. Clapham (eds) *Homelessness: Public policies and private troubles*, London: Cassell, pp 11-28.

King, D. and Wickham-Jones, M. (1999) 'Bridging the Atlantic: the Democratic (Party) origins of 'Welfare to Work'', in M. Powell (ed) *New Labour, new welfare state? The 'third way' in British social policy*, Bristol: The Policy Press, pp 257-80.

Marcuse, P. (1993) 'What's so new about divided cities?', *International Journal of Urban and Regional Studies*, vol 17, no 3, pp 355-65.

Marquand, D. (1998) 'What lies at the heart of the people's project?' *The Guardian*, 20 May.

Marsh, A. and Kennett, P. (1999) 'Exploring the new terrain', in P. Kennett and A. Marsh (eds) *Homelessness: Exploring the new terrain*, Bristol: The Policy Press, pp 1-16.

Paugam, S. (1995) 'The spiral of precariousness: a multidimensional approach to the process of social disqualification in France', in G. Room (ed) *Beyond the threshold: The measurement and analysis of social exclusion*, Bristol: The Policy Press, pp 49-79.

Pleace, N. (1998) 'Single homelessness as social exclusion: the unique and the extreme', *Social Policy and Administration*, vol 32, no 1, pp 46-59.

Pleace, N. and Quilgares, D. (1996) *Health and homelessness in London*, London: King's Fund.

Power, R., French, R., Connelly, J., George, S., Hawes, D., Hinton, T., Klee, H., Robinson, D., Senior, J., Timms, P. and Warner, D. (1999) *Promoting the health of homeless people. Setting a research agenda*, London: Health Education Authority.

Robertson, M.O. (1991) 'Interpreting homelessness: the influence of professional and non-professional service providers', *Urban Anthropology*, vol 20, no 2, pp 141-53.

Ruddick, S. (1996) *Young and homeless in Hollywood: Mapping social identities*, New York: Routledge.

Shelter (2000) *Housing and homelessness in England: The facts* (www.shelter.org.uk).

Shelter (2001) *Millennium Plus year 2*, London: Shelter.

Social Exclusion Unit (1998) *Rough sleeping*, London: SEU.

Wilcox, S. (2001) *Housing finance review 2000/2001*, CIH/CML/JRF, Coventry, London.

TEN

Homelessness in contemporary Japan

Masami Iwata

Introduction

Rough sleepers first began to appear on the streets of Japan's major cities towards the end of 1992. Since then, the term 'homelessness' has been widely used to describe sleeping rough. To begin, this chapter explores the characteristics and production processes of homelessness found in the Tokyo Survey of March 2000 (Iwata, 2000b). It then discusses the meaning of this 'new homelessness' and the response of social policies in the context of recent changes in the socioeconomic structure of Japan.

Although no exact number has been put forward of people who sleep out on the streets and public spaces, the official figure of 20,451 was announced as an estimated number at the end of October 1999 (Ministry of Health and Welfare, 2000). The figure was based on different counts over different periods in 132 cities, including the five major cities – Tokyo (23 wards), Osaka, Yokohama, Kawasaki, and Nagoya. Social and voluntary workers have warned that there may be, in fact, even more people sleeping rough. It is clear that families, women, and young people who have taken refuge with friends, family, or in welfare homes can not have been included in this figure. In any case, contrary to initial expectations, areas where rough sleepers are evident have increased. Nowadays, homeless people are easily found not only in the major cities but also in many other cities throughout Japan.

Until the late 1990s, rough sleepers had not been fully recognised as a significant social problem in Japanese society. They were often considered 'odd' by their visible misery on the streets, or as day labourers who have temporarily lost their jobs due to the recent economic crisis. As their number has increased, however, some cities have begun to confront the difficulties of maintaining public spaces where rough sleepers have settled, and pushed central government into tackling the problem. In 1999, the central and local governments assembled to examine the issue. The term 'homelessness' was formally used as an umbrella term, covering various categories of rough sleepers in each city in Japan.

Recent 'new homelessness' in many industrial countries has been explored in various Western studies of extreme poverty, unemployment, housing problems, sickness or other deprivations in contemporary society (Rossi, 1989; Robertson and Greenblat, 1992; Jencks, 1994). At the same time, it has been discussed that homelessness derives from many problems other than poverty and deprivation. It has been argued that the focus of homelessness has not been the distribution of resources, but rather the deep split in social–physical places between homeless people and other members of contemporary society. From this viewpoint, homelessness has been examined under the concept of citizenship and social exclusion in the post-Fordist era (Kennett, 1999). This viewpoint is also seen in the studies quoting the idea of 'social imaginary significations', through which each society creates its 'identity' and draws a distinction between who 'we' are and who 'they' are[1] (Wright, 1997; Watson, 1999).

The increase in Japanese rough sleeping since the early 1990s requires an examination using this latter approach. Rough sleepers have never been recognised as poor people in Japanese society. In this chapter, the issue is discussed in relation to Japanese society as a whole and how those affected by homelessness have been excluded from its membership. In this discussion, the term 'rough sleeping' is used to represent homelessness, since rough sleepers are the most doubtful and blameworthy of 'our' society, and every day they face the risk of eviction from wherever they live.

Homelessness in Japanese welfare history

Homelessness, in fact, is not a recent phenomenon in Japan. The dawn of modern Japan in the late 1860s was inevitably accompanied by many homeless people in large cities, who lost their bonds of feudal society (Iwata, 1995). Although the Meiji government adopted a policy to return the homeless to their original places, homeless people continued to live in the cities and soon formed large slum areas, swelled also by many poorer people from rural areas. Slum dwellers were roughly divided into three types:

1. the *fixed abode poor*: those who lived in *nagaya* (poor quality terraced houses);
2. the *quasi-fixed abode poor*: those who stayed in flophouses;
3. the *non-fixed abode poor*: those who slept in the open air or drifted around the slums (Kusama, 1978).

In any case, poor people themselves were not considered to be members of modern Japanese society. They were labelled as 'others' that belonged to 'another society' in Japan (Yokoyama, 1949; Tsuda, 1972; Nakagawa, 1985).

Although the government perceived the necessity of integrating these people into modern Japan, no effective social policy was proposed. Therefore, only very limited relief was provided to children, older people and disabled people who could not rely on – or simply did not have – their relatives.

From the 1890s to the 1920s, the Japanese economy prospered and industrial productivity expanded rapidly, including the development of large companies and heavy industry. During this period, some slum dwellers became workers in factories, shops, and other formal industries in the cities and became integrated into mainstream Japanese society as 'ordinary' members of the nation (Nakagawa, 1985). Both social policies and company welfare systems were introduced to the newly growing working class. Slums shrank, and poverty was dispersed among ordinary working families and became invisible.

The migration of impoverished tenant farmers from rural areas to large cities continued. It was uncertain whether new migrants were initially able to find both jobs and houses. If they could not, they were likely to end up sleeping on the streets. From the late 1920s to the early 1930s, the great economic recession added many labourers and farmers to the numbers of people on the street. At this point, then, rough sleeping became an issue associated with the unemployed or job seekers, rather than the slums. In order to prevent it, the public employment bureau and public hostels for job seekers expanded their operation in major cities. Yet, the efforts of these institutions were futile with the outbreak of the Second World War (Iwata, 1995).

Major Japanese cities were destroyed by bombing, and many people, including returning soldiers, faced extreme hardship. Some of them had to live in dugout shelters constructed during wartime, or in barracks built with scraps of junk. Those who could not even find such poor quality shelters slept in stations and under railroad bridges. The deflation policy of the General Headquarters of the Supreme Commander for the Allied Powers (GHQ) also prolonged their hardship until the early 1950s. Homeless people began to build shanties in riverbanks, graveyards and public parks (Iwata, 1995).

In response to homelessness in the immediate postwar period, the central government initially restricted people moving into the major cities from rural areas, but then decided to provide emergency houses. Since the government could not secure sufficient finance, only 100,000 houses were provided nationwide, although 300,000 houses were needed. Instead of a distinct housing policy, local governments provided a small number of welfare hostels to eliminate these people from public spaces (Iwata, 1995). These hostels operated mainly under the 1946 Public Assistance Act (*Seikatu-hogo hou*, revised 1950) and the 1947 Child Welfare Act (*Jido-fukushi ho*), which were introduced as part of the democratisation policy for Japan by GHQ. Although public assistance fundamentally secured a minimum standard of living in cash terms for all members of the nation, homeless people could not claim these cash benefits. They were segregated from the day-to-day administration of welfare offices (Iwata, 1995).

At first, the welfare hostels were filled with people who were homeless for a variety of reasons. However, the 'able-bodied' poor gradually became viewed with suspicion by the welfare administration. Despite the principle that public assistance should be extended to all people, welfare offices and hostels began to refuse admission to those people. Welfare departments in major cities established 'appropriate places' for those able-bodied homeless people: private hostels (flophouses) for day labourers and travelling merchants, and workers' dormitories for rubbish collectors (Iwata, 1995). Such private hostels and workers' dormitories had been problematic elements of slums in pre-war time, but now they were considered as better places for able-bodied homeless people than welfare hostels. Some cities helped to rebuild some private hostels, which were burned down during the war. These hostels absorbed many homeless people in conjunction with the public day-labour programme for unemployed people. Rubbish dealers were also permitted to operate their informal businesses in exchange for taking such people into their dormitories. Homeless women were accommodated in dormitories catering predominantly for prostitutes.

Consequently, rough sleepers were located within the 'segregated places': public welfare hostels, private cheap hostels, and dormitories for workers with informal occupations (Iwata, 1995; Shimodaira, 1998). In this way, these typically run-down and segregated districts became centres for social problems in the 1960s: the *yoseba* districts were generally characterised by mass flophouses and by an open-air labour market mainly for the construction and transportation industries. The origin of the word *yoseba* lies in the name given to the special places in which ex-offenders were gathered together to do manual labour during the Tokugawa (Edo) period (1603-1867)[2]. The *bataya* districts consisted of rubbish collector's shabby dormitories and of workplaces to sort and sell the rubbish that they collected. *Bataya* is an old name for rubbish collectors. Those rubbish collectors were subordinated to rubbish dealers who rented the carts for collecting rubbish and provided shabby dormitories in advance.

During the period from the 1960s to the early 1970s, the Japanese economy maintained a high growth rate, and it brought about wide-scale socioeconomic changes of modernisation, urbanisation, and the transition to an affluent society. In particular, the lives of workers became more affluent and stable. Leading industries absorbed young people straight from schools into long-term employment. People also found many employment opportunities in expanding large cities. The number of people in *bataya* or in welfare hostels declined rapidly during this period (Iwata, 1995; Shimodaira, 1998).

In this context, only *yoseba* districts retained their informality. Since many unskilled workers were rapidly needed in construction and transport industries in large cities, *yoseba* became the storerooms of cheap day labourers for those industries. At the same time, *yoseba* districts were also widely known as the last places for poor people or dropouts to be offered a job and accommodation at the same time. Therefore, *yoseba* continued to serve this population as segregated districts in an increasingly affluent Japan. The number of residents in Sanya, the most famous *yoseba* in Tokyo, amounted to more than 20,000 people, and Kamagasaki in Osaka had more than 30,000 at its peak.

In the 1960s, several riots led by day labourers occurred in both Sanya and Kamagasaki, and the public was forced to pay more attention to the *yoseba* districts. The local governments of both Tokyo and Osaka launched special programmes of social order. As a result, many families were accommodated in public housing, and *yoseba* became unusual districts in the sense that they were populated mostly by single male labourers (Iwata, 1995).

Rough sleeping represented day labourers' precarious everyday life in *yoseba*, even in such an affluent society. For example, one night a person could stay in a hostel due to their income from day labour, but the next day he might need to sleep in a park or riverbank near *yoseba*. In the mid–1970s, however, the average length of rough sleeping extended due to the impact of the oil crisis. In addition, there was an issue of ageing among the *yoseba* residents. In response, some cities strengthened their welfare programmes including the provision of winter shelters for rough sleepers (Iwata, 1995). Yet, this problem was concealed until the 'bubble' economy burst in the early 1990s.

The 'new homelessness' that has emerged since the 1990s has been equated with the habitual rough sleeping of *yoseba*, especially in initial discussions. Certainly, many rough sleepers are likely to come from *yoseba*. It suggests that increasing numbers of rough sleepers are a transient phenomenon of the recent economic recession. However, does the 'new homelessness' mean only an extension of the habitual rough sleeping in *yoseba* as witnessed during the oil crisis in the 1970s? Or, is it an incident of the fundamental changes in the socioeconomic structure of contemporary Japan?

Characteristics and the production process of rough sleepers in Tokyo

The data used for illustrating the characteristics and the production process of rough sleepers were collected in a survey of rough sleepers in Tokyo conducted by the Tokyo Metropolitan Government in March 2000 (Iwata, 2000b). This is one of two comprehensive surveys on rough sleeping in recent years (the other being a survey of Osaka: Study Group on Urban Environment, 2001). Face-to-face interviews were conducted with 1,028 people. A 'street survey' consisted of 710 informants who were selected from parks, riverbanks, and other streets in 23 wards of the Tokyo Metropolitan areas, as well as a 'shelter survey' with 318 respondents who were staying in a winter shelter for men run by the Tokyo ward office on any day between 3 March and 8 March 2000. In the survey, the areas were selected according to their number of rough sleepers observed by the local government of Tokyo, as well as taking into account each area's unique characteristics. Since those in the winter shelter were males only and were selected due to their vulnerability by the welfare office, this analysis will predominantly use the results from the street survey.

The sample's profiles are presented in Table 10.1. The sample was predominantly male and middle-aged. For example, 97.8% of the street sample was male, and 47.5% of the street sample and 43.7% of the shelter sample were in their 50s. Only 15% of rough sleepers in this survey were female, and those who were aged 40 years and younger accounted for 6.7% of the street sample. Educational attainment and marital status were also distinctive: over half of the sample were junior high school graduates who have never been married. Compared to the census data of Tokyo in 1995, rough sleepers were clearly concentrated in the middle-aged, low educated, and unmarried male group.

Table 10.1: Sex, age, education and marital status of rough sleepers in Tokyo (%)

	Street sample (n=710)	Shelter sample (n=318)	Census/Tokyo (1995)
Sex			
male	97.8	100.0	50.1
female	2.2		49.9
Age			*male*
15-19			7.4
20-29	0.6	0.6	23.0
30-39	6.1	3.5	16.8
40-49	19.6	19.2	17.7
50-59	47.9	43.7	15.9
60-69	22.9	28.6	11.7
70 and over	2.9	4.4	7.5
Median Age	54	55.2	36.8
Education			*male 55-59*
Less than junior high school	2.7	0.9	0.1
Junior high school	60.2	55.5	25.1
High school	28.8	33.4	47.8
More than high school	8.4	10.1	23.1
Marital status			*male 55-59*
Married	5.9	1.9	87.8
Divorced/widowed	41.2	46.6	5.9
Never been married	52.9	51.4	4.3

Source: Tokyou-to Rojoseikatusha Jittaichosa (Survey on Rough Sleeping In Tokyo, 2000)

Their characteristics mirrored the stereotype of day labourers in *yoseba*, although over 60% of the street sample did not have any experience of living in *yoseba* (Table 10.2). Since the shelter sample included the clients of the Sanya special welfare programme, the experience rate was slightly higher than the street sample. In each sample, the short–term rough sleepers (less than one year) had less experience in *yoseba* than their long-term counterparts (more than five years). This indicates a shift in the 1990s. Compared with the fact that almost

Table 10.2: Experiences in *yoseba* (%)

Duration of rough sleeping	Yes	No
Street sample (n=710)		
Total	39.7	60.3
Less than one year	29.7	70.3
One to five years	39.2	60.8
Five years and over	53.3	46.7
Shelter sample (n=318)		
Total	45.6	54.4
Less than one year	32.8	67.2
One to five years	46.4	53.6
Five years and over	66.7	33.3

Source: Tokyou-to Rojoseikatusha Jittaichosa (Survey on Rough Sleeping In Tokyo, 2000)

half of rough sleepers in the early 1990s were from *yoseba*, in the late 1990s nearly 70% were from outside of *yoseba*.

How and from where did the respondents come to be rough sleepers? To answer this question, the study examines the term 'place'. In order to live, a person generally needs some 'places' to sleep, eat and work, to purchase goods and services, to communicate and to do other physical activities. Such 'places' are socially distributed to individuals and the family according to their income, wealth, power, prestige, and other social characteristics. Society ranks these places – good or bad, stable or unstable – through a system of 'social imagery significations' that makes each society a united common world (Castoriadis, 1987; Wright, 1997). Consequently, each individual needs to integrate some 'social-physical places' into their everyday life. 'Home' is the fundamental place of such social-physical fabric. The *yoseba* district is considered as a segregated unstable place; however, day labourers have woven their everyday lives based on this unstable home place.

In this survey, information regarding migration, occupation, employment status, and housing situations was collected as a key to understanding the 'places' of rough sleepers. First of all, their 'physical places' are examined: 16.7% of the street sample was born in Tokyo, and 66.1% was born in other prefectures and came to Tokyo in their youth (before they turned 20 years-of-age). This illustrates that over 80% of the sample were long-term residents in Tokyo. Estimating from an average age, the majority moved to Tokyo during the postwar great economic growth period. The average length of residence in Tokyo was 27.3 years among the street sample. There were similar periods for all migrants who moved to Tokyo. Newcomers after the burst of the 'bubble' economy represented only 9% of the street samples. It is evident from these remarks that many rough sleepers in the 1990s had emerged from within Tokyo.

Second, 'social places' are determined by occupation, work status and housing. The information was collected from the street sample at two particular points in their life histories: firstly, when they held their main jobs; and secondly, immediately before they came onto the streets. By 'main job' is meant a job that the person held for the longest term in their earlier life. Table 10.3 indicates the type of occupation, work status and housing situations at these two points.

Following this table, at the first point, the respondents had various types of occupations: 46.6% of the street sample were skilled workers (such as craftsmen, factory, transport and construction workers); 20.3% were unskilled labourers; and 19.5% were engaged in sales or service industries (as cooks, waiters, shop clerks, newspaper agents, cleaners, security service workers and other service workers). Former managers, officials and clerical workers accounted for 10% of the sample. In terms of work status, 55.9% had regular employment, while 21.8% were day labourers.

The employment status can be divided into two categories – stable and unstable. The stable jobs include employers, managers, the self-employed, and regular employees. Indeed, these are considered to be better jobs in Japanese society. By contrast, the unstable jobs often include temporary employees and

Table 10.3: Occupations and types of employment status (%)

(street sample n=710)	Major job	Last job before coming to the street*
Type of occupation		
Managers/professional	4.1	1.9
Clerical	5.9	2.5
Agricultural	1.7	0.6
Skilled worker	46.6	28.9
Sales, service worker	19.5	13.0
Unskilled labourer	20.3	39.9
Others	0.6	0.5
No occupation	0.1	12.7
Unknown	1.1	0.0
Type of status (1)		
Employer, manager	1.7	1.1
Self-employed	5.5	3.5
Employing others	0.8	0.8
Regular employee	55.9	28.1
Temporary employee	11.8	16.2
Day labourer	21.3	44.2
Others	0.7	0.9
Unknown	2.3	5.2
Type of status (2)		
Stable	63.9	33.5
Unstable	33.1	60.4
Type of housing (1)		
Owned house	16.2	8.5
Rented house	29.3	23.4
Public rented house	2.4	1.0
Company house/workers' dormitory	42.0	37.6
Hostel (flophouse)	6.6	15.5
Inn/hotel	1.4	7.3
Others	1.8	5.7
Unknown	0.3	1.1
Type of housing (2)		
Independent house	47.9	32.9
Others	51.8	66.1

day labourers, which are considered to be among the lower ranks of 'places.' Interestingly enough, 63.9% of the street sample once had stable jobs. In other words, many rough sleepers have lived in 'stable places' for a long time, similar to 'ordinary' workers. There was further evidence to suggest the stability of their 'places': 48.9% of the rough sleepers were once covered by social insurance based on their occupations, and 13.8% were covered by social insurance based on their residency (Table 10.4). On the other hand, approximately 30% of the sample had no way of life other than unstable employment including day labour.

In contrast with their employment classification, the type of housing shows very different characteristics of rough sleepers. It is notable that 42% of the sample lived in company houses or workers' dormitories, compared with only

Table 10.4: Experience of social insurance

Type	(%)
Occupational	48.9
Regional	18.3
Day labourers	4.8
No insurance	22.1
Unknown	5.9

Source: Tokyou-to Rojoseikatusha Jittaichosa (Survey on Rough Sleeping In Tokyo, 2000)

3.9% of the total households in the Housing and Land Survey in 1998. Although houses are often independently chosen for people's personal and family needs, these houses are provided by employers in order to meet the needs of their labour management. They had the right to live in such houses as long as they worked for the company. The types of housing can also be classified into two categories: independent housing and other housing. First, 'independent housing' includes owner-occupied houses, and both private and public rented housing. 'Other housing' means company houses, workers' dormitories, hostels, hospitals and so on. Those who lived in independent housing accounted for only 47.5% of the sample, compared with the majority of the total households in the national survey (94.4%). Taking account of the many unmarried respondents, it seems that many homeless people had lived outside of family units and previously devoted the majority of their lives to the company.

Using the data of 660 respondents who answered all questions on employment and housing, a four-dimensional classification of the relationship between job status (stable or unstable) and housing type (independent or other) emerged as indicated in Figure 10.1:

- stable jobs and independent house group accounted for 39.4%;
- stable job and other house accounted for 25.6%;
- unstable job and independent house group accounted for 8.8%;
- unstable job and other house accounted for 26.2%.

At the second point of their earlier lives, the stability of their main job has broken down. The rate between stable and unstable jobs is the opposite of the rate shown at the first point (see Table 10.3). By this point, almost half of the stable people had moved into unstable jobs, either day labouring or other temporary work, while 12.7% of the street sample had no occupation previous to coming to the street. However, it is notable that 33.5% of them still had stable employment. Therefore, although *yoseba* remained as one of the direct sources of rough sleepers, those without an occupation and in both stable and temporary employment also came to the street but not through *yoseba*.

The same observation applies to the type of housing: 32.9% of the street sample

Figure 10.1: Relationship between employment and housing (at the time of main job)[1]

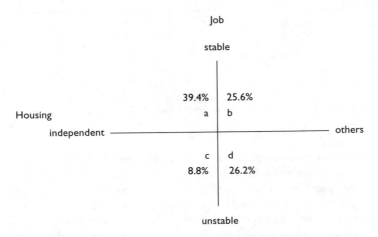

Job

stable

39.4%	25.6%
a	b

Housing

independent ——————————————————————— others

c	d
8.8%	26.2%

unstable

Notes:
[1] Since the percentages in Figures 10.1 and 10.2 were based on 660 respondents who answered all questions, there were slight differences observed from those in Table 10.3 (sample 710).

[2] Type of job: Stable – employers, managers, self-employed, and regular employees; Unstable – temporary employees, day labourers, others.

[3] Type of housing: independent – owner-occupied houses, private rented houses, public rented houses; Others – company houses, workers' dormitories, hostels, hospitals, others.

still lived in 'independent houses' at the second point, while 13% stayed in inns and hospitals or with friends. Those who lived in private hostels for day labourers (flophouses) accounted for only 15.5%.

Figure 10.2 shows the change in the distribution of the four groups that were classified by employment status and housing type between the two points, which also suggests possible routes into homelessness. There were mainly three routes onto the streets. First was the route directly from 'stable places' in independent houses or company houses and dormitories. Second was the route from 'stable places' by way of a short-term stay in 'unstable places' with other housing. And third was from the long-term stay in 'unstable places' with workers' dormitories or hostels. The ratio of the three routes was about even.

The causes of rough sleeping for each individual are likely to be diverse and complex. Almost all of the respondents experienced at least both job loss and housing loss, which resulted in the onset of rough sleeping. As Table 10.5 indicates, 94% had some reason for losing their jobs: 15.1% were either dismissed or their stable job disappeared; and 32.7% did not have a fixed-term contract renewed. Although 29.7% voluntarily left their stable or unstable jobs, they were still not able to find new job opportunities at the point of the interview.

Figure 10.2: Change of the 'places' and routes to the street

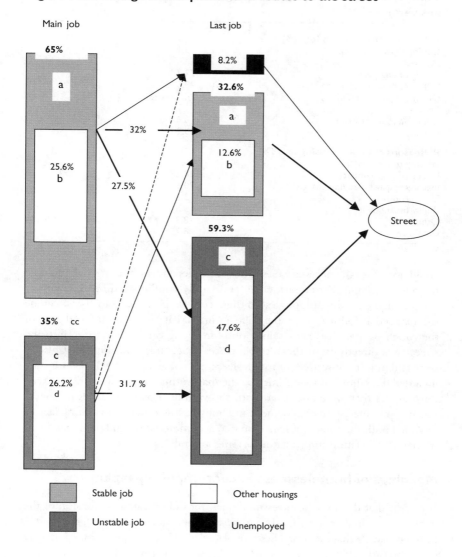

Fourteen per cent of the respondents reported that they were physically or mentally too vulnerable to work.

Possible reasons behind rough sleeping were often linked to the loss of their previous housing. Those in company houses or workers' dormitories came to the streets since they were dismissed or their temporary contract expired, and those who had been staying in hostels or inns became rough sleepers since they

Table 10.5: Causes of rough sleeping (street sample) (multiple answers)

A. Reasons cited for job loss (%)	
Closing of factory/shop	2.1
Dismissal	13.0
Ending of engagement	32.7
Left the job voluntarily	29.5
Old age, injury, sickness	14.0
Others	1.7
Continue (did not lose)	0.8
Unknown	5.2
B. Reasons cited for housing loss (%)	
Inability to pay rent	17.2
Ending of engagement	38.2
Inability to pay hostel/inn charge	20.6
Debt problem	3.3
Family breakdown	5.5
Others	8.3
Unknown	8.2

could not afford the necessary fees. Those in 'independent housing' had multiple reasons, including rent arrears, debts, and family conflicts and breakdown.

Overall, the production process of the recent rough sleepers in Tokyo can be summarised as follows. First, the data confirms that between 60% and 70% of the rough sleepers had held 'stable jobs' for a long time. One route into the streets was directly from these 'stable places'. Second, 'unstable social places' were still important sources of rough sleeping. These 'unstable places' not only included day labour in *yoseba*, but also the many other casual jobs with workers' dormitories that were associated with the various urban industries in Tokyo. Finally, combined with employment and housing loss, other contributing factors included both their heavy reliance on tied accommodation and the breakdown of marriage/relationships (or not forming a family).

Meanings of homelessness in contemporary Japan

It is clear that the 'new homelessness' does not only mean an extension of the habitual rough sleeping found in *yoseba*. One interpretation of the study's findings may be that many 'stable social places' have become precarious generally since the early 1990s, and previous 'unstable social places' including *yoseba* have shrunk, and no longer work as buffer zones for middle-aged people in particular. Moreover, unmarried or divorced middle-aged people may have fewer resources to cope with their unstable lives than those with families, partners or children.

The major factor that overturned the former 'stable social places' was often the change of Japanese employment practices in response to the deep recession. Since the 1960s, Japanese workers had been able to enjoy lifetime employment practices, salary scales based on seniority and company welfare systems. Stability among workers often differed in degree with the size and type of company but not usually in kind. Indeed, such stability was realised at the expense of workers' identities, health and community lives. In other words, Japanese workers were given a 'stable place' but only inside a 'company society'. Although women were often excluded from such stable jobs, they could be in the 'stable places' as wives. The self-employed and small company employers could also be in 'stable places' within the 'company society' as sub-contractors.

The erosion of long-held Japanese business practices, especially employment practices, became essential in order to make the Japanese economy stronger in the light of increasing global competition. The Japanese workers of today are expected to be 'independent workers' and not 'dependent workers', and expected to construct their lives outside the 'company society'. Sub-contractors are also encouraged to be independent parties.

More than a few companies have started advising middle-aged workers to take early retirement, restrict new recruitment, and cut down the welfare costs associated with employees including company houses and subsidies for housing loans. Consequently, the unemployment rate has risen from 2.3% in February 1989 to 5.0% in August 2001, and jumped to the latest record 5.4% in October 2001 (Statistic Bureau, 2001). In a survey conducted in August 2001, approximately 30% of the middle-aged unemployed have been unable to find jobs for more than a year. Various types of casual employment have replaced long-term employment. In 1999, the rate of irregular workers exceeded one fourth of all employees, and this is expected to increase further in the near future (Table 10.6). In such situations, the increasing inequality of income

Table 10.6: Change in regular workers' rates and the unemployment rates

Month/ Year	Employees[a] number (10,000)	Regular workers rate[b] (%)	Unemployment rate[c] (%)
Feb-1989	4,269	80.9	2.3
Feb-1990	4,369	79.8	2.1
Feb-1991	4,536	80.2	2.1
Feb-1992	4,664	79.4	2.2
Feb-1993	4,743	79.2	2.5
Feb-1994	4,776	79.7	2.9
Feb-1995	4,780	79.1	3.2
Feb-1996	4,843	78.5	3.4
Feb-1997	4,963	76.8	3.4
Feb-1998	4,967	76.4	4.1
Feb-1999	4,913	75.1	4.7
Feb-2000	4,903	74.0	4.7
Feb-2001	4,999	72.8	4.8
Aug-2001	4,974	72.3	5.0

[a] Not including executives.
[b] Reguler workers/employees.
[c] Unemployed persons/all labour force.
Source: Tokyou-to Rojoseikatusha Jittaichosa (Survey on Rough Sleeping In Tokyo, 2000)

distribution has become apparent, since the Gini coefficient rose from 0.39 in 1984 to 0.44 in 1997 (Ministry of Health and Welfare, 1997). The 'mass affluent' society of post-war Japan has peaked and is now in decline.

In order to cope with such obstacles of 'stable places', support mechanisms within the family are expected prior to any social support being provided by the government. Housewives have started participating in the unstable labour market more than before, and households have started cutting their living expenses and giving up sending their children to higher education. Families today are becoming increasingly vulnerable due to economic change. Such social and economic pressure has led to an increasing number of suicides and runaways from families in recent years, with over 60% of those being middle-aged males (National Police Agency, 2000).

The previous 'unstable social places' have also been influenced by the same circumstances. Such places were formed by both the surplus labour forces and the labour-intensive industries. In particular, the construction industry, retail and service industries in urban areas depended on large numbers of cheap labourers during periods of economic growth. Therefore, the *yoseba* districts and the dormitories of small shops, restaurants, *pachinko* parlours (popular pinball game centres), inns, and other urban industries could absorb many dropouts. Although these places were precarious and problematic, they could work for many people as buffers from living rough. However, the prolonged recession in the 1990s has resulted in the closing down of many businesses in these industries. For example, almost 320,000 private businesses closed during the three years since 1997: one half of them were retail, wholesale and restaurant businesses (Statistic Bureau, 1999). In 2000, the number of bankruptcies was almost 20,000, and 33% of those were from the construction industry (Tokyo Trade Research, 2001). To compound these difficulties, new technology and management systems have been introduced into these fields. The old day labourers or other casual employees have been replaced with new contingent workers including temporary workers, most of whom are young or female, and can adapt to new technology and systems. In addition, in the construction industry, the percentage of day labourers has fallen from 14.8% in 1975 to 5.5% in 1999. On the contrary, the number of the new temporary workers in this industry in 1999 has increased more than 60% from the number in 1996 (Statistic Bureau, 2000).

In this context, the changes have dramatically affected those who lived in company houses or dormitories, and/or those who did not have a family. In the case of workers living in company houses or dormitories without any family support, unemployment might directly equate with the onset of living rough. It means that those who have depended almost entirely on the 'company society' or specific casual jobs outside of family networks for a long time have faced more difficulties as a result of the recent changes. Although many young people are unemployed today, their precarious lives are concealed within family lives through the support of their parents. In addition, since social welfare services and practices tend to exclude able-bodied males, single middle-aged males are the first victims of the changes. In comparison, homeless women are more likely to be supported in the welfare homes, and are therefore less visible in the streets.

Overall, rough sleeping since the early 1990s is a sign of the general destabilisation of life's 'places', caused by the recent major changes of the Japanese employment system. Traditionally, the family has provided a safety net for those who need support, but now the family is also on the verge of change. The change of the family is indicated by both the decreasing size of households and decreasing rates of marriage. If the family size continues to shrink and the number of unmarried people increases, the visible homeless might extend more to women and younger people.

The response of Japanese society

According to the Tokyo survey, approximately 30% of the rough sleepers slept in parks; 25% under bridges or on riverbanks; and 16.1% around railway stations (Iwata, 2000b). Although they were certainly present in these 'physical places' – and nearly 40% had some temporary shanties made of cardboard boxes or plastic sheets – society does not regard such temporary houses as their 'places.' The rough sleepers are considered by the general public as not having a fixed address and are therefore viewed as squatters. Society had regarded the *yoseba* district as a segregated place for poor people during times of economic growth, whereas nowadays there are not even such segregated places for rough sleepers. Those people sleeping rough "are the people deemed out of place in the eyes of authority" (Wright, 1997, p 1).

The response of Japanese society, both the feelings of its citizens and the social policy, has been more hostile than sympathetic. Major social policy has not yet addressed this issue. The Ministry of Health, Labour and Welfare (formerly the Ministry of Labour) has restricted unemployment insurance provision as the first response to the current recession and has denied the provision of public relief works. The housing authority has also restricted single people from public housing, and indeed, entirely excluded those without a fixed address. Only the public assistance and the temporary welfare provision at local level, which follow the special programmes in *yoseba*, have responded – albeit reluctantly – to this issue. Some residents have put pressure on local governments to remove rough sleepers from public places. Moreover, those who live in the areas with rough sleepers have always opposed the idea of building shelters for rough sleepers, since they view that such facilities would devalue their own communities.

There are some explanations for this. First, it may be that many Japanese, even homeless people themselves, still hold onto the memories of former economic growth, in that jobs were always available for those who are willing to work, or view the present recession as only a temporary phenomenon (Iwata, 2000a). In other words, Japanese society has not become accustomed to long-term unemployment. Moreover, since an incentive to work was – and still is –

viewed as the most important principle of social policy in the past, Japanese society cannot easily accept middle-aged males to be eligible for social support and benefits.

Secondly, Japanese social policy, based on traditional systems, is no longer suitable for the current socioeconomic climate. Such support systems were first developed through the company welfare system during the pre-war period and then further developed along community-based lines in the 1960s (Tamai, 1999). This has continued since the 1960s, except for adjustments made as a result of demographic changes, especially in response to societal ageing. Under this system, regular workers have been entitled to pension and health services according to their employment in the 'company society'. Those who are out of the system, such as temporary workers, the self-employed and family members, have been entitled to benefits at a lower level often based on the family as a unit, as a resident of a municipality. Unemployment benefit is available for those workers who have made contributions based on regular wages, while those workers in less regular employment are often not covered. Day labourers are entitled to the special benefit of unemployment insurance, if they work over 26 days in two months and if they have registered as a resident with local governments. For many people, however, their recent unemployment periods are too long to be qualified for such benefits. Needless to say, unemployed people without a resident card cannot apply either for jobs advertised at job centres or public housing provided by local governments.

The third reason may regard concerns of social membership and social rights. The right to receive benefits in Japan is not based on the equal status of citizenship by which people are integrated into a single nation. Rather, it is based on membership of the family, the company, as well as the local municipality. The day labourers in *yoseba* could have a partial entitlement to welfare benefits as a resident within the segregated districts. Indeed, there is public assistance, which is available to any Japanese national below the poverty line – the public assistance acts as a safety net to secure social rights for all Japanese citizens. However, welfare administration requires strong reasons to explain why a person cannot work and why their family cannot help them. In reality, therefore, public assistance has only a charitable role to provide benefits and services for older people, sick people, people with disabilities, and single mothers. Moreover, since a welfare office belongs to local governments, city officials and social workers prefer to work for residents who are formally registered. Politicians also prefer to work for their electorates, while homeless people usually do not have the right to vote due to the loss of their resident card. Welfare offices often give rough sleepers travel fares so that they can visit a different welfare office. Furthermore, local governments hesitate to provide temporary provision for rough sleepers, since such provision often has the effect of attracting more homeless people into their districts. The recent trends of decentralised government and increased local autonomy have reinforced narrow views of such city officials. Every city wants to restrict their support to deserving formal residents, and they believe that social provision exists mainly for those residents.

In 1999, the central government launched the Independent Living Programme for rough sleepers in some major cities. This programme aims to provide shelter, food, and other services for daily living and some vocational services for those who expect to return to the labour market within approximately three months. The policy response seemingly appeared in another way three years after: the Homeless Act (*Homeless Jiritushien-ho*) was proclaimed without enough discussion. The Act is a provisional legislation with specified duration (10 years) and provides that the central and local government have the duty to survey the homeless problem in each area and to develop adequate policies in order to lead the homeless people from the streets to independent living. In other words, it does not secure homeless people's right to live or housing, but to secure public order in each local area.

The actual measure is not yet developed except the Independent Living Programme of a few major cities. In addition to this, the Independent Living Programme does not cover all rough sleepers. Rough sleepers are obliged to be classified into three different categories: workers, welfare clients and deviants, and only those who are regarded as workers may possibly receive benefit from the programme.

Therefore, the number of rough sleepers has not decreased but has rather expanded either to the periphery of major cities or to small cities. As a result, the central government has had no choice but to encourage the local government to apply the public assistance measures more positively to rough sleepers. In March 2001, the Department of Social Assistance notified local governments of new guidelines for the application of public assistance by rough sleepers. The department stressed that even in cases of a person having the ability to work but no formal place to live, the person should not be excluded from the assistance. However, most local governments hesitate to apply for the public assistance for homeless people since there is not a sufficient number of welfare hostels or shelters to accommodate those in need, and many rough sleepers are not considered as capable of living with outdoor relief.

In order to fill the gap between the state provision and local responses, new businesses have sprung up at the local level. Some private organisations have started operating hostels for homeless people who can afford to pay rent through public assistance. In particular, one organisation is taking advantage of the current recession and converting empty apartments and company houses for sale due to their financial difficulties. Such organisations rent out the accommodations at low rates; furthermore, their staff bring rough sleepers to welfare offices to make sure their potential tenants apply for the public assistance. The profit lies on a difference between rents for such accommodation and housing allowance. Currently, the organisation provides over 2,000 beds for homeless people in the Tokyo Metropolitan area. Neither central nor local governments have yet questioned this practice.

Many homeless people have been evicted from company accommodation or apartments due to the insecurity of employment caused by the current economic crisis. The recession is also the cause behind much empty accommodation. It is therefore ironic that such new welfare business, which emerged due to the recent economic hardship, has also brought some homeless people back to their old places. It is not certain, however, whether or not such accommodation can fulfil rough sleepers' need for 'social places' as a member of a changing society.

Conclusion

Homelessness is defined as the condition of those who have lost their 'social-physical places' and especially the core place of 'home' through which a society regards them as its members. Therefore, the issue of homelessness seems to be a problem of 'others'; that is, those outside the mainstream society. This point distinguishes homelessness from simple poverty or unemployment and highlights that the concept of homelessness is formed in parallel with the concept of membership of a society. Consequently, to resolve this problem, there needs to be a re-evaluation of the concept of membership of a society in order to make new 'places' for those made homeless within a society.

In the Japanese context, although people started to exist outside the 'company society' and other established structures, social policy and services are lagging behind, and unable to prevent the creation of rough sleepers. Japan needs to re-examine the basis of social policy and the concept of membership in the face of the coming 'uncertain society'. In this perspective, it will be ineffective simply to gloss over the problem with the Independent Living Programme, new welfare business, or the public control to maintain the social order.

Notes

[1] The term is explored by Cornelius Castoriadis. He describes it as

> Every society up to now has attempted to give an answer to a few fundamental questions: Who are we as a collectivity? What are we for one another? Where and in what are we? What do we want; what do we desire; what are we lacking? Society must define its identity, its articulation, the world, its relations to the world and to the objects it contains, its needs and its desire. Without the answer to these questions, without these definitions, there can be no human world, no society, no culture – for everything would be an undifferentiated chaos. The role of imagnary significations is to provide an answer to these questions, an answer that, obviously, neither reality, nor rationality can provide. (Castoriadis, 1987, p 147)

[2] This is the latter part of the centralised feudal period ruled by Togugawa.

References

Castoriadis, C. (1987) *The imaginary institution of society*, Cambridge: Polity Press.

Iwata, M. (1995) *Sengo shakai fukushi no tenkai to daitoshi sai-teihen* [*Social welfare and the underclass in the postwar Tokyo*], Kyoto: Minerva Press.

Iwata, M. (1999) 'Homeless toshiteno gendai no shitugyo, hinkon' ['The construction of homelessness in the "Hyper Modern Society"'], in Society for the Study of Social Policy (ed) *Hiyatoi rodosha-homeless to gendai nihon* [*Day labourers and homelessness and contemporary Japan*], Tokyo: Ochanomizu-shobo, pp 3–19.

Iwata, M. (2000a) *Homeless, gendai-shakai, fukushi-kokka* [*Homelessness, modern society, and the welfare state*], Tokyo: Akashi Press.

Iwata, M. (ed) (2000b) *Rojo-seikatusha jittai chosa* [*Report on rough sleeping in Tokyo*], Tokyo: Toshi Seikatu kenkyuukai.

Jencks, C. (1994) *The homeless*, Cambridge, MA: Harvard University Press.

Kennett, P. (1999) 'Homelessness, citizenship and social exclusion', in P. Kennett and A. Marsh (eds) *Homelessness: Exploring the new terrain*, Bristol: Policy Press, pp 37–60.

Kusama, Y. (1978) *Furosha no shosou* [*Vagrants in Tokyo*], (Akashi edn: *Ethnography of the modern underclass I*), Tokyo: Akashi Press.

Nakagawa, K. (1985) *Nihon no toshi kasou* [*Urban lower class*], Tokyo: The Keisoshobo Press.

Ministry of Health and Welfare (1997) *Shotoku sai-bunpai chousa* [*Survey of the redistribution of income*], Tokyo: Ministry of Health and Welfare.

Ministry of Health and Welfare (2000) *Homeless no jiritsu shien ni tuite* [*Support programme for independent life of homeless people*], Tokyo: Ministry of Health and Welfare.

Rossi, P. (1989) *Down and out in America: The origins of homelessness*, Chicago; University of Chicago Press.

Robertson, M.J. and Greenblatt, M. (eds)(1992) *Homelessness: A national perspective*, New York: Plenum Press.

Shimodaira, H. (1998) 'Slums in Tokyo: their changing phases with economic development,' in T. Akimoto (ed) *Shrinkage of urban slums in Asia and their employment aspects*, Bangkok: ILO Regional Office for Asia and the Pacific.

Statistic Bureau (1995) *Kokusei chosa* [*Population census*], Tokyo: Statistic Bureau.

Statistic Bureau (1999) *Jigyousho toukei* [*Establishment and enterprise census*], Tokyo: Statistic Bureau.

Statistic Bureau (2000) *Roudou-ryoku chousa* [*Report on the special survey of the labour force*], Tokyo: Statistic Bureau.

Study Group on Urban Environment (2001) *Report on rough sleepers*, Osaka: Osaka City University.

Tamai, K. (1999) 'The reform of social policy in the latter half of the 20th century in Japan,' *Journal of Economics* (Osaka City University), vol 100, no 1, pp 29-47.

Tokyo Trade Research (2001) *Tousan jyouhou* [*Information on bankruptcy*], Tokyo: Tokyo Trade Research.

Tsuda, M. (1972) *Nihon no toshi kasou shakai* [*Urban under society in Japan*], Kyoto: Minerva Press.

Watson, S. (1999) 'A home is where the heart is: engendering notions of homelessness', P. Kennett and A. Marsh (eds) *Homelessness: Exploring the new terrain*, Bristol: Policy Press, pp 81-100.

Wright, T. (1997) *Out of place: Homeless mobilizations, subcities, and contested landscape*, New York: State University of New York Press.

Yokoyama, G. (1949) *Nihon no kasou shakai* [*The under society in Japan*], (Iwanami edn), Tokyo: Iwanami Press.

ELEVEN

Women's health politics in Japan and Britain: comparative perspectives

Lesley Doyal

Introduction

Japan and Britain are both industrialised countries and have similar health care systems with universal provision. Women have a very high life expectancy in each of these countries, at 85 years-of-age in Japan and 81 in Britain (UNDP, 2001). Yet in both cases they have been critical of the health services they are offered and have campaigned for reforms. At the heart of their criticisms lies a common concern with women's entitlement to effective and appropriate health care. However, closer examination reveals significant differences in the form of these activities as well as their immediate goals. These in turn can be linked to wider differences in the nature of feminist politics in the two countries.

This chapter explores the ways in which living in Japan and Britain has shaped women's perceptions of their health care needs. It reviews the nature of women's health activism in each setting, and concludes with a summary of some of the common challenges now facing women as they fight for a healthier society.

Women's activism in Japan

Japan is often said to be 'backward' when it comes to gender issues. According to the UNDP's Gender Empowerment Index, Japan fell from 38th among the world's nations in 1999 to 41st in 2000 (UNDP, 2001). Women made up only 14% of candidates elected to the parliament, or Diet, in the 2000 General Elections. Furthermore, only 3% of senior managers are female, and the average female wage is still less than half that of men. Therefore, Japan continues to be a 'man's world' especially in economics and business, exhibiting what have been described as 'especially elaborate patterns of gender segregation' (Khor, 1999; Hashimoto, 2001).

Within this context, the building of feminist – or women-centred – politics has been especially challenging. Trends in the development of women's activism in Japan have shown some similarities with those in other parts of the world.

There has been considerable interchange of ideas with the US, for example. However, Japanese feminism does have its own clearly defined characteristics (Mackie, 1988, 1999; Buckley, 1994). According to Diane Khor, these are based on a holistic critique of Japanese society and a commitment to valuing women and their perspectives. In other words, the main aim of Japanese feminism has not been to make women more like men but to ensure that the female is given as much respect as the male (Khor, 1999).

Activists in Japan have therefore worked predominantly in women's spaces with what are seen as women's issues. Of course, this does not mean that there is a single feminist movement. For some women, feminism has meant working to oppose militarism and to support peace movements in Japan and other parts of Asia (Liddle and Nakajima, 2000, ch 1). This has included campaigns to oppose the trafficking of women and other forms of abuse carried out across national boundaries. However, for others the main focus remains domestic concerns, which have traditionally been seen as female terrain. This has been especially evident among *shufu* – housewives – who became a powerful political force in Japan during the postwar period (Matsui, 1990; Liddle and Nakajima, 2000, ch 1). As we shall see, this emphasis on sexuality and motherhood has had a major impact on the nature of women's campaigns in and around the health sector.

Women campaigning in the health sector

In line with the experience of many other countries, health care has been a major interest for Japanese women concerned with the promotion of social change. Many different forms of activism have been evident in the health field, ranging from self-help and support groups to high profile campaigns for legislative change. However, by contrast with other countries, the focus of this campaigning has been relatively narrow, with attention directed mainly at issues relating to sexuality and reproduction. Few attempts have been made to reshape the broader agenda of medicine itself or to reform the ways in which it is delivered through the health service.

A recent review of women's organisations listed in the periodical *Onna No Nettowakingu* (Women's Networking) identified 42 grassroots groups concerned with health issues. Most of these are based on a rejection of the ways in which 'men's ways of thinking' permeate the medical sphere (Khor, 1999). In order to counter this male domination, they have devised ways of affirming women's own experiences and building up their knowledge of their own bodies. Reflecting similar approaches adopted in the US and Britain, these strategies have included self-help groups, consciousness raising and other educational activities. The cross-cultural commonality of many of these issues was highlighted in 1988 with the translation into Japanese of the best-selling US self-help book *Our bodies ourselves*.

Seeking sexual and reproductive rights

Alongside these various networking initiatives, women have also been involved in public campaigns for legislative and regulatory change in the arena of reproductive health. If women are to exercise their right to self-determination, it is essential that they have the capacity to control their own fertility. Unless they can choose whether or not to have children and with whom, they will be able to determine little else about their lives. However, women in Japan have faced particular obstacles in their attempts to guarantee such freedom. This results from the continuing male domination of Japanese society in general and from the absence of women's voices in the medical arena in particular.

Commentators on the Japanese health care system have emphasised its paternalism and the lack of attention paid to the rights of patients as a group (Hall, 2001). This is especially true for women. Only 13% of practising doctors are female (Prime Minister's Office, 1997), and there are very few opportunities for women to express their health care needs either collectively or as individuals. This situation has been exacerbated in recent years by demographic concerns. By 2000 the fertility rate had fallen to only 1.5, raising major fears about the economic and social viability of Japanese society (UNDP, 2001). The term 'parasite singles' has been used to describe those people who choose not to form families (see also Chapter Eight, p 165), and women's desire to control their fertility is frequently lost in this pro-natalist rhetoric (Ogino, 1993; Watts, 2002).

Under these circumstances, it is not surprising that sexual and reproductive health issues have been central to the concerns of most health activists of all political perspectives. The need for effective reproductive health care is self-evident both to traditionalists (who see motherhood as the 'natural' sphere of women) and to radicals (who are concerned with deconstructing the links between social roles and biological reproduction). As we shall see later in this chapter, the recognition of this reality has led many women into campaigns to ensure that appropriate methods of fertility control are available and affordable to all those who wish to use them.

Contests over the acceptability of the termination of pregnancy have a long history in Japan. Under the 1907 Criminal Abortion Law, both the woman who had an abortion and the person who carried it out risked imprisonment. This law remains in place, although it was amended under the 1948 Eugenic Protection Law, which permitted terminations in order to avoid 'inferior offspring', to protect the mother's health, and to end a pregnancy conceived as the result of rape. In 1996 it was further amended to remove the eugenics clauses and it is now termed the Law for Northern Mother's Bodies.

In the 1970s and 1980s, a number of attempts were made by Shinto fundamentalists to return to more stringent controls. In response, a coalition of more than 70 women's groups formed the League Against the Revision of the Eugenic Protection Law (*Yusei-hogo-ho kaiaku soshi renmei*) to resist these moves and to replace the existing legislation with a rights-based law (Liddle and Nakajima, 2000, p 10).

Alongside the fight to maintain and extend abortion rights, women have also attempted to improve contraceptive provision. There is currently no national policy on population or family planning in Japan. The Law for the Protection of Mothers' Bodies regulates the provision of contraceptive services, and the Ministry of Health and Welfare has overall responsibility for planning them. However, they are not a government priority and insufficient facilities are provided to meet the needs of Japanese women (IPPF, 2002). The complex politics behind this reality and their implications for the reproductive health of Japanese women can be illustrated through the history of low dose oral contraceptives.

Low dose oral contraceptives: a case study

Unlike women in other developed countries Japanese women were long denied the right to low dose oral contraceptives (OCs). Although their use spread around the world from the 1960s onwards, it was not until June 1999 that these drugs were finally approved for use in Japan (Goto et al, 1999). The reasons given for this 35-year delay have been many and they have varied over time. They include scientific concerns about the possibility of adverse cardiovascular effects, fear of deterioration in sexual morality and increased rates of STDs, and possible risks of environmental pollution through the water supply. In reality, however, the perceived interests of the various stakeholders seem to have been taken more seriously than the health needs of women themselves (Norgren, 2001).

The possible approval of low dose OCs was viewed with suspicion in many quarters of Japanese society. Very broadly, these drugs could be seen as a threat to existing gender relations since they shifted the responsibility for contraception more clearly towards women. Although this was rarely spelled out explicitly, it is clear that a move from male–controlled condoms (still used by about 80% of couples) to female controlled hormonal methods would represent a significant cultural shift. At the same time, such a move would directly threaten the interests of family-planning associations and other voluntary bodies supplying condoms, as well as those of the private doctors who made large sums of money from induced abortions (Goto et al, 1999). A recent study has suggested that private doctors currently earn around $400 million (£250 million) annually from such work (Maruyama et al, 1996).

The impact of the delay of OCs was certainly bad for women's health. In the absence of the low dose option, many chose to use the combined high dose alternatives, which, paradoxically, remained available throughout the whole period[1]. These drugs are known to have adverse effects on the cardiovascular system and their used is especially risky for older women. According to a recent report, however, they have been used regularly by between 500,000 and 800,000 Japanese women (IPPF, 2002). A study carried out in the Gifu

Prefecture in 1997 showed that high dose OCs were being used by around 1.3% of women over the age of 35, and that 7.1% of women had used them at some time or other (Nagata et al, 1997).

Figures also show that Japan has continued to have a very high rate of unwanted pregnancies throughout the postwar period. In 1999, the proportion of such pregnancies was as high as 52%, compared with 19% in France and 30% in the US (Alan Guttmacher Institute, 1999). Not surprisingly, this is also reflected in Japan's very high rates of induced abortion. Unlike the situation in comparable countries where terminations are much higher among the young, older married women in Japan continue to make up a significant proportion of those wishing to end pregnancies. Therefore, the lack of appropriate and effective contraception has imposed severe limitations on Japanese women's capacity to control their own fertility (Goto et al, 2000).

Despite these difficulties, women's responses to the unavailability of low dose OCs have been varied. Many have been happy to accept the delay, feeling no need to challenge the medical and other authorities making decisions on their behalf. Indeed, even after the drugs were authorised, many were still reluctant to use them since official sources of information had always stressed the potential risks rather than potential benefits. However, a campaign to make them available gathered strength following the UN Conference on Population and Development (ICPD) held in Cairo in 1994.

In 1995, a women's group, including 24 members of the Diet, joined with sympathetic professionals to lobby the Ministry of Health and Welfare. This was followed in 1997 by the formation of the Professional Women's Coalition for Sexuality and Health. The main aim of this group was to gain approval for low dose OCs, while also making more information available on issues related to both women and health workers. Activities of this kind played a major part in ensuring the drug's eventual approval in 1999. A number of commentators have drawn comparisons between the long and complex history of low dose OCs and the speedy introduction of sildenafil citrate or Viagra which was approved for use in Japan after only six months (Kamimura, 1999).

Since the Cairo Platform for Action, women's health advocates in Japan have increasingly framed their demands within the rhetoric of sexual and reproductive rights (Ashino, 1997). Official acceptance of this terminology was evident in the *Plan for gender equality 2000*, published by the Japanese government in 1996 (available in English online at www.gender.go.jp/tzoudou/contents.html). However, the practical implications of these linguistic changes appear to have been limited. As a number of Japanese NGOs have pointed out, government spending remains heavily biased towards maternal and child health: children are given the highest priority, women still have to get their husband's consent to abortion and many report pressure to undergo fertility treatment (Japan NGO Report Preparatory Committee, 1999).

As well as facing legal and regulatory constraints on their access to reproductive health care, it is also clear that Japanese women face significant obstacles in individual medical encounters. Little research has yet been undertaken into the experiential dimensions of clinical practice in Japan. However, it is clear that gynaecological consultations in particular can be very demeaning. In many large institutions, patients continue to be examined on a bed with a curtain over their abdomen and their legs facing outwards. Health workers can then walk up and down the row examining the bodies of women who are not even aware of what is being done to them. Among Japanese women aged 30 years and older, only 14.8% received Pap smears in 1996, and a survey revealed that the majority cited embarrassment as a major barrier (Goto et al, 1999). Change is therefore needed at a number of different levels if Japanese women's experiences of health care are to be improved.

Women's activism in Britain

By contrast with women in Japan, those in Britain have been more direct in their criticisms of the British National Health Service (NHS). Moreover, their concerns have extended well beyond the arena of sexual and reproductive health to include a range of other clinical specialties as well as wider economic and social issues (Doyal, 1998). As a result, they have challenged some of the more fundamental aspects of medical knowledge and practice. Again these differences in priorities need to be understood by reference to the particular nature of feminist politics in Britain.

The second wave of organised feminism in Britain has been extremely diverse. Some organisations have concentrated on the need to affirm women's own values and practices while others have pushed for greater equality with men through anti-discrimination and equal pay legislation (Rowbotham et al, 1979; Kanter et al, 1984; Rowbotham, 1989). Issues of similarity and difference between women have been high on the agenda, with women choosing to join groups that reflected their ethnicity, sexual preference or a range of other characteristics. In the past decade in particular, many British women have been involved in campaigns to support women in less developed parts of the world. These different strands of British feminism have all been reflected in health campaigns.

Women campaigning for change in the NHS

When the NHS was set up in 1948 it received widespread acclaim as the first example of a universal health care system financed by general taxation. Yet, women have long claimed that the service treats them unfairly (Doyal, 1983, 1998; Roberts, 1985). Women were clearly major beneficiaries of a system that gave many of them access to free health care for the first time in their lives, but at the same time considerable evidence has now been amassed to show that women are treated differently to men in ways that are to their objective disadvantage.

Some of these inequalities are similar to those identified in the Japanese context. Therefore, women in Britain have also reported that they are treated with less respect and attention than male patients (Graham and Oakley, 1981; Roberts, 1985; O'Sullivan, 1987). However, the critics of medicine have now gone beyond these experiential concerns to identify gender bias in the technical quality of care they are offered. Drawing on findings from Britain and beyond, they have attempted to explain these patterns of discrimination with reference to the broader inequalities in status and power that continue to characterise medical practice in general and the workings of the NHS in particular.

Gender inequalities in care in the NHS: the experiential dimension

The early phase of feminist health campaigning in Britain consisted of several interconnected strands (Doyal, 1983). The core concern of these activities was the overthrowing of the medical perception of women as inferior and 'sickly' creatures, and replacing it with the reality that they are normal healthy human beings. At the same time, there was a growing awareness that certain areas of knowledge had been monopolised by doctors. Hence, strategies were developed to make this information more available to women. One of these was the publication in 1971 of the British version of *Our bodies ourselves* (Boston Women's Health Book Collective, 1978).

Like women in Japan, British activists have been especially concerned with reproductive health care. The 1967 Abortion Act marked the liberalisation of abortion provision in Britain and remains in place as an important part of the legislative provision guaranteeing a high level of reproductive freedom. However, during the 1970s women and their advocates had to resist several attempts to limit these rights. The fight to open up women's access to contraception was also fought much earlier in Britain than in Japan. Campaigns during the late 19th and early 20th centuries paved the way for the wider range of provision offered after the creation of the NHS. Yet again, however, women have needed to be active in ensuring that services are sustained as the priorities of the NHS shift (Kennir, 1990).

Although the legal battles have been won, a woman's ability to choose a contraceptive may still be constrained by the doctor's unwillingness to take her preferences seriously. These limits on autonomy have also been identified beyond the reproductive arena. For example, many women have reported feelings of disempowerment in the context of decision making about breast cancer surgery. While men may also experience a lack of power in their medical encounters, many female patients are doubly disadvantaged as a result of prevailing sexist attitudes. In order to tackle such discrimination, women from both patient groups and professioanl organisations have called for the reshaping of medical education to give doctors and other health workers a clearer understanding of the significance of gender issues in the therapeutic process. They have also worked on education and advocacy initiatives to give women themselves better information and more support in making their choices (Doyal, 1998).

Gender inequalities in care: the clinical dimension

Concerns about the qualitative aspects of care continue to be high on the agenda of women's health advocates in Britain. Alongside these, however, there has been a growing concern about the technical quality of the care offered to many women. These concerns were initially focused on fertility control (Mintzes, 1992). Questions were raised, for example, about the broader health implications of the newer injectable contraceptives such as Depo Provera, which were being offered most often to poor women and to those from ethnic minorities. However, it is the situation of women in developing countries that has received most attention: women's health advocates in Britain are supporting global campaigns to ensure the availability of safer and more acceptable methods[2].

Moving beyond the arena of reproductive technology, women have also become increasingly critical of other aspects of clinical care they are offered in the NHS. Breast cancer treatment has come under particular scrutiny as a growing body of evidence shows that many women are continuing to die unnecessarily. Though the incidence of the disease in Britain is not especially high, the mortality rate from breast cancer is the highest in the world. In 1992, there were nearly 40 deaths per 100,000 of the population, compared with a rate of 34 per 100,000 in the US. Yet the US has an incidence of 89 cases per 100,000 compared with Britain's rate of only 56 (House of Commons Health Committee, 1995).

A recent report concluded that most of these differences were due to the way care is currently organised in the NHS, particularly the huge variations in women's access to specialist treatment (House of Commons Health Committee, 1995). This makes the deaths potentially preventable were all patients able to take advantage of existing knowledge and skills. In response to such findings, many women have been involved in campaigning for more resources for breast cancer research and for all women to have equal access to specialist care and to the most effective therapies.

In recent years, concerns about gender inequalities in clinical care have been extended further still to include comparisons of the treatment received by women and men suffering from the same conditions. A recent review of 138 studies of specialist care in eight countries (including Britain) concluded that men were more likely than women to undergo non-invasive investigations for coronary heart disease, to be given renal transplantation, and to receive anti-retroviral therapy for HIV infection (Raine, 2000). More work is needed to assess the extent to which differences of their kind found in the NHS are the result of gender bias in clinical judgement (Khaw, 1993; Petticrew, 1993; Farrer et al, 1997). In the meantime, however, British women are following the lead of women in the US in demanding that more attention is paid to these apparent inequalities in the treatment they receive (Sharp, 1998).

Studies in both the US and Britain have also demonstrated the existence of gender bias in the conduct of research (LaRosa and Pinn, 1993; Rosser, 1994; Bandyopadhyay et al, 2001). Many epidemiological studies and clinical trials have been conducted with all-male samples or have included too few women to make a scientific assessment of relevant biological or social differences. Yet the findings are then used as the basis for treating both women and men. In the US, campaigns to remove these evident inequalities led to a change in the law and applicants for federal funding now have to demonstrate that their sample reflects an appropriate balance of women and men (Auerbach and Figert, 1995). Drawing on these experiences, women in Britain are beginning to call for greater sensitivity towards sex and gender in the conduct of medical research. However, this is unlikely to be achieved without more fundamental changes in the gendered balance of power within the NHS in general and the medical profession in particular.

Gender inequalities in status and power in the NHS

Many critics of the NHS have drawn attention to women's lack of influence in a system where 75% of workers are female, and women comprise the majority of its users (Doyal, 1998). Most of the power remains with the medical profession and with senior managers, the majority of whom are male. During the last few years, changes in the way the NHS is managed have seen a marked curtailment of the 'clinical freedom' of doctors. However, they still exercise a significant degree of control both over medical research and over the allocation of scarce medical resources. They also have a major influence on the quality of the treatment given to individuals. It is unlikely that an increase in the numbers of women in senior positions in the NHS would lead on its own to dramatic improvements in the treatment of female patients (Pringle, 1998, ch 10). However, the pursuit of this goal continues to be seen as one element of the campaign to promote gender equity in health care.

As a result of hard-won battles, women now make up over 50% of the medical student body. For many years, they were not permitted to study medicine at all, and it was not until the 1960s that 'quotas' on the number of female students began to be lifted (Pringle, 1998). The numbers of women in medical practice are increasing sharply as new entrants move through the system. However, they are still unable to compete on equal terms with their male colleagues (Witz, 1992; Pringle, 1998). They are less likely than men to achieve consultant status and continue to be concentrated in the less prestigious specialties. In surgery, for example, women still make up only about 6% of consultants (McManus and Sproston, 2000). They also continue to be under-represented on powerful professional bodies, such as the General Medical Council, and the committees of the royal colleges.

Women within the profession have campaigned for changes in the organisation of medical work to make it more family-friendly for both women and men. Organisations such as the Medical Women's Federation and Women in Medicine have set up support groups and developed information packs to help female colleagues to develop their careers. Spurred on by their female members, the Royal College of Surgeons set up Women in Surgery (WIST) in 1991. The aim of the scheme is to increase the number of women in surgery to 20% by the year 2010. The Royal College of Physicians followed suit with a major investigation into the obstacles women doctors face in pursuing their careers (Royal College of Physicians, 2001).

Progress is therefore being made in restructuring medical careers within the NHS and in facilitating women's competition with men on equal terms. However, many aspects of medical culture remain profoundly male-dominated, and discriminatory practices will not be removed by equal opportunities policies alone. The needs of women patients have also begun to move up the NHS agenda. However, changes are still needed to ensure that health care itself is more sensitive to the needs of both male and female service users.

Conclusion

Common challenges for women health activists in Britain and Japan

As this chapter has shown, women in Britain and Japan have pursued broadly similar goals in their attempts to reform health care. However, differences in the position of women in the two countries have shaped the ways in which these goals are pursued. These differences in approach are likely to continue, but there is also evidence of convergence since Japanese and British women face common challenges. Three of these are discussed here: rationalisation in health care; the impact of demographic change on the demand for services; and increasing recognition of the social and economic constraints on women's health.

Commentators in both Japan and Britain have highlighted the potential dangers of health sector reform for women. In both countries, governments have been heavily involved in attempts to control public expenditure (Robinson and Le Grand, 1993; Tsuda et al, 1994; Ikegami et al, 1999). Unless women are able to make their voices heard, there is a real danger that their interests may be ignored in the push for rationalisation. The authors of a recent Japanese NGO report highlighted this problem (Japan NGO Report Preparatory Committee, 1999). They focused in particular on the plight of women in underpopulated areas where services are being closed, and on the discrimination against those from minority groups, such as the *buraku* whose access to services is increasingly restricted.

In Britain, women have drawn attention to the reductions in the availability of well-woman services and family-planning clinics and the growing geographical inequalities in access to drugs for conditions such as breast cancer (Doyal, 1998). However, they have also used the opportunities offered by restructuring to try and increase their influence in the NHS. As the medical profession has been increasingly regulated and its power limited in pursuit of greater efficiency, more spaces have been opened up for public consultation. Women are increasingly using those spaces to highlight the particularity of their own needs, as well as emphasising the rights of health service users in general (Doyal, 1998).

One factor pushing up the cost of health care in both countries is the increasing numbers of older people in their populations. This trend again poses particular challenges for women, since they live longer than men, and are therefore the major users of services for older people. In Japan, 60% of the population aged 65+ are women, and a much higher proportion of those aged 80 and older. Research has shown that many of the problems faced by older women are different from those of their male compatriots (Krause et al, 1998; Higuchi, 2001). A recent report from Japanese NGOs criticised the government for failing to develop specialist services for this group. It also stressed the financial problems facing many older women and called for special insurance schemes for those with low incomes (Japan NGO Report Preparatory Committee, 1999).

In Britain, the health of older women has also been given very little attention. However, voluntary organisations are now beginning to draw attention to the double discrimination of ageism and sexism and to the poor quality of care older women too often receive (Gilchrist, 1999). A particular focus of concern has been the failure to include women aged 60+ in the NHS breast-screening programmes. In Britain as in Japan, it is clear that the combination of demographic change and health care restructuring has put particular pressure on informal carers (Lloyd, 1999). Although British men appear to be more involved in caring than their Japanese counterparts, looking after older people still remains a predominantly female activity. Campaigns have highlighted the health needs of carers themselves and this has been reflected in a number of legislative and policy initiatives.

Finally, it is significant that women in both Japan and Britain are beginning to move beyond concerns with health care, and are exploring the wider impact of gender relations on health itself. These developments are less advanced in Japan than in Britain, but a broadening of the agenda is evident in a number of areas. For instance, recent work has explored the impact of work and of housing on the health of women (Saito et al, 1993; Nohara and Kagawa, 2000). Most importantly perhaps, domestic violence has been identified as a major public health issue and its aetiology has been clearly located within the realm of gender relations (Kozu, 1999; Yoshihama, 1999; Weingourt et al, 2001; see also Chapters Five and Six of this volume).

The first survey of domestic violence in Japan was carried out in 1992 by the Domestic Violence Research and Action Group, and it revealed very high levels of abuse (Kozu, 1999). Commentators have related these to the continuation of patriarchal power relations within marriage, a reluctance on the part of women to bring shame on the family by disclosing abuse, as well as a tendency within the wider society to continue to condone marital violence. As more evidence of the scale of violence has emerged, campaigns to support the survivors have increased. These resulted in 2001 in the passing of the Law on Prevention of Spouse Violence and Protection of the Victim. This includes provision for restraining orders and eviction of offenders as well as the funding of shelters and other support services (see Chapter Six of this volume).

In Britain too, the prevention of domestic violence had been a goal for campaigners and the past two decades have seen major changes in legislation and in policy making. However, other aspects of gender inequality have also been identified as constraints on women's health. The large numbers of women living in poverty have received particular attention. Studies have identified the problems many women (often single mothers) face in bringing up children on very low incomes. They have explored the impact of poor housing and inadequate diets on both physical and mental health, and have made important links between the stresses of daily life and unhealthy habits such as tobacco smoking (Graham, 1993). As poor women become the major consumers of cigarettes, health campaigners in Britain have highlighted the links between smoking and gender inequality and have called for gender specific health promotion programmes.

In both Britain and Japan, women are continuing their campaigns for more gender-sensitive health care. At the same time, they are beginning to campaign for changes in the wider society to enable both women and men to realise their potential for health. The comparisons presented here have highlighted some of the differences between the two countries. However, they have also identified those common goals that are shared, not just by women in Britain and Japan, but by all those engaged in the global pursuit of gender equity in health and health care.

Notes

[1] These drugs were allowed for uses other than contraception, but the evidence shows that, whatever the ostensible reason for the prescription, many women were taking them to control their fertility (Nagata et al, 1997).

[2] Regular information on these campaigns and on related matters can be found in the British-based publication *Reproductive health matters* (Elsevier Science).

References

Allan Guttmacher Institute (1999) *Sharing responsibility*, New York: Allan Guttmacher Institute.

Ashino, Y. (1997) 'Sexual and reproductive rights/health: a challenge for women in Japan', *Yokahama Women's Centre for Networking and Communication Newsletter in English*, no 8.

Auerbach, J. and Figert, A. (1995) 'Women's health research: public policy and sociology', *Journal of Health and Social Behaviour* (extra issue), pp 115-31.

Bandyopadhyay, S., Bayer, A. and O'Mahony, M. (2001) 'Age and gender bias in Statin trials', *QJM*, vol 94, no 3, pp 127-32.

Boston Women's Health Book Collective (1978) *Our bodies ourselves: A health book by and for women*, British edition edited by A. Phillips and J. Rakufen, Harmondsworth: Penguin.

Buckley, J. (1994) 'A short history of the feminist movement in Japan', in J. Gelb and M. Palley (eds) *Women of Japan and Korea: Continuity and change*, Philadelphia: Temple University Press.

Doyal, L. (1983) 'Women, health and the sexual division of labour in Britain', *Critical Social Policy*, vol 7, pp 21-33.

Doyal, L. (ed) (1998) *Women and health services: An agenda for change*, Buckingham: Open University Press.

Farrer, M., Skinner, J., Alberti, K. and Adams, P. (1997) 'Outcome after coronary artery surgery in women and men', *QJM*, vol 90, no 3, pp 203-11.

Gilchrist, C. (1999) *Turning your back on us: Older people and the NHS*, London: Age Concern.

Goto, A., Reich, M. and Aitken, I. (1999) 'Oral contraceptives and women's health in Japan', *Journal of the American Medical Association*, vol 282, no 22, pp 2173-7.

Goto, A., Fujiyama-Koriyama, C. and Reich, M. (2000) 'Abortion trends in Japan 1975-1995', *Studies in Family Planning*, vol 31, no 4, pp 301-08.

Graham, H. (1993) *Hardship and health in women's lives*, London: Harvester Wheatsheaf.

Graham, H. and Oakley, A. (1981) 'Competing ideologies of reproduction: medical and maternal perspectives on pregnancy', in H. Roberts (ed) *Women, health and reproduction*, London: Routledge & Kegan Paul.

Hall, W. (2001) 'Patient patients', (www.japaninc.net/mag/comp/2001/02/feb01_reports_js.html).

Hashimoto, H. (2001) 'Men's involvement in gender equality movements in Japan', Women in Action, no 1, (www.isiswomen.org/pub/wia/wia101/japan.html).

Higuchi, K. (2001) http://wom-jp.ovg/e/jwomen/kaigo.html (accessed 6 November 2002).

House of Commons Health Committee (1995) *Breast cancer services*, vol 1, London: HMSO.

Ikegami, N. and Campbell, J. (1999) 'Health care reform in Japan: the virtues of muddling through', *Health Affairs*, vol 18, no 3, pp 56-75.

International Planned Parenthood Federation (2002) *Country profile: Japan*, (ippfnet.ippf.org/pub/IPPF_Regions/IPPF_CountryProfile.asp.html).

Japan NGO Report Preparatory Committee (1999) 'Women 2000', (www.jca.ax.apc.org/fem/bpfa/NGOreport?C_en_Health.html).

Kamimura, K. (1999) 'Japan approves pill after nearly decade of debate', (www.cnn.com/HEALTH/women/9906/02/japan.pill.02/).

Kanter, H., Lefanu, S. and Spedding, C. (1984) *Sweeping statements: Writings from the years 1981-1983*, London: Women's Press.

Kennir, B. (1990) *Family planning clinic cuts: A survey of NHS family planning clinics in Greater London*, London: Family Planning Association.

Khaw, K. (1993) 'Where are women in studies of coronary heart disease?', *British Medical Journal*, vol 306, pp 1145-6.

Khor, D. (1999) 'Organizing for change: women's grass roots activism in Japan', *Feminist Studies* Fall, pp 633-70.

Kozu, J. (1999) 'Domestic violence in Japan', *American Psychologist*, vol 54, no 1, pp 50-54.

Krause, N., Liang, J., Jain, A. and Sugisawa, H. (1998) 'Gender differences in health among the Japanese elderly', *Archives of Gerontology and Geriatrics*, vol 26, no 2, pp 141-59.

LaRosa, J. and Pinn, V. (1993) 'Gender bias in biomedical research', *Journal of the American Medical Women's Association*, vol 48, no 5, pp 145-51.

Liddle, J. and Nakajima, S. (2000) *Rising suns and rising daughters: Gender, class and power in Japan*, London: Zed Press.

Lloyd, L. (1999) 'The wellbeing of carers', in N. Daykin and L. Doyal (eds) *Health and work: Critical perspectives*, London: Macmillan.

Mackie, V. (1988) 'Feminist politics in Japan', *New Left Review*, vol 167, pp 53-76.

Mackie, V. (1999) 'Dialogue, distance and difference: feminism in contemporary Japan', *Women's Studies International Forum*, vol 21, no 6, pp 599-615.

Maruyama, H., Raphael, J. and Djerassi, C. (1996) 'Why Japan ought to legalise the pill', *Nature*, vol 379, pp 579-80.

Matsui, M. (1990) 'Evolution of the feminist movement in Japan', *National Women's Studies Association Journal*, vol 2, no 3, pp 435-49.

McManus, I. and Sproston, K. (2000) 'Women in hospital medicine in the United Kingdom: glass ceiling, preference prejudice or cohort effect', *Journal of Epidemiology and Community Health*, vol 54, pp 10-16.

Mintzes, B. (ed) (1992) *A question of control: Women's perspectives on the development and use of contraceptive technology*, Amsterdam: Women and Pharmaceuticals Project, Health Action International and WEMOS.

Nagata, C., Matsushita, Y., Inaba, S., Kawakami, N. and Shimizu, H. (1997) 'Unapproved use of high-dose combined pill in Japan: a study on prevalence and health characteristics of users', *Preventive Medicine*, vol 26, pp 565-9.

Nohara, N. and Kagawa, J. (2000) 'The health care system for female workers and its current status in Japan', *International Archives of Environmental Health*, vol 73, pp 581-86.

Norgren, T. (2001) *Abortion before birth control: The politics of reproduction in postwar Japan*, Princeton, NJ: Princeton University Press.

Ogino, M. (1993) 'Japanese women and the decline of the birth rate', *Reproductive Health Matters*, vol 1, pp 78-84.

O'Sullivan, S. (1987) *Women's health: A spare rib reader*, London: Pandora Press.

Petticrew, M., McKee, M. and Jones, J. (1993) 'Coronary artery surgery: are women discriminated against?', *British Medical Journal*, vol 306, pp 1164-6.

Prime Minister's Office (1997) *Present status and plans for the national plans of action for a gender-equal society* (in Japanese), Tokyo: Ministry of Finance Press.

Pringle, R. (1998) *Sex and medicine: Gender, power and authority in the medical profession*, Cambridge: Cambridge University Press.

Raine, R. (2000) 'Does gender bias exist in the use of specialist services?', *Journal of Health Services Research and Policy*, vol 5, no 4, pp 237-49.

Roberts, H. (1985) *The patient patients: Women and their doctors*, London: Pandora Press.

Robinson, R. and Le Grand, J. (1993) *Evaluating the NHS reforms*, London: Kings Fund.

Rosser, S. (1994) 'Gender bias in clinical research: the difference it makes', in A. Dan (ed) *Reframing women's health: Multidisciplinary research and practice*, London: Sage Publications.

Rowbotham, S. (1989) *The past is before us*: Feminism in action, Boston: Beacon Press.

Rowbotham, S., Segal, L. and Wainwright, H. (1979) *Feminism and the making of socialism*, London: Merlin.

Royal College of Physicians (2001) *Women in hospital medicine: Career challenges and opportunities. Report of a working party*, London: Royal College of Physicians.

Saito, K., Iwata, N., Hosakawa, T. and Ohi, G. (1993) 'Housing factors and perceived health status among Japanese women', *International Journal of Health Services*, vol 23, no 3, pp 541-54.

Sharp, I. (1998) 'Gender issues in the prevention and treatment of coronary heart disease', in L. Doyal (ed) *Women and health services: An agenda for change*, Buckingham: Open University Press, pp 100-12.

Tsuda, T., Aoyama, H. and Froome, J. (1994) 'Primary health care in Japan and the United States', *Social Science and Medicine*, vol 38, no 4, pp 489-95.

United Nations Development Programme (UNDP) (2000) *Human development report 2001*, New York: UNDP.

Watts, J. (2002) 'Birth dearth can turn Japan into nation of ancients', *The Observer*, 6 February.

Weingourt, R., Maruyama, T., Sawada, I. and Yoshimo, J. (2001) 'Domestic violence and women's mental health', *Japan International Nursing Review*, vol 48, no 2, pp 102-08.

Witz, A. (1992) *Professions and patriarchy*, London: Routledge.

Yoshihama, N. (1999) 'Domestic violence: Japan's hidden crime', *Japan Quarterly*, vol 46, no 3, pp 76-82.

TWELVE

Women and health in Japan: sexuality after breast cancer

Miyako Takahashi

Introduction

Cancer has been the primary cause of death in Japan since 1981 (Ministry of Health, Labour and Welfare, 2000). The Japanese word for cancer – *gan* – was once associated with the image of death, or with severe physical and psychological distress. However, thanks to the recent development of medical technology and treatment, patients' survival rates have been dramatically improved and the diagnosis of cancer is no longer regarded as a virtual death sentence. This fact has directed people's attention from mere survival to how to achieve a better quality of life (QOL) following a cancer diagnosis (Osoba, 1991; Kawano, 1995).

In spite of the fact that cancer survival rates have increased, sexuality after having cancer remains a taboo topic in both the clinical and research setting of many countries. Research on sexuality after cancer in the context of psychosocial rehabilitation began in the 1980s (Andersen, 1985; Schain, 1988; Burbie and Polinski, 1992). In Japan, the reluctance to raise the topic seems to be even greater. There, sexuality was rarely included in cancer QOL scales. Also, when sexuality was discussed in the clinical setting, it was always related to pathological aspects, such as an infection route of sexually transmissible infections, or impotence as a complication of diabetes. Sex after having specific illnesses was rarely discussed in the context of pleasure or undergoing post-treatment rehabilitation.

This chapter focuses primarily on women's sexuality after having breast cancer, and discusses how this long-neglected issue is influenced by both the socio-cultural context and the health care system in Japan. However, the chapter first presents an overview of the health status of Japanese people and the Japanese health care system in general.

Overview of health status and health care system in Japan

Health status of people in Japan

The current life expectancy of people in Japan is the longest in the world. As of 1999, the average life expectancy at birth was 77.1 years for men and 84.0 years for women (Ministry of Health, Labour and Welfare, 2000). Figure 12.1 shows the changes in mortality rates according to the cause of death in Japan since 1950. After infectious diseases such as tuberculosis were successfully controlled in the 1920s and 1930s, cerebro-vascular diseases (CVD), heart diseases and malignant tumours have been the three major causes of death. Malignant tumours overrode CVD in 1981, and have remained the primary cause of death since then. The mortality rate according to cancer shows a remarkable decrease in stomach cancer, although it still remains in the primary position for women and second for men. On the other hand, the mortality rate of lung, colon and breast cancers have increased steadily.

Other health indices, such as the infant mortality rate and neonatal mortality rate, have improved remarkably during the last 50 years. The infant mortality rate, which used to be as high as 60.1 per 1,000 births in 1950, dropped to 3.2 in 2000. This is among the lowest in the world (Table 12.1). Similarly, the neonatal mortality rate has dropped from 27.4 to 1.8 per 1,000 births during the same period (Ministry of Health, Labour and Welfare, 2001). When it comes to health care spending in Japan, the percentage of total health expenditure is approximately 7% of GDP, which is no more than the OECD average, despite a high standard of health (Figure 12.2).

Table 12.1: Infant mortality rate: deaths per 1,000 live births

	1960	1970	1980	1990	1998
Australia	20.2	17.9	10.7	8.2	5.0
Canada	27.3	18.8	10.4	6.8	–
France	27.5	18.2	10.0	7.3	4.6
Germany	33.8	23.6	12.6	7.0	4.7
Greece	40.1	29.6	17.9	9.7	5.7
Italy	43.9	29.6	14.6	8.2	5.3
Japan	30.7	13.1	7.5	4.6	3.6
Spain	43.7	28.1	12.3	7.6	5.7
Sweden	16.6	11.0	6.9	6.0	3.5
Switzerland	21.1	15.1	9.1	6.8	4.8
UK	22.5	18.5	12.1	7.9	5.7
US	26.0	20.0	12.6	9.2	7.2

Source: OECD Health Data 2001 (2001)

Figure 12.1: Trend in leading cause of death in Japan during 1950-99

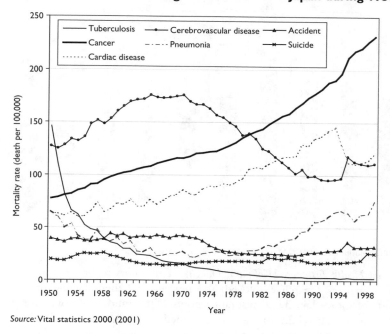

Source: Vital statistics 2000 (2001)

The Japanese universal health insurance system

One of the major factors that has enabled good health status without excessive cost is the universal health insurance system, which keeps patients' co-payments low, thereby maintaining good access to health care. All Japanese citizens and registered international residents are covered by the Japanese universal health insurance system[1].

The insurance can be classified into four major categories as follows:

- *Society-Managed Health Insurance [Kumiai Hoken]*. This insurance covers the employees of large companies with more than 300 employees and their dependants. It consists of about 1,800 insurance pools at the company level, administered by management-labour committees. The revenue resource consists of employee and employer premiums.
- *Government–Managed Health Insurance [Seifu Kansho Hoken]*. This covers the employees of small and medium-sized companies with more than four and fewer than 300 employees, as well as their employees' dependants. It has a single pool at the national level managed by the Ministry of Health, Labour and Welfare. Similar to the Society-Managed Health Insurance, the revenue resource is provided by employee and employer premiums. However, reflecting the lower incomes of these employees, the government subsidises a fixed percentage of expenses.

Figure 12.2: Total expenditure on health in ratio to GDP in 1998

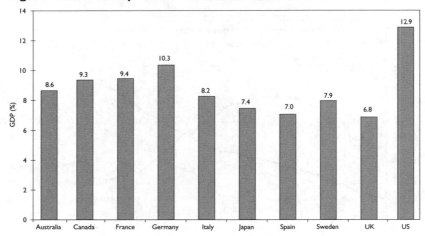

Source: OECD Health Data 2001 (2001)

- *National Health Insurance* [*Kokumin Hoken*]. This caters to non-employees, such as farmers, the self-employed, and retirees, and their dependants. It consists of more than 3,000 insurance pools at the municipal government level. About half of the outlays are provided by premiums, which varies somewhat according to each local government with the rest subsidised by the general revenue.
- *Mutual Aid Associations* [*Kyosai Kumiai Hoken*]. This insurance is for public employees, private-school teachers and staff, and their dependants. It consists of about 80 insurance pools administered by the mutual aid association.

Health insurance plans finance medical and dental care, hospitalisation, nursing, rehabilitation, and other welfare and public health services. The insured is charged a co-payment that varies between 20% and 30% of the total expense according to the insurance cover. A ceiling is also set on household co-payments to fill a 'catastrophic gap'; a family whose co-payment exceeds ¥63,000 (£315) per month – ¥200 = £1 – due to major illnesses is exempt from paying the excess. Medical facilities send bills for all patients to intermediary review and payment organisations. The organisations review the bills and send them to the insurers that cover each patient. The insurer pays the total amount of reimbursement to the intermediary organisation, which is then paid to the medical facility.

A special feature of this health insurance system is the fact that the cost of each medical procedure and product is set by the national fee schedule (*shinryo hoshu*). The fee schedule, which is revised every two years, lists the price of all medical procedures and products, including pharmaceuticals, that will be covered by health insurance. Since the same fee schedule is applied to all medical facilities, both public and private, all patients who receive the same treatment pay the same amount of money based on the fee schedule regardless of the kind of insurance they have and the hospital they go to. Campbell (1998, p 18) points out that this system is extremely egalitarian, since various mechanisms – premiums as a percentage of income, differential tax subsidies, direct cross-subsidisation among insurance carriers – ensure that premium levels are adjusted to the patient's ability to pay.

It is also noteworthy that patients are allowed to go to any medical facilities of their choice. This leads to the tendency among patients to choose major hospitals, such as university medical centres with sophisticated laboratory facilities. In order to prevent the outpatient clinics of major hospitals becoming overcrowded with patients suffering from minor illnesses, the government decided in 1996 to put an extra fee on those who visit a major hospital with certain criteria without a reference from a primary-care physician. However, this strategy has not worked well, since the extra fee, which is paid only at the initial visit and varies from ¥2,000 to ¥4,000 (£100 to £200) depending on the hospital, is not expensive enough to deter people from their first-choice hospitals.

Mass health screening

Mass health screening tests – which are conducted in workplaces, schools and the community – may also explain the healthy status of people in Japan. According to the Industrial Safety and Health Law (*Rodo anzen eisei ho*), it is mandatory for an employer to provide employees, including part-time workers, with a free annual health check-up. For employees who deal with hazardous substances, such as organic solvents, lead and so on, the employer provides extra health check-ups. In schools, the School Health Law (*Gakko hoken ho*) states that schools, both public and private, should conduct an annual check-up that includes screening by a general physician, an ophthalmologist, an ear, nose and throat specialist, and a dentist. At the community level, based on the Health and Medical Service Law for the Elderly (*Rojin hoken ho*), local government provides free cancer screening programmes and free general check-ups for older residents.

Publicly subscribed health checks are supplemented by health check clinics – the so-called 'human dry dock' (*ningen dokku*) – which are quite popular among middle-aged business people. Many hospitals provide various half-day and day packages for the 'human dry dock' that include a clinical examination, detailed blood tests, chest X-rays, upper gastrointestinal X-rays, electrocardiograms, abdominal ultrasounds, mammography, Pap smears, and so on. However, since these supplements are not covered by national health insurance, each hospital can set its own price resulting in high profitability. The average expense for a half-day package is about ¥50,000 (£250). In many cases, employers subsidise a part of the expense. Moreover, the 'human dry dock' provides a potential patient to the hospital since a positive result often results in further examinations at the hospital affiliated to the 'dry dock' facility.

These conditions motivate hospital administrators to expand business in this area, leading to more campaigns to promote preventive medicine.

Despite a health system that provides few barriers to accessing preventive and clinical medicine, a number of problems exist. The problem that is most frequently raised by patients is the long waiting time for short consultation time in large hospitals. Under a universal health insurance system that fixes the price of each medical procedure by the uniform fee schedule, profits motivate doctors to see as many patients as possible. As a result, the consultation time in an outpatient clinic is extremely short – five minutes at most for a returning patient, sometimes less. This situation is often ridiculed in the press as 'seeing a doctor for three minutes after waiting for three hours'. In addition, the layout of a consultation room in a hospital is designed to facilitate patient turnover: sometimes patients are asked to wait 'outside' the consultation space, when all that divides it from the waiting space is a curtain. Naturally, patients overhear the conversations between other patients and the doctor; this makes them self-conscious about what to discuss at the clinic once their turn comes. Such a time constraint and the lack of privacy in the clinical setting discourages patients from raising complicated psychosocial issues such as sensitive or sexual aspects of their treatment, and forces them to focus on physical aspects only.

Sexuality after a cancer diagnosis: the Japanese context

Japanese women and breast cancer

When we look at age adjusted mortality rates according to the cancer site, the three common cancers are: stomach, colon, and lung. Breast cancer is fourth but with a considerably lower mortality rate compared with that of European and North American countries (Table 12.2). However, the age-adjusted

Table 12.2: Age-adjusted mortality rate of women's breast cancer

(Deaths/100,000 women)

	1960	1970	1980	1990	1995
Australia	24.4	25.7	24.9	26.3	25.1
Canada	30.4	30.2	29.5	31.1	27.7
France	20.7	21.9	23.5	25.4	25.2
Germany	21.4	24.8	27.0	29.8	28.7
Italy	18.7	22.1	24.2	26.5	25.5
Japan	4.7	5.3	6.6	7.4	8.9
Spain	10.6	–	17.2	21.8	22.2
Sweden	25.7	24.3	25.2	22.9	22.5
UK	30.4	33.1	35.9	36.4	32.6
US	27.5	28.4	27.9	29.1	26.8

Source: OECD Health Data 2001 (2001)

incidence rate calculated using population-based cancer registration data (supplied by The Research Group for Population-based Cancer Registration in Japan, 1999) indicates that breast cancer has been the most common cancer among women in Japan since 1994. It is estimated that approximately 30,000 Japanese women are newly diagnosed with breast cancer each year.

Breast cancer has a unique feature among cancers in Japan. Patients are often not disclosed the true diagnosis of cancer (Uchitomi, 1997). Both doctors and families are reluctant to tell the truth since they are afraid of upsetting the patient, and try to 'protect' the person from the fear of death. Although research has observed a pronounced tendency toward truth telling in the last decade, Japanese doctors still have a strong hesitancy to tell a patient their pessimistic prognosis (Akabayashi, 1999). Most women with breast cancer have, however, been told the truth of their diagnosis due to the relatively good prognosis of the disease. Women with breast cancer, who lead their everyday lives knowing they have a life-threatening illness, have been the most active and visible cancer survivors in Japan. Self-help groups for breast cancer survivors have been established nationwide to promote mutual and tangible support for survivors.

Why is the topic taboo?

It is universal that the sexual aspects of having cancer have long been neglected in both the research and clinical setting. Some researchers have pointed out certain barriers to the discussion of sexual issues. Related to medical professionals' hesitancy, Auchincloss (1990) has pointed out four barriers:

- medical professionals define their responsibilities as treatment centred;
- lack of information about what can be done for sexual problems;
- the perception that the patient is mainly concerned with having cancer, not sexual issues;
- embarrassment in raising the topic.

From the point of view of patients, they often felt embarrassed and guilty to be thinking about sex when they 'should be grateful' for being alive (Kaplan, 1992). They also tried to be 'the good patient' and let the doctor determine when, if ever, sex should be discussed (Auchincloss, 1990).

In Japan, similar hesitation by health professionals and patients has been reported. A questionnaire conducted by Takahashi et al (1999) revealed that Japanese breast surgeons considered themselves responsible mainly for medical treatment, and expected other support resources – such as families and nurses – to take care of psychosocial issues. Less than 40% of respondents considered it a role of the surgeon to deal with a patient's body image and sexuality-related issues.

A survey by Ishihara et al (1993) pointed out four major reasons that prevented Japanese women with cancer from raising the topic in the clinical setting:

- hesitation in bothering medical professionals that always seem to be busy;
- lack of privacy in the hospital;
- hesitation in 'monopolising' a doctor when many other patients are waiting;
- lack of signals from medical staff to the effect that questions related to sexuality would be welcomed (Ishihara et al, 1993).

The hesitation among patients strongly reflects the time constraints and lack of privacy in outpatient clinics in Japan. Given the hesitancy on the part of both medical professionals and patients, it is understandable why the topic has not reached a high profile in the clinical setting.

The focus on the specific organ and gender

Another problem is that research on sexuality and cancer conducted in Japan has focused on sexual intercourse and reproduction. Most research looks at sexual dysfunction caused by urological, gynaecological and colorectal cancers, describing the impact of surgery on penis-in-vagina intercourse. Studies on the sexual impact of cancer treatments that involve other parts of the body, such as head and neck surgery, laryngectomy and limb amputation, were not found in a database of medical articles in Japan. Studies on breast cancer and sexuality are surprisingly few, despite the fact that the breast is the body part that has been explored most in connection with sexuality and women's cancers by researchers in the West[2]. Studies on the influence of adjuvant therapies, such as chemotherapy, hormone therapy and radiation, are also extremely scarce. When the influence of adjuvant therapies was discussed, it was always related to reproduction issues, such as the possibility of pregnancy and the necessity of contraception.

It was also noteworthy that, with the exception of gynaecological cancers, the subjects in most studies were men. The most likely explanation is that it is easier to assess the severity of the symptom and the effect of a treatment by erectile function. In the case of women – without having such an obvious indicator – it is extremely difficult to assess accurately the changes in sexual desire and arousal in primary-care settings. Consequently, Japanese health care providers and researchers seemed to underestimate the sexual impact of cancer treatments as far as sexual intercourse itself was physically possible.

Breast surgeons' optimism

This underestimation may account for Japanese breast surgeons' optimism regarding the sexual complications of breast cancer treatments. One prominent Japanese surgeon wrote:

> Mastectomy itself never leads to sexual impairment or loss of desire. However, patients' belief that their sexuality is impaired damages their intact endocrine

organs. Thus, patients can control their situation by changing their attitude. (Tominaga, 1995, p 266)

Other articles and books by Japanese surgeons, with few exceptions, comment mainly on the impact of treatments on sexual intercourse and fertility issues, and conclude that mastectomy per se never leads to sexual impairment (Seno and Izuo, 1994; Fukutomi, 1996; Kusama, 1998). The Cancer Information Service, the most comprehensive on-line information service for the general public provided by the National Cancer Center in Japan (www.info.ncc.go.jp/NCC-CIS), also states in relation to breast cancer that "there is no problem at all regarding sexual life. However, because breast cancer is associated with hormones, there is some period you should avoid pregnancy. Please consult your doctor on this issue". These optimistic views are totally inconsistent with the findings of academic research that reports sexual changes such as reduced frequency of sex, loss of libido, and reduced sexual pleasure after breast cancer (Jamison et al, 1978; Andersen, 1985; Schover, 1991, 1997). In addition, the descriptions by Japanese breast cancer survivors themselves that mention sexual and marital problems further highlight these inconsistencies (Watt, 1987; Nakamura, 1993).

Interviews with Japanese breast cancer survivors

What really happens to Japanese women's sexuality after breast cancer? In order to answer this question from women's point of view, I conducted qualitative, semi-structured interviews with 21 Japanese breast cancer survivors in 1998 and 1999 (Takahashi, 2000). Most of the informants had modified radical mastectomy or breast-conserving surgery for relatively early-stage breast cancer. Each had some kind of adjuvant therapy such as radiation, oral or intravenous chemotherapy, and hormone therapy.

Physical and psychological factors intertwined

The time it took before resuming sex after surgery varied considerably, from just several days to ten months. Not surprisingly, most of the informants stated that sex after surgery was accompanied by various physical discomforts. The most frequently mentioned was painful intercourse due to decreased lubrication of the vagina. All of the women who mentioned this had either hormone therapy or intravenous chemotherapy that damaged ovarian functions. The research also revealed that women experienced various physical discomforts other than painful intercourse. Some women suffered extreme discomfort when the area around the operated or radiated area of the breast was caressed. One woman stated that she was afraid of her partner pressing on the operated side of her body. Another said that she was afraid of her partner's unpredictable movements – such as suddenly grabbing and moving her arm during sex – since her arm had not yet regained its full mobility after surgery. Indeed, these uncomfortable sensations disturbed the women's concentration on their sexual pleasure, hence indirectly leading to painful intercourse. It was obvious that women's physical discomfort was induced, not only by psychological factors, but also by physical and physiological changes induced by treatments including mastectomy itself:

> "It's painful ... and my vagina is so vulnerable. I have vaginal discharge like a period for many days after having sex. I tried a lubricant jelly several times, but (it didn't work) .... I'm very reluctant to have sex if it hurts like that. I can't be positive about it, and I want to avoid it, if possible." (37 years-of-age, 16 months after surgery)

Many other informants referred to a reluctance to have sex during and after treatments. In addition to the secondary effects caused by physical discomfort, they mentioned other reasons such as loss of physical and/or psychological energy due to subsequent treatments, fear of getting pregnant, and fear of the partner's rejection. Some women decided to cover their operation scars with camisoles or T-shirts during sex because they were afraid of upsetting their partners by the altered appearance of their breast:

> "I'm determined not to show the scar to my husband because I'm very afraid to turn him off.... There is something delicate and sensitive about men, don't you think? I thought I'd better not show him something like my scar. I am concerned that he may lose sexual interest toward me by seeing it." (54 years-of-age, three years and 11 months after surgery)

Women's fear of rejection seemed to be strongly influenced by the psychological impact of their altered breast appearance and their own acceptance of the scar. Although there were some women who kept covering the scar long after surgery, many said they gradually 'got accustomed to' their scar by seeing it everyday and became less nervous about showing it to their partner. In addition, there were some women who did not seem to hesitate so much to show the scar to their partner from the beginning. They were either quite satisfied with the appearance of their post-surgery breast or they did not regard their breast as the symbol of their femininity. A woman who had a mastectomy states:

> "As a woman, I don't have a particularly strong feeling toward the specific organ. It is just that I don't want a mastectomy when cancer returns in the opposite breast. It's not because I give a special meaning to my remaining breast as a woman. I just don't want to lose balance of my body function, because the human body is made so exquisitely." (48 years-of-age, three years and nine months after surgery)

Some informants stated that it was their partner, not themselves, who had become very passive regarding sex after surgery. According to them, partners seemed to fear that sex would hurt the women physically, although those partners were not willing to share their concerns.

Hesitation in raising sexual issues

Most of the women who had sexual changes took some active measures to improve the situation. They tried to seek their partner's understanding through active communication. However, assertiveness of the informants varied significantly. Some women hesitated to speak out since they had not talked about their sexuality frankly with their partner before having cancer. It was only when they could not stand the discomfort any longer that they finally tried to speak out:

> "I understand that my husband and I should talk about sex more frankly. But in our relationship, we didn't think that the sexual aspects were so important. Couples like us are too shy to raise the topic and discuss it." (38 years-of-age, five years and eight months after surgery)

The hesitation to consult health care providers about sexual problems was even stronger. Consistently, the professionals' response was totally disappointing. According to one informant, a gynaecologist gave her lubricant jelly saying, "Your husband would have a mistress unless you have sex with him". Another informant said a nurse she consulted simply replied, "You should just do it!" Clearly, these health care providers imposed their own biased opinions even though they were asked to give professional advice. The rest of the informants hesitated to talk about sex, especially with a male surgeon, and said "it's too embarrassing" or "doctors would be at a loss for an answer". They were also hesitant to consult surgeons about problems that imply sexual activities, such as contraception and early menopause. Many expressed a wish for a brochure, or informal counselling by a health care provider of the same gender:

> "I can't consult my doctor about sex. Don't you agree? He is certainly a good doctor, … but I can't raise such a topic! I wish I could talk with a nurse and have some information. I suppose many women have the same reluctance to verbalise certain problems. So, it must be much easier for us to read a brochure or something than asking questions." (45 years-of-age, 18 months after surgery)

Interaction with a partner

The long-term outcome of the sexual relationship was largely influenced by the attitude of partners. Sexual changes, such as reduced frequency of sex and physical distress, did not seem to result in a serious crisis so long as the partner was understanding and respected the woman's intentions regarding the sexual aspect of the relationship. It was a great relief for women when the partner patiently waited until she gained enough energy to resume sex, or if the partner was thoughtful enough towards her physical distress.

> "My husband is always considerate toward my condition. He never forces me when I feel uncomfortable. Although the frequency of sex has decreased, I can say our emotional bond is as strong as ever." (44 years-of-age, 18 months after surgery)

Unfortunately, there were several women who were forced to have sex, resulting in severe physical and emotional pain. In one case, a woman's partner refused to see her operation scar, and forced her to cover it with a T-shirt. After enduring the situation for six months she finally refused to have sex with him:

> "With or without breasts, inside myself I am unchanged. I wanted him to see my whole body, because it is my own body and it is what I looked like after surgery. Being forced to hide my scar, I felt as if I had been raped by my own husband. The lower half of my body was exposed and he tried to satisfy only his desire. So, I refused.... Afterwards, he confessed that it was too emotionally painful for him to see my body." (43 years-of-age, four years and four months after surgery)

The deep disappointment in the partner and the loss of trust in him crucially damaged the whole relationship.

Moving forward: implications to clinical practice and policies

The interviews revealed notable findings regarding sex after breast cancer in a Japanese context. First, contrary to the optimism of Japanese breast surgeons, the majority of informants referred to sexual changes caused by breast cancer. The changes were associated with physical and physiological factors as well as psychological ones, so the situation was not something that patients can control 'by changing their attitude'. It may be that the optimistic attitude of surgeons reflects their intention to encourage post-surgery patients to have sex without hesitation. However, such comments can be interpreted by women with breast cancer to mean that it is abnormal to have sexual problems after treatment, resulting in even more suppression to raise the topic. Detailed information and discussion of various ways to deal with sexual complications need to be provided to women.

Second, the informants displayed a strong psychological resistance to consult health care providers, especially male surgeons, about sexual issues. Even though the percentage of female doctors is steadily increasing in Japan[3], it is still considerably lower than other countries (Table 12.3). Moreover, the data in 1996 indicates that only 2.9% of all female doctors in Japan specialise in surgery (Ministry of Health, Labor and Welfare, 1998). Other factors, such as the

Table 12.3: Percentage of female physicians

Australia (1998)	27.8	Japan (1998)	13.9
Austria (1998)	31.6	Luxembourg (1998)	24.5
Belgium (1995)	25.3	Netherlands (1998)	33.7
Canada (1998)	29.8	New Zealand (1998)	31.3
Czech Republic (1998)	53.7	Norway (1995)	27.4
Finland (1998)	49.5	Poland (1998)	54.7
France (1998)	34.6	Portugal (1998)	43.6
Germany (1995)	35.5	Spain (1998)	36.4
Greece (1995)	31.3	Sweden (1998)	37.6
Hungary (1998)	49.1	Switzerland (1998)	27.8
Ireland (1998)	34.6	UK (1998)	33.1
Italy (1998)	29.1	US (1998)	23.2

Source: OECD Health Data 2001 (2001)

hierarchy of power between patient and doctor, lack of privacy and time constraints in outpatient clinics, only add to the problem. I strongly recommend the involvement of other health care providers, such as nurses and medical social workers, and the provision of a secure environment in the hospital where sexual problems can be discussed with patients. Also, in order to promote questions from patients in the clinical setting, health care providers need to reassure patients that topics related to sex are welcomed. It would be helpful to provide women with a booklet that contains information about resources on sexuality and that might encourage them to ask questions.

Third, even when women did raise the topic, health care providers often imposed their own biased views on patients. The books and articles published internationally often advise patients and their partners to try self-help strategies, and encourage them to consult medical professionals when self-help measures do not work (Kaplan, 1992; Kneece, 1995; Maldonado, 1995; Schover, 1997). In Japan, however, it may be difficult to find health professionals who consider it their role to deal with the sexual issues of patients: the majority of health professionals do not regard this role as a part of their job. Moreover, the specialised profession of sex therapist has not yet been recognised; consequently, they are few and far between. Even when a woman has the courage to consult a medical professional, she may not obtain effective support. It is an urgent matter to promote understanding about sexual complications among health care providers in general.

General health care providers do not need to be experts in sex counselling. Rather, they need to know the sexual impact of treatments and learn some basic sex counselling techniques, such as listening to sexual issues, without evoking a feeling of shame in a client. It is desirable to train health care providers to take an individualistic approach according to the wide variety of contexts that each couple experiences, rather than applying uniform standards.

In Japan, it is necessary to increase the number of specialists with whom women and general health care providers can turn to when problems occur. No more than 50 hospitals currently offer sex counselling (Japanese Society of Sexual Science, 1995). With the exception of some clinical psychologists and psychiatrists, the majority of sex therapists are gynaecologists or urologists who are mainly interested in the diseases related to their own medical speciality. Therefore, it is necessary to train more sex therapists who can deal with a broad range of sexual issues including those caused by cancers and chronic illnesses.

Fourth, the attitude of partners has a great impact on a couple's long-term sexual relationship. A couple's sexuality is the product of interaction between the two. In the research, informants who could communicate frankly with their partners about their various sexual concerns could adjust better to an altered sexual relationship after surgery. For couples with sexual difficulties, efforts to articulate one's own feelings regarding the sexual aspects of the relationship would be much more necessary than before. Partners should always be involved when considering support interventions into the sexual aspects of the lives of patients. Health care providers should take a stronger role in the facilitating of communication between the patient and their partner, and help couples find a way of having a sexual relationship that is satisfactory to each partner.

Finally, the Japanese government, which presently prioritises preventive medicine and screening programmes, needs to recognise the importance of psychosocial care for people with cancer and their families, including the sexual aspects. For example, the fee schedule, which allows only psychiatrists to do psychological counselling, discourages hospital administrators from hiring psychologists and medical social workers since they do not contribute to a hospital in terms of profits. At present, sex counselling or psychotherapy in general from a clinical psychologist is provided at a patient's own expense. Increased person-power to cater to women's psychosocial needs and the financial backup for these activities are ultimately necessary. In order to support the activities of cancer self-help groups and grassroots non-profit organisations that have been trying hard to fill in the gap between the needs of women and insufficient psychosocial care in the clinical setting, it is strongly desirable to establish a national organisation that reaches out to cancer survivors and develops and distributes education materials on life after cancer.

Overall, sexuality after cancer deserves much more attention. We need to accumulate more research on women with cancer that goes beyond penis-in-vagina intercourse and reproduction in order to understand this complicated and multidimensional phenomenon. More research that acknowledges sexual pleasures and the options for psychosocial support and rehabilitation is necessary. In order to support the sexual life of women after having cancer, it is an urgent matter at both national and local level to provide an appropriate environment including resources and quality of care under the Japanese health care system.

Notes

[1] International residents with a valid visa, and those registered to live in Japan for more than one year, are entitled to the universal health insurance system. It should be noted that the following description in the text is simplified. For further details of the universal health insurance system in Japan, see Powell and Anesaki, 1990; Okimoto and Yoshikawa, 1993; Yoshikawa et al, 1996; Campbell and Ikegami, 1998.

[2] In US culture especially, the size and shape of a woman's breast have been regarded as the standards of physical and sexual attractiveness (Kasper, 1995; Altman, 1996; Latteier, 1998). Researchers therefore paid attention to the impact of mastectomy on the sexual relationship, and the earliest publications related to this topic can be traced back to the 1950s (Renneker and Cutler, 1952; Bard and Sutherland, 1955).

[3] According to the Ministry of Health, Labour and Welfare (2000), women accounted for 13.9% of all medical doctors in Japan in 1998. For doctors aged 29 and younger, the percentage was as high as 28.4%.

References

Akabayashi, A. (1999) 'Truth telling in the case of a pessimistic diagnosis in Japan', *Lancet*, vol 354, p 1263.

Altman, R. (1996) *Waking up, fighting back: The politics of breast cancer*, Boston: Little, Brown & Company.

Andersen, B.L. (1985) 'Sexual functioning morbidity among cancer survivors: current status and future research directions', *Cancer*, vol 55, pp 1835-42.

Auchincloss, S. (1990) 'Sexual dysfunction in cancer patients: issues in evaluation and treatment', in J.C. Holland and J.H. Rawland (eds) *Handbook of psychooncology*, New York: Oxford University Press, pp 383-413.

Bard, M. and Sutherland, A.M. (1955) 'Psychological impact of cancer and its treatment: IV adaptation to radical mastectomy', *Cancer*, vol 8, pp 656-72.

Burbie, G.E. and Polinski, M.L. (1992) 'Intimacy and sexuality after cancer treatment', *Journal of Psychosocial Oncology*, vol 10, pp 19-33.

Campbell, J.C. (1998) 'Low health-care spending in Japan', in J.C. Campbell and N. Ikegami (eds) *The art of balance in health policy: Maintaining Japan's low-cost, egalitarian system*, Cambridge: Cambridge University Press, pp 1-20.

Campbell, J.C. and Ikegami, N. (1998) *The art of balance in health policy: Maintaining Japan's low-cost, egalitarian system*, Cambridge: Cambridge University Press.

Fukutomi, T. (1996) *Nyugan kaunserinngu: Kokomade ha kannja ni tsutaetai kisochishiki* [*Breast cancer counselling: The basic knowledge patients need to know*], Tokyo: Nankodo.

Ishihara, K., Yamada, Y. and Harikae, S. (1993) 'Akusei-shuyo kanja no jutsugo no sei-kino shogai kaihuku he no enjo ni kansuru kenkyu' ['Research on the support practices for post-surgery cancer patients with sexual dysfunction'], *Kokurits gan senta kango kenkyukai shuroku* [*A report of the National Cancer Center meeting for nursing research*], pp 19-25.

Jamison, K.R., Wellisch, D.K. and Pasnau, R.O. (1978) 'Psychosocial aspects of mastectomy: I. The woman's perspective', *American Journal of Psychiatry*, vol 135, pp 432-36.

Japanese Society of Sexual Science (1995) 'An appendix: a list of hospitals that offer sex counselling in Japan', *Sekkusu kaunseringu nyumon* [*Introduction to sex counselling*], Tokyo: Kanehara shuppan.

Kaplan, H.S. (1992) 'A neglected issue: the sexual side effects of current treatment for breast cancer', *Journal of Sex and Marital Therapy*, vol 18, pp 3-19.

Kasper A.S. (1995) 'The social construct of breast loss and reconstruction', *Women's Health*, vol 1, pp 197-219.

Kawano, H. (1995) 'Saikoonkoroji no rekishi to gainen' ['The history and conception of psychooncology'], in H. Kawano and N. Kamishiro (eds) *Saikoonkoroji nyumon* [*Introduction to psychooncology*], Tokyo: Nihon Hyoron Sha, pp 1-20.

Kneece, J.C. (1995) *Helping your mate face breast cancer: Tips for becoming an effective support partner*, Columbia: Edu Care Publishing.

Kusama, M. (1998) *Mune no shikori ga kininaruhito ga yomu honn* [*A book for a woman who is concerned about a lump in the breast*], Tokyo: Fusosha.

Latteier, C. (1998) *Breasts: The women's perspective on an American obsession*, New York: The Hawarth Press.

Maldonado, R. (1995) 'Mastectomy and sexual identity: the reconstruction of self-image', *Trends in Healthcare, Law and Ethics*, vol 10, pp 45-52.

Ministry of Health, Labour and Welfare (1998) *A survey on medical doctors dentists and pharmacists 1996*, Tokyo: Ministry of Health, Labour and Welfare.

Ministry of Health, Labour and Welfare (2000) *A survey on medical doctors dentists and pharmacists 1998*, Tokyo: Ministry of Health, Labour and Welfare.

Ministry of Health, Labour and Welfare (2001) *Vital statistics 2000*, Tokyo: Ministry of Health, Labour and Welfare.

Nakamura, M. (1993) 'Kanjakai kara mita onzon ryoho' ['Breast-conserving surgery from the perspective of a cancer self-help group'], *Sexual Science*, vol 2, pp 20-22.

OECD (2001) *OECD health data 2001*, Paris: OECD.

Okimoto, D.I. and Yoshikawa, A. (1993) *Japan's health system: Efficiency and effectiveness in universal care*, New York: Faulkner & Gray.

Osoba, D. (1991) 'Measuring the effect of cancer on quality of life', in D. Osoba (ed) *Effect of cancer on quality of life,* Boca Raton: CRC Press, pp 25-40.

Powell, M. and Anesaki, M. (1990) *Healthcare in Japan,* London: Routledge.

Renneker, R. and Cutler, M. (1952) 'Psychological problems of adjustment to cancer of the breast', *Journal of American Medical Association,* vol 148, pp 833-38.

Schain, W.S. (1988) 'The sexual and intimate consequences of breast cancer treatment', *Cancer Journal for Clinicians,* vol 38, pp 154-61.

Schover, L.R. (1991) 'The impact of breast cancer on sexuality, body image, and intimate relationship', *Cancer Journal for Clinicians,* vol 41, pp 112-20.

Schover, L.R. (1997) *Sexuality and fertility after cancer,* New York: John Wiley and Sons.

Seno, T. and Izuo, M. (1994) *Nyusen shikkan manyuaru [Manual of breast diseases],* Tokyo: Kanehara shuppan.

Takahashi, M. (2000) *Qualitative research on Japanese women's sexuality after having breast cancer: The processes of change and coping,* Unpublished PhD, University of Tokyo, Tokyo.

Takahashi, M., Kai, I., Akabayashi, A., Kasumi, F., Higashi, Y., Koinuma, N., Hisata, M., Shima, Y. and Ohi, G. (1999) 'Nyugan kanja heno shinri-shakaiteki shien ni kansuru gekai no ishiki' ['Who should meet the needs of breast cancer patients?: A questionnaire survey of Japanese surgeons'], *Nyugan no Rinsho [Japanese Journal of Breast Cancer],* vol 14, pp 495-502.

The Research Group for Population-based Cancer Registration in Japan (1999) 'Estimates based on data from seven population-based cancer registries', *Japanese Journal of Clinical Oncology,* vol 29, pp 361-64.

Tominaga, K. (1995) 'Nyugan shujutsu to sei-kino shougai' ['Breast cancer surgery and sexual dysfunction'], in Japanese Society of Sexual Science (ed) *Sekkusu Kaunseringu Nyumon [Introduction to Sex Counselling],* Tokyo: Kanehara shuppan, pp 264-68.

Uchitomi, Y. (1997) 'Truth-telling practice in cancer care in Japan', *Annals of the New York Academy of Sciences,* vol 809, pp 290-99.

Watt, T. (1987) *Gan kanja ni okuru 87 no yuki [87 courageous messages for cancer survivors],* Tokyo: Soshisha.

Yoshikawa, A., Bhattacharya, J. and Vogt, W.B. (1996) *Health economics of Japan: Patients, doctors and hospitals under a universal health insurance system,* Tokyo: University of Tokyo Press.

Index

Page references for figures and tables are in italics; those for notes are followed by n

Also available from The Policy Press

Changing labour markets, welfare policies and citizenship
Edited by Jørgen Goul Andersen and Per H. Jensen
Paperback £18.99 US$29.95
ISBN 1 86134 272 1
Hardback £45.00 US$59.95
ISBN 1 86134 273 X
216 x 148mm 320 pages
January 2002

Europe's new state of welfare
Unemployment, employment policies and citizenship
Edited by Jørgen Goul Andersen, Jochen Clasen, Wim van Oorschot and Knut Halvorsen
Paperback £17.99 US$35.00
ISBN 1 86134 314 0
Hardback £55.00 US$79.95
ISBN 1 86134 315 9
216 x 148mm 308 pages
November 2002

Active social policies in Europe
Inclusion through participation
Edited by Rik van Berkel and Iver Hornemann Møller
Paperback £19.99 US$32.50
ISBN 1 86134 280 2
Hardback £50.00 US$75.00
ISBN 1 86134 281 0
234 x 156mm 240 pages
September 2002

Lone parents, employment and social policy
Cross-national comparisons
Edited by Jane Millar and Karen Rowlingson
Paperback £16.99 US$28.95
ISBN 1 86134 320 5
Hardback £45.00 US$59.95
ISBN 1 86134 321 3
216 x 148mm 320 pages
November 2001

What future for social security?
Debates and reforms in national and cross-national perspective
Jochen Clasen
Paperback £18.99 US$29.95
ISBN 1 86134 410 4
234 x 156mm 292 pages
July 2002
Hardback edition published by Kluwer Law International in 2001

The welfare we want?
The British challenge for American reform
Robert Walker and Michael Wiseman
Paperback £18.99 US$29.95
ISBN 1 86134 407 4
Hardback £50.00 US$59.95
ISBN 1 86134 408 2
234 x 156mm 192 pages tbc
May 2003

For further information about these and other titles published by The Policy Press, please visit our website at:
www.policypress.org.uk

To order titles, please contact:
Marston Book Services
PO Box 269 • Abingdon
Oxon OX14 4YN • UK
Tel: +44 (0)1235 465500
Fax: +44 (0)1235 465556
E-mail: direct.orders@marston.co.uk